Possessed

Possessed

A Cultural History of Hoarding

Rebecca R. Falkoff

Cornell University Press

Ithaca and London

First published 2021 by Cornell University Press

Library of Congress Cataloging-in-Publication Data

Names: Falkoff, Rebecca R., 1976– author.
Title: Possessed : a cultural history of hoarding / Rebecca R. Falkoff.
Description: Ithaca [New York] : Cornell University Press, 2021. |
    Includes bibliographical references and index.
Identifiers: LCCN 2020025167 (print) | LCCN 2020025168 (ebook) |
    ISBN 9781501752803 (paperback) | ISBN 9781501752827 (ebook) |
    ISBN 9781501752810 (pdf)
Subjects: LCSH: Compulsive hoarding—Social aspects—History. |
    Hoarders—History. | Compulsive hoarding—Philosophy.
Classification: LCC RC569.5.H63 F35 2021 (print) | LCC RC569.5.H63
    (ebook) | DDC 616.85/227—dc23
LC record available at https://lccn.loc.gov/2020025167
LC ebook record available at https://lccn.loc.gov/2020025168

In memory of my grandmother,
Fontaine Maverick Falkoff,
A poet, hoarder, and maverick.

Fall from Grace

While casing the flea markets
For fabulous finds
Priced for the penurious,
I've felt little quick
Subcultural
Darts of desire
For those delightful things.

Avon bottles, I mean.
Perfume bottles shaped like poodles,
Turtles of aftershave, ships at sea,
The rosebud with the honeybee.

Well, today I fell from Grace.
It cost me a dollar:
Two green glass parakeets,
Shining likenesses,
Their screw-on heads of amber glass,
And one still full of perfume.

Is there shame on my face?
No, I've a gleam in my eye.
I see them as great emeralds,
The very essence of parakeet.
I think, now, I'll be collecting
All that shimmers,
Dazzles and dazes,
The daydreams of
Demented artisans.

This will be
One of my phases.
                    —Fontaine Maverick Falkoff

Contents

Figures

Preface

A BOOK AND TWO HOARDS

The first two decades of the twenty-first century have seen an outpouring of interest in hoarding, and in those whose accumulated possessions overwhelm their living spaces, rendering them unusable and often unsafe. Fatal accidents and residential fires across the United States drew considerable attention to hoarding, and cities and towns throughout the nation assembled task forces charged with reducing related safety risks. Hoarding is the subject of documentary and feature films; novels, memoirs, and plays; guides for clinicians and self-help books; installation art, painting, and photography; stand-up and late-night comedy acts; episodes of television forensic dramas, sitcoms, and reality series; academic work in psychology and cultural studies.[1] With the increasing visibility of hoarding, many who had long considered themselves to be packrats, savers, collectors, and clutter bugs began to form support groups and seek out professional help. Others retreated into their barricaded isolation—now proud of their monumental lots, now embittered by the scorn of their thriftless neighbors, still helpless, still alone. Family members, too, saw their experience reflected in all the talk of hoarding, and founded organizations like "Children of Hoarders" and "Squalor Survivors."[2]

I count myself among their numbers; my father is a hoarder, as was my paternal grandmother. Because of this personal connection, I have been following the cultural discourse with an acute interest that oscillates between: "So that's what that is!" and "Well, it isn't quite like that." As a child, I saw adventure in hoarding; my father and I spent weekends going to yard sales and flea markets. On trash days we would drive around looking for treasure, with mixed results. Once we found a Pepsi machine from the 1950s, which we restored to again dispense glass bottles for a dime. Another time, as I was climbing through some promising curbside heap, my leg was gashed open by something razor-sharp. My grandmother, Fontaine, used to make regular pilgrimages to the town dump down the street from her summer home in Jefferson, Maine. Once she found a box with dozens of pairs of new canvas sneakers in black, white, and orange, and in sizes sufficient to outfit me and my cousins through our walking years of youth. Last time I went to Fontaine's house in Maine—more than thirty years after the wondrous boon—there were still a couple of mismatched shoes left in the closet.

Fontaine died in 2005, leaving behind two houses brimming with the accumulated passion of her life. It had been years since she let anyone into her Auburndale, Massachusetts, home, and its months-long clean out after her death required the labor of her five sons, three daughters-in-law, sixteen grandchildren, as well as the lease of a forty-yard dumpster. We found a rattlesnake's rattle and seventeenth-century ecclesiastical books; stacks indiscriminate with junk mail and stock certificates; decomposing vermin and rotting food buried under creaky antiques. Although Fontaine's eccentricities were a source of laughter at family gatherings, we occasionally recognized something sinister in her accumulations. As when she contracted spinal meningitis from the filth that surrounded her, or when my father found her body, comatose, at the foot of a too-cluttered staircase. For all its quirky fascination, there is horror in the hoard, and I shudder to think of the disaster that looms over my father's house, with its exterior dominated by a rotting wood porch crumbling under the weight of salvaged plywood and bookcases, a dozen bicycles, a lawnmower, and the soundboard of a piano; and its interior strewn with the makeshift electrical fixes of overextended extension cords.[3] Most academic writing grows from personal obsession or intimate pain; my own betrays these roots more materially than some.

I began to explore these roots in writing in January 2010, when I launched *If I Were a Hoarder.* I conceived of the Tumblr blog as a compendium of all the intriguing detritus, all the irresistible bargains, and all the wondrous objects that would clutter my Berkeley apartment if I were a hoarder. I imagined the site as an exercise in restraint and empathy, a chronicle of my effort to understand the allure of objects, to heed the call of things. I figured I would save money and space—if not time—by transforming this call into writing. Almost immediately, the medium eclipsed the message. Tumblr is a microblogging and social networking platform. Users post video, audio, text, links, and other content that can be easily reposted by others.[4] Almost 80 percent of Tumblr posts are image files, and I quickly learned that images and videos were more effective in engaging other users than essayistic posts dedicated to appealing objects, my family history, or reflections on the cultural discourse of hoarding. The blog distended haphazardly to include virtually any digital content I stumbled upon that seemed somehow relevant. Hoarders mingled with ragpickers, gleaners, scavengers, misers, fetishists, collectors, archivists, and makers. Discussions of academic works of new materialism, historical materialism, discard studies, and thing theory were punctuated by images of abandoned objects, cabinets of curiosity, and cluttered spaces. Photographs of landfills, junkyards, and brimming dumpsters attested to the allure of the broken, the threadbare, and the obsolete.

Though initially intended to ward off what I feared was an inexorable disposition toward hoarding, I soon realized that the unwieldy accumulation of content reproduced the logic of a hoard. *If I Were a Hoarder*, like many hoards, is an aesthetic object that results from the ceding of authorial or curatorial intention to a series of chance encounters with miscellaneous stuff. The posts were organized according to the date that I chanced upon them and deemed them relevant enough to repost. If I periodically attempted to impose some structure with hashtags, the evolving assortment of such markers and their inconsistent implementation shook its foundations. Any order that might be discerned from properties intrinsic to the posts themselves was secondary to the one established by the chronology of my encounter with them.

Disorganized abundance, which may torment all who write a first book long in the making, is particularly cruel to those who write about accumulation. Writing about hoarding has led me to a range of texts, disciplines, historical periods, and national traditions. I returned to the abandoned spaces of the Tumblr blog and attempted to communicate its meaning without reproducing its logic. If, in this book, I manage to give form to the unbounded content of *If I Were a Hoarder*, that is an achievement diminished by a personal failure as I have not been able to help my father. I fear that he will not be spared the fate that awaits so many who live in hoards: to be consumed by raging flames or crushed by a domestic avalanche.

Acknowledgments

I would not have been able to complete this book without the support and encouragement of family, friends, and colleagues whose belief in this project and my abilities sustained me when my own faltered. Nor would it have been possible for me to write this book without the material resources provided by the institutions with which I have been affiliated. For the better part of a decade, I have been fortunate to call the Casa Italiana Zerilli-Marimò at New York University home, and to have worked under department chairs who encouraged me to write the book I wanted to write. At New York University, my work has been supported by a Goddard Junior Faculty Fellowship and a Global Research Initiative Faculty Fellowship at NYU-Florence, a Dean for Humanities First Book Colloquium Program Award and a Humanities Faculty Writing Collaborative stipend.

I am beholden to the Wolf Humanities Center at the University of Pennsylvania and to members of the 2018–19 Mellon Seminar for the lively yearlong dialogue about "Stuff" and for their comments on the introduction.

Essential research was conducted at the Archivio Bonsanti Gabinetto Vieusseux, the Biblioteca Nazionale Centrale di Firenze, the Fondo Manoscritti in Pavia, the New York Public Library, and NYU's Bobst Library. The Watertown Free Public Library in Massachusetts and the Bibliothèque Richelieu-Louvois provided sanctuary spaces for writing at critical moments. I thank Cesare de Seta, director of the Archivio Fotografico Giuseppe Pagano; the Fratelli Alinari Archives; the Estate of André Kertész; the Bibliothèque nationale de France; and the Association Atelier André Breton for the photographs in chapter 2.

In the years in which I have been researching hoarding, I have found vital interlocutors in a community of scholars and writers who have taken up the subject: Kimberly Adams, William Davies King, Jessie Sholl, and Barry Yourgrau. I also thank readers of *If I Were a Hoarder* and members of the Children of Hoarders Yahoo! and Facebook groups.

I am grateful to many students, colleagues, mentors, friends, and family members who have offered insight and perspective: Gianna Albaum, Emily Antenucci, Maria Luisa Ardizzone, Albert Ascoli, Ruth Ben-Ghiat, Lisa Bombardieri, Elizabeth Ainsley Campbell, Valeria Castelli, Christina Chalmers, Nicola Cipani, Giuseppe Civitarese, Elizabeth Cohen, Judy Cohen, Jonathan Combs-Shilling, Alison Cornish, Virginia Cox, Brian de Grazia, Bruce Edelstein, my extended Falkoff family, Aileen Feng, Gregory Flaxman, Elisa Fox, Mia Fuller, Andrea Gadberry, Mollie, Lynda, and Richard Goldstein, Stephanie Malia Hom, Michael Immerso, Serenella Iovino, Paola Italia, Janet Jameson, Anna Lapenna, Janaya Lasker, Wendy Lee, Giancarlo Lombardi, Maria Anna Mariani, Anthony Martire, Valerie McGuire, Stiliana Milkova, Scott Millspaugh, Erica Moretti, Julie Napolin, Elena Past, Federica Pedriali, Deborah Peterson, Lisa Regan, Eugenio Refini, Alessia Ricciardi, Marco Ruffini,

Arielle Saiber, Diane Santas, Susan Shachner-Schultz, Barbara Spackman, Joni Spigler, Genevieve Stamper, Justin Steinberg, Tom Sugrue, Paola Ureni, Silvia Valisa, Giorgio Van Straten, J. David Velleman, Melissa Vise, Sarah Wasserman, Rhiannon Welch, and Mahnaz Yousefzadeh.

To David Forgacs and Marisa Escolar I am particularly indebted. David has been a generous and compassionate mentor and advocate, reading and commenting on multiple drafts and insisting on necessary deadlines. Marisa has also read and commented on multiple drafts and has provided a model of strength, resilience, and intellectual rigor that I can only hope to emulate.

My editor at Cornell University Press, Mahinder Kingra, has been enthusiastic about this project from the start and has offered necessary guidance at critical stages. I am also grateful for the meticulous work of my copy editor, Irina Burns, and my production editor, Karen Laun. The constructive feedback I received from three anonymous readers helped to shape the book into its current form.

Most important, I thank my brother, Sam, and my parents, Susan and Mike for their unwavering support and for their thoughtful engagement with this project.

Possessed

Introduction to Hoardiculture

On the morning of March 21, 1947, New York police headquarters received a call reporting that there was a dead body in the Collyer Mansion. The caller did not need to give the address; the rundown 2078 Fifth Avenue brownstone and the eccentric brothers who lived there, Homer and Langley, were local legends. Since 1938, when the journalist Helen Worden Erskine wrote about the "Hermits of Harlem" in the *New York World-Telegram*, the mansion had become a neighborhood attraction. Ongoing squabbles with Consolidated Edison, the Bowery Savings Bank, city officials, and developers resulted in memorable scenes: solicitors banging on the door, Langley shouting at them from an upstairs window. Everyone seemed to have a theory about what was inside the dilapidated brownstone. Neighborhood children insisted that the place was haunted and that Langley lived there with the decomposing cadavers of his father, his mother, and his older brother, Homer, who was blind and had not been seen outside since 1936. Some said there was a car in the basement (there was a Model T that Langley had attempted to rig to generate electricity), a rowboat in the attic (it was a broken canoe), and countless grand pianos (there were fourteen). Others said there were piles of money; rumors of their vast fortunes circulated in the neighborhood, unaffected by regular sightings of Langley rummaging through garbage cans and appealing to butchers and grocers for scraps.

After the mysterious call, an emergency squad was dispatched to the Fifth Avenue address. Performing for a crowd of hundreds of gawkers, the first responders tried to get in through the front door and a basement grate. Unsteady barricades of newspapers blocked both. Eventually, they were able to enter through a second-floor window. There, they found the emaciated corpse of Homer nestled into an alcove amid piles of debris. He had become paraplegic in his final years; the autopsy determined that he had died of starvation-induced heart failure. A frenzied search began for Langley, with the *Daily News* and the *Daily Mirror* making competing bids for exclusive information leading to his discovery.[1] The tip lines rang off the hook: Langley was reportedly spotted eating frozen custard in Newark, hitchhiking in North Carolina, trout fishing in the Adirondacks, and riding the subway in Brooklyn.[2] The search continued for another two and a half weeks, expanding into nine states. Meanwhile on Fifth Avenue, the public administrator, H. Walter Skidmore, led preliminary efforts to clear out the town-house. Cats scurried about, lured by shelter or mice or perhaps the "queer odor" whose source was discovered, on April 8, to be the decomposing, rat-gnawed corpse of Langley.[3] The younger Collyer brother had been dead for about a month; he was bringing food to Homer when he set off one of the many boobytraps he had rigged to deter intruders. He was crushed by bales of newspapers and died of asphyxiation; "a victim of fear," Worden Erskine writes, "killed by his invention."[4]

More than 120 tons of stuff—the bulk of which was combustible debris—were removed from the Collyer Mansion. Magazines, newspapers, wood, and other combustibles were carted off by the Department of Sanitation and burned.[5] The clean out yielded the detritus Langley scavenged when he went out walking at night and the remaining effects of the brothers' childhood and their ancestors, an intricate potato peeler, a beaded lampshade, a toy airplane, a drugstore cologne display, and a jar containing a two-headed human fetus preserved in formaldehyde.[6] The fourteen pianos were put up for auction in the fetid, dusty parlor as bidders stumbled over "battered cartons and bottles" and covered their noses with handkerchiefs; only four sold.[7] Tattered rugs, stopped clocks, musical instruments, toys, furniture, pictures, linens, and clothing—wares described even by the auctioneer's aide as "junk I wouldn't pay a dime for"—were removed from the mansion and sold at auction, bringing in the disappointing sum of $1,800.[8] Max Schaffer, the impresario for Hubert's Dime Museum and Flea Circus on 42nd Street, spent $300 on a carpet, a crib, a coffee grinder, Homer's old school desk, two cornets, a bugle, three rusty bayonets, and some pictures. Another big spender, Jacob Lubetkin, owner of Ye Olde Treasure Shoppe in Greenwich Village, spent $310 on a 200-pound, nine-foot-tall musical clock.[9] Both men correctly recognized that however banged up or broken down their purchases may have been, relics of the legendary hoard would attract customers to their businesses.

The Collyer brothers' reclusive lives and horrible deaths may be "the ultimate New York cautionary tale," as Lidz writes, without specifying what that tale is about, or against what it cautions.[10] Sorting through Collyer curiosa in 1947, Skidmore discovered an unmailed letter from Langley to one of his students describing the anguish he felt when she stopped her music lessons with him. With that evidence, the public administrator imagined a love story to be at the origin of the brothers' "frightful and puzzling end."[11] Worden Erskine traces the source of their ills to a different love story, that between their parents, who were first cousins, and whose union she therefore considered a "diluting of the blood by inbreeding." As an alternate hypothesis, she names the "dominant character" of their mother, speculating that her "overpowering devotion" to her sons rendered them helpless.[12] Dozens of writers have since taken up the story of the Collyer brothers—notable titles include Marcia Davenport's *My Brother's Keeper* (1954), Andrew Scott's *The Dazzle* (2002), Lidz's *Ghosty Men* (2003), and E. L. Doctorow's *Homer and Langley* (2009)—to explore horrifying codependence of a devoted caretaker or a deranged prison-keeper and his helpless charge, or unchecked materialism, paranoia, or misanthropy.[13] The joys and sorrows, attachments and estrangements that conducted the brothers to their crushing end will likely remain opaque despite the efforts of psychologists, playwrights, novelists, and even cultural critics.[14]

Hoarding Today

However iconic the death of the Collyer brothers may be, stories like theirs are not uncommon. In July 2010, similar events unfolded when firefighters were called to the 5400 block of Foster Street in Skokie, Illinois. There they discovered the corpse of the seventy-nine-year old Marie Davis buried under heaps of domestic debris. To remove her body, first responders had to drill into the roof and create a tunnel through the possessions that were piled up to three feet from the ceiling.[15] The cause of Davis's death—heart failure—was not directly related to the state of her home, but it was the latter that made her death local news. Or rather, the state of her home and the time of her death: years marked by a spike in cultural interest in hoarding evidenced in literary and visual culture, medical research, and academic works of cultural criticism. In 2009, A&E aired its first episode of *Hoarders*, a series that has been credited with establishing narrative formulas and iconographies of the phenomenon.[16] Four years later, the American Psychiatric Association included the new diagnostic category of "hoarding disorder" in the fifth revision of its standard reference work, the *Diagnostic and Statistical Manual of Mental Disorders (DSM-5)*.

The *DSM-5* defines hoarding as a "persistent difficulty discarding or parting with possessions, *regardless of their actual value*."[17] The emphasized qualification suggests that hoarding is rooted in conflicting perspectives about value. Hoarding thus resembles fetishism, a concept that figures prominently in the fields of anthropology, economics, and psychology; naming, in each discipline, a misrecognition of value—religious, commercial, or sexual.[18] Unlike Freudian fetishism, which is generally experienced by the afflicted as a welcome expedient to erotic life, the contemporary psychiatric diagnosis of hoarding requires that the difficulty discarding results in "clinically significant distress or impairment in social, occupational, or other important areas of functioning."[19]

The wording of this specification is generic; it is used to designate the threshold of disorder in multiple entries of the *DSM-5*. The authors explain that without "clear biological markers" or "clinically useful measurements of severity," "it has not been possible to completely separate normal and pathological symptom expressions contained in diagnostic criteria."[20] The formulation "clinically significant distress" thus replaces a gap in information, a representational lacuna: the absence of a measurable difference between normal and pathological symptom expressions. A substitute for something that is not there is also Freud's basic formula for the fetish: "To put it more plainly: the fetish is a substitute for the woman's (the mother's) penis that the little boy once believed in and—for reasons familiar to us—does not want to give up."[21]

Hoarding amplifies and multiplies fetishism, not only because both are predicated on clashing perspectives about value, but also because both the diagnostic category of hoarding disorder and the hoard itself are structured like the fetish. The disorder and the hoard are substitutes for something that cannot be seen: a measurable difference between normal and pathological conditions. This doubleness infects hoarding discourse, raising its ambivalences to the third power.

Among disorders included in the *DSM-5*, hoarding is unique because its diagnosis requires the existence of a material entity external to the patient's psychic reality: the hoard.[22] However fatal its magnitude, the hoard is an aesthetic object produced by a clash in perspectives about the meaning or value of objects; it is caught between phenomenology, aesthetics, and ontology. This bears a significant implication: the hoarder resembles an artist or an artisan whose identity as such is a function of the (composite) artifact he produces—*facit artem*. Diagnosis is, in part, an aesthetic problem. Hoarding experts Randy Frost and Gail Steketee have even developed aesthetic standards with which to evaluate a hoard, an assessment tool they named the Clutter Image Rating (CIR). The CIR is composed of three series of nine photographs of increasingly cluttered staged domestic spaces—a kitchen, a bedroom, and a living room (see figure 0.1).[23] Intended to address the absence of a clinically useful measurement of severity, the assessment tool makes the reality of the diagnosis of hoarding disorder derive from an index (a photograph) of a realist representation (a mise-en-scène) of an analogy (a hypothesized likeness to the hoarder's dwelling). Hoarding disorder, diagnosed as such, is a malady in which "objective reality" is both essential to the diagnosis and incredibly elusive.

The CIR is useful not only as a measure of the severity of hoarding but also as a document of what makes and unmakes sense

Clutter Image Rating: Living Room

Please select the photo below that most accurately reflects the amount of clutter in your room.

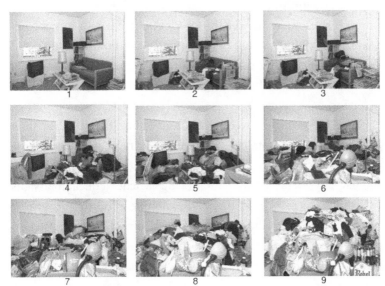

FIGURE 0.1
Clutter Image Rating, Living Room

in living spaces. At what point do room assemblages denote not bad housekeeping or bad taste but something pathological, and accordingly, irrational and inexplicable? What supplementary narratives or economic rationales could redomesticate the images to the realm of sense? Economic theories of hoarding focus on those who accumulate bullion, money, or necessity goods to manipulate market conditions and enhance their wealth, whereas the accumulations that define hoarding in clinical psychology are of no direct economic consequence outside the hoarded home. That contemporary capitalist culture makes a mental disorder of irrational economic choices is consonant with the broader encroachments of a present characterized by "the non-state sphere of economy permeating everything" or "the commodification of everything."[24] The pathologization of irrational decisions about the allocation of limited resources may be the most extreme form of this permeation, demonstrating that "all conduct is economic conduct" and corroborating Gary Becker's claim that "the economic approach provides a useful framework for understanding all human behavior."[25]

The relationship between economic elaborations of hoarding and free market capitalism, however, is more nuanced and more essential. Drawing on mid-eighteenth-century writings by the French physiocrat Louis Paul Abeille, Michel Foucault assigns hoarding a critical role in the development of the governing rationality or "governmentality" of the liberal state. Reflecting on grain markets, Abeille argues that by allowing hoarding, the state entrusts the regulation of supply and demand to the free market, thus rendering scarcity a chimera.[26] True, Abeille concedes, some without means may die of hunger, but these are "people," distinguished from the "population," composed of rational economic actors who produce, buy, store, or sell in profitable syncopation with the market.[27] Instead of administrative fiat, the liberal state abandons to a hungry fate the people without the means to benefit from the market's freedoms. It is through this abandonment that a caesura is drawn between the "population" and those excluded, the "people." By allowing hoarding, the liberal state transfers the burden of grain storage to the population, performing the ideological work of spinning the failure of the free market to nourish all as a failure of those who lack nourishment. Hoarding, as such, is the limit case of classical liberalism: a test of the idea that individuals acting rationally in their own best interest constitute a beneficent "invisible hand." The increasingly skewed distribution of wealth but one testament to the treacherous iniquity of this idea.

In Marx's account, the clashing perspectives about value that define hoarding manifest in Sisyphean immobility that stills even the most motile matter: exchange value.[28] He focuses on bullion and money rather than grain, presenting the hoarder as a miser and a "martyr [to] exchange-value" who forgoes use in a practice defined through an impressive concatenation of contradictions: "He dreams of exchange-value and he therefore does not exchange. The [liquid] form of wealth and its petrification, the elixir of life and [the philosopher's stone] madly haunt each other in alchemic fashion."[29] Marx frames these contradictions as a tension between the infinite potential of money and the finitude of any actual sum. "This contradiction between the quantitative limitation and the qualitative lack of limitation of money keeps driving the hoarder [*Schatzbildner*] back to his Sisyphean task: accumulation."[30] The stasis-producing tension between quantitative limitation and qualitative boundlessness is also one between petrified and liquid value, and between materiality and immateriality.

Though histories of capitalism tend to distinguish between three stages (market, monopoly, late), its story can be retold as one of an ongoing dematerialization of value that begins when an "ordinary, sensuous thing"—a table, say—is transformed into a commodity.[31] Value performs an acrobatic feat, leaping from the ligneous form of the table-in-use to the general equivalent, where it can be exchanged and stored. This leap is a dematerialization, whether value lands in gold or representative moneys, or in the more manifestly intangible form of digital currencies.

The ubiquity of hoarding in the twenty-first century is due in some part to the unprecedented availability of cheap consumer goods, but the tensions between petrification and liquidity and between materiality and immateriality that Marx isolates are also decisive. Deregulation has enabled further alienation of value from material forms by stimulating investment in derivative financial markets. The bursting of the housing bubble inflated by the bundling of subprime mortgages into mortgage-backed financial products in 2007–8 was a testament to the precarity of these markets.[32] The securitized subprime mortgages that triggered the global financial crisis demonstrated that even the most material of possessions—the home—was as if made of air and could burst like a bubble. The same years saw the permeation of network technologies into everyday life through smartphone use. These were years in which the meanings of materiality and immateriality were particularly unstable, years in which it became clear, for example, that a lifetime of photographs could disappear with the click of a mouse, a tilt of a teapot, or update of an operating system. Though these fraught and fickle notions of materiality and immateriality have galvanized hoarding discourse in the twenty-first century, the essential features of the praxis develop concomitantly with the market economy and more broadly, modernity.

In addition to the upsurge in hoarding discourse, the first two decades of the twenty-first century have seen spate of scholarly interventions in new materialism, thing theory, object-oriented ontology, and vital materialism. Although this cultural history engages sporadically with these theories, new materialist thought is neither my focus nor my doctrine; more important theoretical interlocutors are pillars of modern thought: Marx, Freud, and Walter Benjamin. The literary and visual texts I discuss include those that are frequently named in studies of hoarding: Nikolai Gogol's *Dead Souls*, Arthur Conan Doyle's "The Adventure of the Musgrave Ritual," Song Dong's *Waste Not*, and E. L. Doctorow's *Homer and Langley*.[33] To this corpus, I add Italian texts that have been neglected outside of Italy and excluded from this developing canon of precursors to contemporary hoarding discourse. I devote particular attention to the work of sui generis modernist Carlo Emilio Gadda, a self-declared *archiviomane* (archiveaholic). Gadda's biography is cluttered with the stuff of hoarding, and his personal, poetic, and political sympathies and enmities are often expressed through judgments about functionality and resource allocation.

Hoarding is too ubiquitous and entrenched to be dismembered by the boundaries of national tradition or discipline. A study of hoardiculture must take a hoardicritical approach, registering anachronic presences and unlikely resonances.[34] The examples of hoarding in this cultural history come primarily from Italian, French, British, Russian, and American texts from the late eighteenth to the early twenty-first century to, from the age of reason to the Anthropocene. I initially set out to trace the transformation of hoarding across disciplines—between its psychiatric and economic elaborations—but soon realized that to do so would be to obscure the essential ways in which hoarding entangles the disciplines. Instead, *Possessed* is loosely organized around sites where value is particularly unstable, and where clashing perspectives about the meaning and value of things abound: the personal library, the flea market, the crime scene, the dustheap, and the digital archive.

The first chapter traces a history of hoarding to the early nineteenth century, to the intersection of medical science and literary history in the personal library. Bibliomania becomes, variously, a symptom of bad taste, an effect of ego-dystonic compulsion, the basis of new literary forms, and precursor to a series of other "object-oriented manias," including kleptomania and various "collectomanias."

Ostensibly about economies of hoarding, chapter 2 focuses on flea markets—emporia at which classical economic principles governing the allocation of limited resources are unsettled by wildly unpredictable expressions of value. Gathering places for objects of elusive provenance that seem to have outlasted their use and value, markets seem the *oikos* of the transient, the fleeting, and the contingent—that is, modernity, according to Charles Baudelaire's emblematic formulation. The labor that makes these markets—that of recognizing potential value and awaiting the alchemical union of chance and desire—resembles the work that defines representative conceptions of the modern artist, poet, historian, and, I add, the hoarder.

Chapter 3 investigates the overlap between the epistemological foundations of the detective story and the extraordinary attunement to marginal detail observed in those who hoard. While the detective abstracts minor details from a crime scene and uses them to put together a narrative bound by causality, those who hoard remain overwhelmed by the unrelenting tempo of their perception of detail.

The homology between narrative and material conceptions of waste is central to chapter 4, which considers hoarding from the perspective of an *oikos* situated in the environment rather than the market, in ecology rather than the economy. Noting that hoarding is often understood as a resolute avoidance of waste, the chapter looks at narratives that present hoarding as a way of countering scarcity not by making use of objects but by suspending them in a bounded space of potential.

This cultural history concludes by returning to the split between materiality and immateriality that defines, for Marx, the Sisyphean drive to hoard. Charting conceptual entanglements of hoarding in key sites of praxis, this book shows how hoarding entangles psychic and political economies and troubles the boundaries between material and immaterial, rational and irrational, individual and aggregate, present and future. The hoarder emerges from my readings as a personification of the psychic, economic, epistemological, and ecological conditions of modernity and an agent of their undoing. These conditions begin to emerge, as chapter 1 shows, in separation between the materiality of the book and the immateriality of the reproducible text that informs early denunciations of bibliomania.

1

Psychologies

THE PERSONAL LIBRARY

In his short documentary, *Possessed* (2008), Martin Hampton captures the struggles of members of an Obsessive-Compulsive Disorder Action Hoarding support group in London—people who self-identify as compulsive hoarders.[1] The film is divided into four parts, each composed of a monologue by one group member who leads the camera operator through a cluttered dwelling, giving an account of his or her experience of hoarding. The hoarder in "Control," the first of the four segments, describes the intricately cross-referenced catalogs he maintains to index the books and videocassettes neatly shelved four-deep, up to the ceiling, and across every surface in his apartment. He seems proud of his personal library, if also apprehensive about the lack of space: "I like having books to look at . . . I like having lots of stuff. Like if I had a three-bedroom house then it wouldn't be a problem, cause I'd have enough room for all the stuff I've got, so I'd be quite happy." Despite the meticulous record keeping, the expanding library takes on an almost supernatural power and begins to elude his control. He explains: "It's not the way it should be. It's starting to take over. And that's sort of a bit spooky." The contentment afforded by his collection is offset by an awareness of the slow approach of disaster: "At the moment it's not too bad, but it's very close to becoming a real real problem." His control over the books and videocassettes is precarious—he situates disaster in the not too distant future—"ten, fifteen years": "It's like the walls of the flat are sort of closing in. It's a bit like that thing in *Star Wars*, where they end up in the trash compactor. And the walls are coming in!" To inhabit a present structured by the dread of a domestic avalanche or some similar catastrophe is a recital of what it means to be human in the Anthropocene, living in anticipation of an apocalypse of our own making.

The second segment presents a different affective orientation: "Submission." The hoarded space brims with consumer goods destined for prompt desuetude: cellular phones, computers, digital cameras, external hard drives—most still in their original packaging—as well as kitschy figurines, plush toys, and office supplies. The hoarder describes these purchases as the result of a dream-like state: "You see something and you want it so much. You've got no choice but to buy it. So, I suppose I don't feel like I can, sometimes, *not* buy things." As if hypnotized by flashes of opportunity, he is unable to resist a bargain. And when the embarrassment of riches arouses distressing indecision, he buys whole lots. He confesses haltingly to having racked up credit card debt of more than £40,000: "That's more than my mortgage. And it's just basically everything you see around you." He describes the sense of panic he feels when visiting the post office, fearing the arrival of another order: "I recognize I can't trust myself." While the hoarder of "Control" relishes in the presence of his possessions, for the subject of "Submission," the objects have lost their luster; they accumulate like an unwelcome residue of his helplessness. Like the dangerous environment the hoarder of "Control" has created, which seems to be exceptional and yet engenders an Anthropocenic sense of doom, the hoarder's

indebtedness in the "Submission" segment is the norm for subjects of contemporary capitalism.[2]

If the juxtaposition of "Control" and "Submission" appears to
mirror that between subject and object of the verb "to possess,"
the documentary—and its title, *Possessed*—suggests that even in
exercising control over things, we are possessed by them. Hoarding
marks a dangerous threshold at which control over objects cedes to
a sense of helplessness before the material world. That threshold—
between control and submission, between the subject and object
of the verb "possess"—may be used to draw a distinction between
collecting and hoarding—a tantalizing exercise that finds provi-
sional resolution in considerations of value.[3] But such resolution is
necessarily fleeting; value is unstable and hoarding, like fetishism,
is rooted in conflicting perspectives about value. The ambivalence
expressed by the subjects of *Possessed* shows how these conflicts
take root not only between individuals but also within them, and
over time.

The ambivalence is particularly evident in "Control" and "Submission" in the ascription of increasing agency to objects: "It's
starting to take over" becomes an uncanny refrain in the film. In
a different idiom, new materialism takes up the ways in which
matter eludes human agency and cognition.[4] Broadly speaking,
new materialist thought attempts to escape binaries that structure
Western metaphysics and capitalism and to put critical pressure
on the cultural turn that seemed—in caricature—to render the
materiality of the world an effect of language. Jane Bennett's vital
materialism, for example, proposes a world composed not of inert
matter transformed by human labor but of "actants" that can produce effects and change the course of events. In place of hoarder
and hoard, Bennett sees a "hoard-assemblage" marked by porous
boundaries between human and nonhuman matter. Bill Brown's

thing theory, and more broadly, his decades-long attention to the "material unconscious" of literary and visual texts, is better able to speak to the practices of acquiring and keeping that result in hoards because he maintains some distinction between human and nonhuman matter and between subject and object, even as he troubles the threshold between the two. In his introduction to the 2001 special issue of *Critical Inquiry* titled "Things," Brown distinguishes between an *object*, which participates unobtrusively in the experience of being-in the-world, and a *thing*, which provokes a confrontation with materiality. The "thingness" latent in every object becomes evident on contingent occasions when its materiality intrudes. A pen that runs out of ink, a printer that jams, or a picture that tilts confronts us with a materiality that exceeds our intentionality and use.

Brown understands modernism—across literary and visual arts—as the aesthetic work of attending to or provoking the intrusions of material, of liberating thingness from the "fetters of modernity."[5] Modernity, he argues, subjugates matter to human ends; modernism is the aesthetic project of making manifest the indomitability of matter to reveal the limits of modernity. That formulation helps to explain the compatibility between the push and pull of modernity and its artistic movements and the scenes of control and submission that Hampton documents in *Possessed* and that characterize obsessive-compulsive and impulse-control disorders. The disruptions of use and order represented by what Brown calls "thinging"—bringing out the thingness of an object (i.e., its alterity)—are *symptomatically* vexing to those who suffer from obsessive-compulsive and related disorders.[6] Given that the intrusions of "thingness" that define modernism for Brown overlap with the irregularities intolerable to those who suffer from obsessive-compulsive and related disorders, it is unsurprising that scholars have proposed strong correlations between obsession and modernity. Lennard Davis, for example, writes: "To be obsessive is . . . to be modern."[7] He underscores the exceptional concentration of energy that is associated with success in a range of areas: "We live in a culture that wants its love affairs obsessive, its artists obsessed, its genius fixated, its music driven, its athletes devoted."[8] Davis understands obsession as an extraordinary concentration of energy, a monomaniacal passion. But as Hampton's film, and the other texts I discuss in this chapter show, that concentration of energy, that consuming passion, consumes the impassioned in cases of hoarding and its precursors, beginning with bibliomania.

Bibliomania to Monomania

The sense of being possessed by possessions becomes increasingly insistent beginning in the nineteenth century, as collections spilled forth from curiosity cabinets, grand galleries, and the personal libraries of bibliomaniacs into the annals of medicine, where all sorts of object-oriented manias and maniacs began to accumulate.[9] Those "possessed" by the material world appeared to early nineteenth-century psychiatrists to be suffering from some form of the ailment Jean-Étienne Dominique Esquirol named "monomania."[10] The French psychiatrist began using the term in around 1810 to describe repetitive and intrusive thoughts or actions: obsessions and compulsions.[11] Monomania, like its precursor, "partial insanity," left mental functioning unimpaired in all but one area.[12] It was a form of insanity that could affect a large segment of the population, even those who appeared to be in full possession of their mental faculties.[13] This relegation of madness to some small corner of the mind held great appeal for contemporary writers, as did the linguistic affinity between "monomania" and "bibliomania," which had been in use for more than 150 years to describe the passionate, disordered extremes of book collecting. Monomania quickly swept through literary circles in France and beyond; writers began using the word to refer to a harmless quirk in the form of a fanatical enthusiasm for one subject.[14] Despite the speedy diffusion of monomania in nonspecialist writings, the term was soon replaced in psychiatric writings by a spate of subtypes: manias and phobias "enriched by nearly all the roots of the Greek dictionary" in what Max Nordau dismissed as an exercise of "philologico-medical trifling."[15] Some of these ills relate specifically to objects and overlap considerably with hoarding: in addition to bibliomania, there was kleptomania (first called klopemania), oniomania (compulsive shopping), and various collecting manias.[16] Psychiatrists after Esquirol diagnosed kleptomania, oniomania, collectomania, and klepto-collecting in people who seemed unable to control themselves around objects; they, like the hoarder of "Submission," could not help but to steal, buy, or gather. In these manias, the exercise of the aesthetic judgment of taste is transformed into something ego-dystonic—that is, discordant with ego aims and ideals—something "sort of a bit spooky," as the subject of Hampton's "Control" describes it.

The emergence of so many object-oriented manias in the course of the long nineteenth century attests to anxiety about agency that haunts the willful subject of modernity in his confrontation with stuff. This chapter traces that anxiety about agency from bibliomania to hoarding disorder. My attention to this history of object-oriented manias marks a departure from recent studies of hoarding in the humanities and social sciences, which have settled on a genealogy of the diagnostic criteria that begins with the 1993 publication of "The Hoarding of Possessions" by Randy Frost and Rachel Gross. While that article introduces questions of etiology and classification that chart a clear pathway to the inclusion of hoarding disorder in the *DSM-5* in 2013, my attention to the longer, interdisciplinary history of the diagnostic category brings into focus heterogenous thematic threads entangled in hoarding today. I demonstrate the conflation, in hoarding discourse, of the poetic disposition that defines modernism for Brown with the faltering will of the subject of modernity. Before Virginia Woolf, James Joyce, and Carlo Emilio Gadda made literary praxes of hoarding, fin-de-siècle psychiatrists Giovanni Mingazzini and Sante de Sanctis observed obsessive forms of collecting in patients who were seized by inexplicable urges to gather up and stash away twigs and other worthless items.[17]

At the intersection of bibliomania and monomania and of literary and scientific texts, the drama of a will that falters before the object world begins to unfold. Physiologists, alienists, philosophers, and criminologists came up with various explanations for such weakened wills—degeneration and hysteria (along with menstruation, pregnancy, and lactation) were the most common.[18] After surveying these theories, I turn to Freud, who sets aside physiological explanations to develop psychodynamic—that is, narrative—accounts of obsessions and phobias. In an 1895 paper written in French, Freud makes obsessions and phobias a product of mental disordering, a mésalliance of mismatching of ideas, feelings, and actions.

In his 1752 article on bibliomania for the *Encyclopédie*, Jean-Baptiste le Rond d'Alembert makes disordered keeping a function of disuse.[19] The modern history of bibliomania heralded by the encyclopedia entry is apposite to a study of hoarding today because of the distinct relationship between a book's use, which resides primarily in the immaterial, reproducible text, and its material form, which is what captivates collectors, maniacal, and otherwise.[20] For

Walter Benjamin, use is fundamentally at odds with collecting—no matter what the object. "What is decisive in collecting," he writes, "is that the object is detached from all its original functions to enter into the closest conceivable relation with objects of the same kind. This relation is the diametric opposite of utility."[21] Printed books are notable as collectors' objects because their use—reading the reproducible text—is already divorced from the material form of any single copy. The rift between the medium and message—that is, between the possession and use of books—is redoubled in literary texts about bibliomania that relate the travails of the bibliomaniac to the heroic feats narrated in the pages of his tomes.

Whereas the problem with bibliomania for enlightenment writers—for example, d'Alembert and Cesare Beccaria—rests primarily in its removal of books from use, in early nineteenth-century Britain, Romantics relished in the discerning taste of book collectors. By the 1830s, the popularization of the diagnostic category Esquirol invented is evident in literary treatments of bibliomania. Both Gustave Flaubert and Charles Nodier write of bibliomaniacs ruined—financially, socially, and morally—by their unrestrained passions. Already in fourteenth-century Florence, Petrarch recognized that reading too many books can be edifying or dangerous, leading some to knowledge and others to madness.[22] The modern history of bibliomania reveals the extent to which too many books, as physical objects, are no less able to reap refinement and ruin.

In his *Encyclopédie* article, d'Alembert defines bibliomania as "the mad desire to own books and to [amass] them." For the collector who lacks discernment, d'Alembert writes, the love of books—as objects removed from use—results in bizarre amassments rooted in a misrecognition of value: "It would be a little like the madness of a man who piles up five or six diamonds under a heap of stones." Although bibliomania is, for d'Alembert, more disorder than madness, it is close enough to merit the comparison. D'Alembert's primary objection to the bibliomaniac rests in his failure to use books "as a philosopher does."[23] To appreciate the "true value" of a book is to recognize what is good and what is bad in the words and ideas it delivers. Whereas Richard Heber (1773–1833), an avid British book collector and the dedicatee of multiple early nineteenth-century works about bibliomania, claimed that it was not possible to live comfortably without three copies of each book (one for display, one for use, and one to make available to friends), d'Alembert approves of books used only for reading or sharing with friends. He reserves particular scorn for the collector who declines to use his own books, and so ends up borrowing from friends copies of books that he already owns. D'Alembert's assessment of such behavior as a "highly sordid avarice" is predicated on the idea that use would diminish the value of books and that, therefore, their value rests primarily in the material form that is subject to wear.

In contrast to such greed, d'Alembert offers the example of "one of the brightest minds of this century," who managed to acquire a "highly select library" that consisted only of what was worth reading.[24] The discriminating librarian d'Alembert commends would reduce, for example, a twelve-volume work to a mere six pages, throwing the rest to the fire. D'Alembert praises this approach: "This way of forming a library would suit me very well."[25] That might seem like a bizarre statement for the coeditor of a seventeen-volume encyclopedia to make, but the encyclopedia itself is one such library, a distillation of all of human knowledge into a concise and useful form.

Not long after the publication of the Italian translation of the *Encyclopédie*, Beccaria, best known for his treatise *Of Crimes and Punishments*, wrote a short poem titled "Il bibliomane."[26] Like d'Alembert, Beccaria took issue with bibliomania because it entailed making books decorative objects rather than reading and studying them. For the Enlightenment thinker, the thick darkness of so many piled up books seemed an affront to the luminosity contained within: "What value is there, if amidst such bright luminaries / He delights only in thick darkness / If, of the countless volumes / He contents himself with the external cover / Without ever having read or touched them / And sates his eyes with their ornaments and colors alone?"[27] Like his contemporaries in France, Beccaria scorns the bibliomaniac's attention to the physical properties of books: covers, ornaments, and colors. But the engagement with books that Beccaria urges is also rooted in an appreciation of the material form—in addition to reading the immaterial text, the true book lover establishes contact between his body and the physical form of the book by penetrating its cover and touching its pages.

The first decade of the nineteenth century in Britain saw the emergence of an elite culture of book collecting. Rather than disdaining bibliomaniacs for failing to make proper use of books by reading them, writers celebrated the zeal and good taste of passionate collectors. In 1809, the Scottish doctor John Ferriar dedicated a mock-heroic poem to Heber, titled *The Bibliomania*. The poem begins by asking, "What wild desires, what restless torments seize the hapless man, who feels the book-disease?"[28] Ferriar likens book collecting to erotic conquest, describing the wistful glances and aching eyes of the dedicatee, and the "tempting charms" and sumptuous attire of volumes robed in blue and gold, or red morocco.[29] The private library becomes a stage for romance; ubiquitous comparisons between book acquisition and erotic conquest forge homosocial bonds between male collectors.[30] Although he medicalizes bibliomania, calling it "the book-disease," Ferriar also heaps ironic praise on Heber, whom he considers to be blessed "with talents, wealth and taste." Ferriar playfully names his dedicatee the beneficiary of the labor of scribes and bookbinders: "For you the Monk illum'd his pictur'd page, / For you the press defies the Spoils of age," as well as the toils of literary heroes and philosophers: "FAUSTUS for you infernal tortures bore, / For you ERASMUS starv'd on Adria's shore."[31] At once the hero of romantic and epic feats of collecting and the ultimate object of the toils of Faust, Erasmus, scribe and illuminator, the bibliomaniac occupies an overdetermined morphological position. The fictional world of the poem spills forth from tomes, saturating reality with a material and narrative plenitude. The bibliomaniac is hero and prize, subject and object, lover and beloved; an actor in the worlds of fiction and reality. Bibliomania saturates the mock epic with indecision that anticipates Freudian fetishism, collapsing boundaries between the fictional world and reality.

The same year that Ferriar published his mock-heroic poem, the English bibliographer Thomas Frognall Dibdin responded with an epistle to Heber in the form of a mock treatise *The Bibliomania; or, Book-Madness; Containing Some Account of the History, Symptoms, and Cure of This Fatal Disease.* In the preface, Dibdin praises Ferriar for recognizing an illness that had escaped the sagacity of "ancient and modern Physicians," and for depicting it with such pleasing rhymes. He finds the poem disappointing, however, because it lacks "rules for the choice of books," as well as "curious, apposite, and amusing anecdotes."[32] The work Dibdin pens surpasses Ferriar's mock-heroic poem both in its pseudo-medical sketch of book collecting and, more important, in its copious detail: example after example of accomplished collectors and fine manuscripts. Dibdin's style, marked by a stringing together of digression after digression, a piling up of text atop "confused and indigested [foot] notes"—embodies, in less than one hundred pages, a poetics of accumulation.[33] The text thematizes, performs, and even nurtures bibliomania, offering counsel for novice and expert bibliophiles.

The structural mania of Dibdin's work is evident, for example, in a sentence acknowledging the charms of poetry that vexed his decision to write in prose. The sentence spreads across five pages, hovering above the ample notes it prompts (referenced here with parenthetical numbers): "Whoever undertakes to write down the follies which grow out of an excessive attachment to any particular pursuit, be that pursuit horses (3), hawks, dogs, guns, snuff boxes (4), old china, coins, or rusty armor, may be thought to have little consulted the best means of ensuring success for his labors, when he adopts the dull vehicle of *Prose* for the communication of his ideas; not considering that from *Poetry* ten thousand bright scintillations are struck off, which please and convince while they attract and astonish." The note on horses, which includes material on hawks, is composed of more than 500 words. The note names the first British book on sports of the field, *Hunting and Hawking*, and commends the perfect copy owned by Lord Spencer, who would later hire Dibdin to purchase books for the library at Althorp.[34] After praising the collection of Frederick the Great, the note on snuffboxes surveys other prized curiosities: "It may gratify a Bibliographer to find that there are other MANIAS beside that of the book." All manias seem to lead Dibdin back to that of the book: the collection of curiosities of John White of Newgate Street, addressed in the same note, for example, included "some very uncommon books."[35] In notes like this one, books intrude, conveying an insistent, obsessive quality of bibliomania.

The tendency toward amplification that distinguishes the style of the 1809 treatise—with all its digressions and notes—is made explicit in the conclusion, a flippant call for collaboration: "Let it be the task of more experienced bibliographers to correct and amplify the forgoing outline!"[36] Two years after the publication of *The Bibliomania*, the call for amplification is realized in a second volume bearing a similar title, *Bibliomania, or, Book Madness: A Bibliographical Romance, in Six Parts*, which counts more than 700 pages, including the reproduction of the first *Bibliomania*, as well as extensive indexes and notes. The longer *Bibliographical Romance* is organized into a series of dialogues set in spaces full of books. In the preliminary chapter, "An Evening Walk," two gentlemen, Lysander and Philemon, arrive at a country estate and begin discussing books and reading with their host. Their conversation continues in the cabinet, the auction room, library, drawing room, and alcove. The dialogues are overwhelmed by the bibliographic notes, which list both the books found in the spaces and those that arise in conversation. The abundance of books crowding the spaces is mimed by the typography, which deluges the dialogue with references.

Dibdin's bibliographic writings foster a mode of reading prone to interruptions and calculated to elicit the desires of aspiring bibliophiles. Both works on bibliomania play a critical role in defining and propagating the culture of book collecting and endowing it with the luster of a noble pursuit. Just as Ferriar noted Heber's wealth (along with his talent and taste), the bibliomania Dibdin diagnoses affects "higher and middling classes of society" and is "almost uniformly confined to the male sex."[37] Not only does bibliomania afflict the aristocracy; but, like other forms of collecting, it is harmonious with the temporal idea of aristocracy: time ennobles people and lends value to things, rather than enfeebling people and degrading things.[38]

The idea of book collecting Dibdin develops rests not only in the wealth and good taste he attributes to those who practice it but also in the potential for prodigious finds, chance encounters that result in unexpected riches. For d'Alembert, the bibliomaniac resembles the madman who keeps a couple of diamonds mixed up in a pile of stones, whereas for Dibdin, the bibliomaniac is a cunning connoisseur blessed by chance. The tantalizing union, in *Bibliomania*, of the collector's good taste and the gambler's good luck helped to create wild anticipation for the 1812 auctions of the library of the Duke of Roxburghe, who had died in 1804. In the 1811 work, Dibdin gives an account of the provenance of the most valuable volume in the Roxburghe collection, a copy of Giovanni Boccaccio's *Decameron*, printed by Christophorus Valdarfer in 1471:

> In one of the libraries abroad, belonging to the Jesuits, there was a volume entitled, on the back of it, *"Concilium Tridenti"*: The searching eye and active hands of a well-educated Bibliomaniac discovered and opened this volume—when lo! instead of the Council of Trent, appeared the *First*, and almost unknown, edition of the *Decameron* of Boccaccio! This precious volume is now reposing upon the deserted shelves of the late Duke of Roxburghe's library; and, at the forth-coming sale of the same, it will be most rigorously contended for by all the higher and more knowing powers of the bibliographical world![39]

Dibdin's advertisement seems to have worked: the Marquis of Blandford—winning a bidding war against his cousin, the 2nd Earl Spencer—paid the record-breaking price of £2,260 for the Valdarfer *Decameron*.[40] The evening of the sale, several prominent book collectors—including Dibdin, Spencer, and Blandford—founded the Roxburghe Club, an elite association whose membership would also include Heber. Walter Scott, who joined the Club in 1822, recognized Dibdin's essential role in spreading bibliomania: "I fear you are a bad physician and rather encourage the disease than cure it."[41] Dibdin remained a prominent bard of bibliomania, even writing a *Bibliographical Decameron* in 1817 with anecdotes of rare books and momentous sales, including that of the Valdarfer *Decameron*.[42] In his 1832 *Bibliophobia,* written under the pseudonym Mercurius Rusticus, Dibdin happily relates a sequel to the Roxburghe auction: the 2nd Earl Spencer purchased the volume in 1819 for less than half the sum paid by his rival five years earlier.[43]

In addition to helping to make bibliomania fashionable in an elite British milieu in the early 1800s, Dibdin develops a style suited to the subject, in which the reader's attention to the immaterial text is frequently interrupted by the insistence of the material one. The typographical result of the "confused and indigested notes" advertised in the 1809 treatise is a mésalliance of text and note so that reading requires an unusual frequency of turning back and forth between pages. The work is hoard-like not only in its magnitude and in its disorder—the mismatching of text and note—but also in its "possessive realism"; Dibdin indexes a material world that is available for ownership. Although he reserves scorn for the book vendor who authors grandiloquent catalogs: "a great and bold carpenter of words: overcharging the description of his own volumes with tropes, metaphors, flourishes, and common place authorities,"[44] his bibliographical works are no less full of flourish, nor are they any less calculated to excite the desires of collectors.

Dibdin's writings are not catalogs, but the synecdochic the mode of reading they elicit is similar to that which art critic and collector Mario Praz conveys with superlative: "I assure you that no reading has ever compelled me to such quick and decisive action as the reading of an interesting catalogue."[45] Umberto Eco—himself an avid book collector whose passion verged on mania—describes the roguish pleasure he finds in such reading: "To read catalogs means to discover unintended details, and so to switch from a pulp detective novel in which the killer is the butler to the unpublished crime story in which the writer is the victim and the reader is the gentleman thief."[46] In the mystery of the catalog, the victim is the naive narrator who has unwittingly exposed a secret treasure, a scenario that recalls the discovery of the Valdarfer *Decameron* by the "searching eye and active hands of well-educated Bibliomaniac."[47] Catalogs, like Dibdin's bibliographical writings, elicit a kind of reading that resembles fetishism insofar as it privileges part over whole and entails zeroing in on a particular detail.[48]

Dibdin and Ferriar treat bibliomania with playful ambivalence, characterizing it as a heroic—or at least worthy—endeavor, more eccentricity than illness. Two decades later, in France, bibliomania—and the literature it inspires—transforms to coincide more closely with the increasingly widespread diagnosis of monomania. While in Ferriar and Dibdin's Britain, the bibliomaniac is an aesthete whose diagnostic sobriquet conveys friendly jest, Nodier and Flaubert present bibliomaniacs with wonder and pity. In 1836, when he was almost fifteen, Flaubert wrote "Bibliomanie," a story based on a report published earlier that year in the *Gazette des tribunaux* about the murder trial of a monk who owned an antiquarian bookshop in Barcelona. During the trial, the defendant was alerted to the existence of a second copy of an incunabulum he owned and thought to be unique; he flew into a rage so terrible as to convince the judge of his guilt.[49] In Flaubert's telling, the bibliomaniac conforms to the medical profile of monomania: "This passion had entirely absorbed him. He scarcely ate, he no longer slept, but he dreamed whole days and nights of his fixed idea: books."[50] Bibliomania, for Flaubert, was not the learned passion of a cultural elite whose collections were testament to refinement. Rather, he returns to the enlightenment disdain of book collecting as a passion divorced from the use of books: "He scarcely knew how to read." Flaubert's bibliomaniac is a Faustian figure who abandons God for books, and then hands over even his soul: "He had been a monk, and for books he had abandoned God. Later he sacrificed for them that which men hold dearest after their God: money. Then he gave to books that which people treasure next to money: his soul."[51] Though convicted of murder, the defendant in Flaubert's story is guilty only of being so devoted to books that he cannot muster the energy to defend himself. After the verdict is delivered, the bibliomaniac borrows the second copy of the incunabulum from his defense attorney and, weeping, tears it up.

In 1831, Nodier published the short story "Le Bibliomane," which begins: "You all remember good Théodore, upon whose grave I just placed flowers."[52] Nodier's bibliomaniac—like the books he pursues—is a relic of the past, one worthy of commemoration. In life, Théodore was so consumed by his passion for books that all other interests dissolved into the single fixation, and so he becomes a caricature of monomania. If he glanced at a woman, it was only to take note of what she wore on her feet, and then to lament the waste of fine leather that might have been used to bind books. He considers global diplomacy only in relation to the resulting fluctuations in the price of leather and paper.

Nine years later, Nodier published "The Book Lover," setting out a taxonomy of characters of the "age of paper": bouquinistes, bibliophiles, bibliophobes, and bibliomaniacs. Through a series of aphorisms, he distinguishes bibliophilia from bibliomania as selection to accumulation, order to disorder, care to neglect, and minutia to mass—binaries that recur in recent attempts to distinguish between collecting and hoarding: "The bibliophile selects books; the bibliomaniac amasses them. The bibliophile examines each book carefully and keeps it in its place on the shelf; the bibliomaniac piles up book upon book, without even looking at them. . . . The bibliophile works with a magnifying glass, the bibliomaniac with a measuring stick."[53]

The restraint of bibliophilia can give way to the excesses of mania: "The bibliophile often becomes a bibliomaniac when his mind deteriorates or his fortunes increase—two grave afflictions suffered by the best of men, though the first is much more common than the second." Making wealth analogous to mental deterioration as a causal factor, Nodier scoffs at the prestige bibliomania had achieved among British Romantics. His disdain anticipates the strengthened associations between aristocracy and degeneration that will take shape over the course of the century, as well as their fin-de-siècle literary and aesthetic correlates, decadence and *crepuscolarismo* (the twilight school). For Nodier, the decay of the bibliophile's mind is mirrored by a civilizational decline: "The bibliophile is no longer found among the elevated classes of our *progressing* society (and I beg your pardon for using this hideous gerund)."[54]

Nodier draws attention to books as physical objects dangerous in their ensemble. He names one book collector in particular: Antoine-Marie-Henri Boulard, once a "sensitive and scrupulous bibliophile," who descended into the throes of bibliomania and amassed some 600,000 volumes in his six-story Paris home. In Nodier's description, the books transform into precarious building materials: "piled like the stones of Cyclopean walls" to form "poorly supported obelisks." Nodier recalls a frightening visit to the bibliomaniac's home when, in response to a question about a particular title, "Boulard looked at me fixedly, with that gracious and humorous air of good-fellowship which was characteristic of him, and, rapping with his gold-headed cane on one of the huge stacks (*rudis indigestaque moles*) [rough and undigested mass], then on a second and third, said, 'It's there—or there—or there.'"[55] Quoting Ovid's description of Chaos, Nodier emphasizes that the tomes have become indistinguishable, but also suggests that they hold potential both as sources of learning and as raw material for metamorphoses.

> The gigantic stacks, their uncertain equilibrium shaken by the tapping of M. Boulard's cane, were swaying threateningly on their bases, the summits vibrating like the pinnacles of a Gothic cathedral at the sound of the bells or the impact of a storm. Dragging M. Boulard with me, I fled before Ossa could collapse upon Pelion. Even today, when I think how near I came to being struck by a whole series of the Bollandist publications on my head from a height of twenty feet, I cannot recall the danger I was in without pious horror. It would be an abuse of the word to apply the name "library" to menacing mountains of books which have to be attacked with a miner's pick and held in place by stanchions![56]

Bibliomania remakes fine books as raw materials used in unsteady constructions; they are Cyclopean walls, insecure obelisks, Gothic towers, and mines. When bibliophilia deteriorates into bibliomania, it becomes "an acute illness bordering on delirium." When it reaches that fatal point of paroxysm, all connection to the intellect is severed, and the accumulation of books could be mistaken for any other mania.[57] At this point, what once appeared to be an intellectual exercise of taste becomes a manifestation of anatomical difference. Nodier calls on phrenologists to "discover the collector's instinct . . . within the encasing of bone that houses our poor brain."[58]

The medical community took note: just two years later, in *La Médecine des Passions* (*Medicine of the Passions*), the French physician Jean Baptiste Félix Descuret cites Nodier's essay and expands on his account of Boulard.[59] Nodier is more interested in the menacing amassment that results from Boulard's obsession with books, but Descuret focuses on the praxis of the mania and its etiology. He considers bibliomania to be the slowest to lead to complete ruin and the most seductive among the collecting manias, which include passions for stamps, military pins, porcelain tableware, coins, snuffboxes, and shells. Boulard, in Descuret's account, was a religious man of good taste and learning, a highly respected notary who left his practice to his son and dedicated himself to books. Collecting became a daily routine: he would wander among stalls and stores and would never return home without a stack of books. Boulard's sensible wife urged him to read at least some of the books on his shelves before purchasing more, but the bibliomaniac would not listen. He became sullen and crotchety and began buying books on credit and hiding his purchases from his wife. Once, he stayed out all night out of shame at having ordered three carts worth of books. When he finally returned home, his wife made him swear off any further purchases. Boulard agreed, but abstaining from his one passion, he lost his appetite and fell seriously ill. Only his physician suspected that the cause of the mysterious illness was nostalgia for book buying. To cure the ailing bibliomaniac, Boulard's wife and doctor devised a plan; they invited a vendor to set up a stall and call out his wares just below the patient's window.[60] The siren's call gave Boulard the strength needed to rise from bed; he visited the stall and joyfully returned to his old ways.

Descuret emphasizes the economic futility of Boulard's bibliomania: the 600,000 or so volumes on which the former notary squandered most of his fortune were sold for next to nothing after his death in 1825. The physician also notes, contradictorily, that for years after Boulard's death, his books flooded the Parisian market, causing a drop in prices. The account concludes with a detail that Descuret deems most interesting from a medical perspective: one room in the home had been barricaded shut; when movers broke down the door, they discovered obscene and morally corrupt works. The physician concludes that Boulard, a religious man, had purchased the vile works with the intention of burning them. Because of his passion for books, however, he had put off the unbearable act of penance indefinitely. At the core of the notable case of bibliomania, then, is the tragedy of a hero whose moral rectitude is undone by his fatal flaw of loving too much. In Descuret's interpretation, the bibliomania is constitutional, Boulard's failure to burn the obscene books is but a symptom. But one might just as well have reached a conclusion that reverses the causality; the drive to acquire ever-more tomes was the result of a desire to bury ever-deeper the shameful secret at its core. Boulard became a cause célèbre in Paris; the awe-inspiring magnitude of his collection and the obsession from which it resulted still generated interest in literary and medical communities long after his death; Flaubert even gave the name Boulard to the bookseller who sends a parcel to the convalescent Emma Bovary.[61]

Object-Oriented Manias

The compulsive, all-consuming nature of Boulard's bibliomania is also evident in forms of kleptomania. In 1816, the Swiss psychiatrist André Matthey first diagnosed the monomania, naming it "klopemania." Though subsequent writers rename the diagnosis "kleptomania," "the stealing monomania," and then "magasinitis," some basic features remain unchanged: the compulsion to steal is divorced from need and generally experienced as ego-dystonic.[62] The first case Matthey relates is that of a wealthy young woman endowed with a healthy spirit and a good character, save for her frequent impulses to take whatever crossed her path: gloves, handkerchiefs, and various other knickknacks. Fearful of discovery and ashamed of her habit, she prayed to God to help her stop, but remained helpless when an opportunity presented itself. Matthey's other examples include King Victor Amadeus of Sardinia, the wife of a German physician and chemist, and a well-raised Alsatian soldier who was hanged for his petty thieving. Matthey discusses one case marked by pathologized keeping as well as taking. A government employee in Vienna stole so many household utensils that he had to rent two extra rooms for them; he never used the stolen goods, nor did he have any intention of selling them. Though he does not offer much detail about the etiology of klopemania, Matthey emphasizes that it is a form of partial insanity exhibited by people who otherwise appear to be in full possession of their faculties.

The sixth, and last, of Matthey's examples is drawn from Johann Kaspar Lavater's *Essays on Physiognomy*, published between 1775 and 1778. Lavater describes the case of a physician who suffered from an inexplicable compulsion to steal from his patients. So unwitting were the doctor's misdeeds that he would forget about the keys, snuffboxes, scissors, thimbles, spectacles, buckles, spoons, and other trinkets that ended up in his possession. Lavater declares the physician to be unfortunate rather than wicked, assuring his readers that the involuntary, mechanical gestures would be as innocent, in the eyes of God, as any other "indifferent, thoughtless action."[63] He speculates that the compulsion could be traced to the physician's mother, who must have been afflicted with a strong urge to steal while she was pregnant.[64] Although Matthey offers four examples of male thieves and only two of women, kleptomania subsequently comes to be associated almost exclusively with young women of means who could afford to buy the things they stole.[65] Physicians and psychiatrists attributed the urge to steal to the hormonal fluctuations of pregnancy, lactation, menstruation, and menopause.[66]

Both Lavater and Matthey write before department stores changed the scale and scope of shopping as a leisure activity. Like contemporary forms of hoarding, the compulsive stealing Matthey describes does not have immediate commercial relevance.[67] In 1840, C. C. H. Marc introduced kleptomania as a possible mitigating factor in legal proceedings as kleptomaniacs bear little or no responsibility for their unwitting behavior. This medicalization of stealing contributes to the reproduction of social hierarchies; irrationality is reserved for those of means. As Wilhelm Stekel writes: "Cynics have maintained that theft is kleptomania if the offender is rich or has political influence."[68]

The French psychiatrist Valentin Magnan coined "oniomania"— from the Greek *ónios* for sell, and *mania*—to name an uncontrollable, obsessive urge to buy things.[69] Magnan's buying mania was a hereditary affliction, transmitted with increasing intensity, in his example, from grandmother to father to son.[70] Oniomania is an important precursor to hoarding in part because Nordau writes that the pathology Magnan identified offers a new way of understanding excessive acquisition not as an exercise of taste, but as evidence of degeneration: "The present rage for collecting, the piling up, in dwellings, of aimless bric-a-brac, . . . appear[s] to us in a completely new light."[71] Nordau contrasts oniomaniacs to those who "fancy themselves millionaires," whose spending is a conscious expression of their aspirations and their "delusion as to their own greatness"—in short, those whose shopping is ego-syntonic. The oniomaniac, for Nordau, is instead someone who, like the hoarder of "Submission," is "simply unable to pass by any lumber without feeling an impulse to acquire it."[72]

In his study of the gathering and keeping practices among patients confined in an asylum, Mingazzini brings the growing scholarship on kleptomania to bear on irrational forms of collecting. He classifies the obsessive behaviors he observes based on whether the objects gathered and kept were of one kind or many—"mono-klepto-collecting," "poli-klepto-collecting," and "poli-klepto-mono-collecting." Unlike the kleptomania that afflicted bourgeois young women in major city centers where shopping had become a popular leisure activity, the klepto-collecting Mingazzini observes directly is limited to the things of little or no value—twigs, strings, leaves—available to his subjects, who were confined in asylums. He emphasizes the prevalence of gathering practices among the institutionalized: "It is well known to all who possess even limited experience with asylums that there are inmates who exhibit a constant tendency to gather the most useless objects that have been abandoned in their dwellings."[73] Mingazzini concurs with the diagnosis of kleptomania in cases where the stolen goods are abandoned or returned to the rightful owner as soon as the patient comes to his senses—that is, in cases in which kleptomania seems to be not only limited in scope (as in partial insanity), but also in time (as in temporary insanity). He also notices that a number of patients at the asylum stash away whatever odds and ends they pick up. The conclusion Mingazzini reaches from the study of eighty-eight patients—that degeneration is in large part to blame for the object practices he observes—is consistent with the theories of his contemporaries. What is remarkable about his study is its ambit: Mingazzini considers practices of getting and keeping various objects, noting the age, gender, and diagnosis of the patients, as well as whether they experience agitation or distress when the objects are taken away.

Sante de Sanctis offers a different interpretation of ego-dystonic forms of collecting in an 1897 paper titled "Collezionismo e impulsi collezionistici" ("Collecting and Compulsive Collecting"), which establishes a link between alcohol consumption and compulsive collecting. The paper centers on the case of a sixty-three-year-old woman who had long suffered from nervous disorders, but who sought treatment for a bizarre habit she had developed. About four months earlier, she had been seized by a compulsion to gather all sorts of detritus—scraps of food, hair, bones, straw, rags—which she stored in a secret area of her home. The collecting was ego-dystonic—she considered it to be madness and dismissed the items she saved as "all that crap."[74] She also confessed—reluctantly, and with some shame—that she often stashed things away out of a fear that her neighbors might use them against her in some act of witchcraft. Although she knew that this was not possible, she nonetheless could not rid herself of the idea that she had to keep the detritus from ending up in the wrong hands. Such details led de Sanctis to suspect that her "compulsive fixation on gathering" is different from other forms of collecting; it was something "primitive," a sort of "psychic tic." De Sanctis's patient collects useless filthy detritus because she is seized by a mania to do so and cannot help it.

Pressing for more details about the "curious, inexplicable phenomenon," de Sanctis learns that his patient had found wine to be a useful remedy for ongoing anxiety and that she had been drinking wine every day since roughly the time that the strange collecting behaviors began. Noting that "obsessions and ... compulsions develop in minds weakened by intoxication," de Sanctis prescribes complete abstention from alcohol.[75] Within fifteen to twenty days, the collecting stopped, though the patient continued to feel urges to gather things and continued to suspect her neighbors of ill will.

De Sanctis remains troubled by the case. Because the patient's paranoid thoughts and accompanying compulsion to collect persist even after she stops drinking and collecting, he realizes that alcohol was not the cause of the "collectomania" but only an exacerbating factor. What causes this ego-dystonic form of collecting, then? De Sanctis distinguishes between "instinctive" collecting, found in "animals, idiots, the insane, epileptics, drunks, children, and the senile" and "collecting with obsessive ideas and rationales" like the patient's paranoid fantasies about her neighbors.[76] In such cases, collecting is a symptom of something opaque; it cannot be attributed to hormones, degeneration, or alcohol nor can it be considered an exercise of taste. De Sanctis offers no definitive explanation, and the case opens onto a disordered psychic expanse governed not by the ego or by physiological factors but, as Freud will aver, by the significance of particular objects and by obsession-generating mésalliances.[77]

Objects and Obsessions

In his writing about possessions, Freud tends to be more interested in the significance of single objects than in collections or accumulations. In *The Interpretation of Dreams* (1899), collecting seems so unremarkable a diversion of libidinal energy that it serves as a paradigm of obviousness. "When a lonely maid transfers her affection to animals; or a bachelor becomes an enthusiastic collector," Freud explains, "these are instances of psychical displacements to which we raise no objection."[78] Though these ego-syntonic attachments may represent diversions of libidinal energy from the narrow road to genital sexuality, they move along well-cleared pathways. Perhaps these substitutes—animals instead of a husband, objects instead of a wife—also seemed unremarkable to Freud since he was a passionate collector of more than 3,000 Greek, Roman, Egyptian, and Chinese figurines and other objects.[79] The clutter of antiquities in his office was sufficient to make some visitors nervous. In *The Psychopathology of Everyday Life* (1901), he writes: "Shortage of space in my study has often forced me to handle a number of pottery and stone antiquities (of which I have a small collection) in the most uncomfortable positions, so that onlookers have expressed anxiety that I should knock something down and break it." As a rule, Freud dismisses their concerns—"That however has never happened"— though he provides examples of exceptional occasions when he did break objects in symptomatic "accidents," as when he knocked the marble cover off his inkpot. Just a few hours earlier, his sister had visited and remarked: "Your writing table looks really attractive now; only the inkstand doesn't match. You must get a nicer one."[80] Freud interpreted her words to signal an intention to give him a new inkstand, and so he performed the seemingly clumsy but actually "exceedingly adroit and well-directed" movement that shattered the marble cover. He offers other examples of targets for such "accidental" acts of destruction; in each case, they are motivated by the significance of the object rather than the cumbersome abundance.

Although these examples deal explicitly with collecting, Freud's discussions of obsessional-neuroses and obsessional symptoms (including fetishism) are more pertinent to the object-oriented manias charted above and to the recent emergence of hoarding as a disorder and a symptom. In 1895, Freud began to challenge the hegemony of degeneration as a causal explanation for various mental processes, noting that relevant symptoms could be more productively understood through the detective work of tracing affects back to the thoughts and memories from which they originated.[81] He proposed that persistent, unwanted ideas—obsessions and phobias—result not from degeneration but from a mésalliance. To ward off a distressing idea, the neurotic separates it from the associated emotions. The idea is repressed and the free-floating affect is left to attach itself to another idea which, charged with this "false connection," becomes obsessional. The mismatching of thoughts and feelings—the disorder itself—is generative; it rouses the intrusive, unwanted force of obsession.

Neurotics, for Freud, are not susceptible to "possession" because of degeneration, intoxication, or just having a uterus and all that goes with it, but because of the disorder of thoughts, feelings, and actions, mismatched, and in cluttered disarray. When, for example, a medical student reproaches himself for all sorts of immoral acts—murder, incest, arson—Freud surmises that feelings of guilt were prompted by his having read in a medical textbook that masturbation causes moral degradation. The student blamed himself for the depraved acts in place of the one of which he was actually guilty. In 1905, Freud announced a definitive rejection of the utility of the concept of degeneration: "It has become the fashion to regard any symptom which is not obviously due to trauma or infection as a sign of degeneracy. . . . It may well be asked whether an attribution of degeneracy is of any value or adds anything to our knowledge."[82]

Freud returns to obsessions in his 1909 *Notes Upon a Case of Obsessional Neurosis* to develop a theory of intrusive thoughts and compulsive behaviors as representations of opposing ideas in a plastic form. *Notes* details the treatment of "Rat Man," a "clear-headed and shrewd"[83] young university-educated army officer afflicted with compulsions and obsessions, including intrusive thoughts about a torture involving rats.[84] The case pivots on the affective orientations of control and submission registered in the first two segments of Hampton's film, as the patient is "possessed" by fears that something awful might happen to his father or to the woman he loves. Cast in a paternal role through transference, and performing it with the gusto of strong countertransference, Freud explains the mésalliance that powers obsessive thoughts and compulsive actions with an analogy suited to the themes developing in the analysis: "We are not used to feeling strong affects without their having any ideational content, and therefore, if the content is missing, we seize as a substitute upon another content which is in some way suitable, much as our police, when they cannot catch the right murderer, arrest a wrong one instead."[85] The violence of a police state resonates with the Rat Man's obsessional idiom and professional life, and of course, with the experiences of analyst and patient—both Jewish—in Karl Lueger's Vienna.[86] The example also speaks more broadly to the experience of the modern subject, rendered helpless—according nineteenth-century psychiatry—by hormones, degeneration, intoxication, the phantasmagoria of the arcades; or even, as in Freud's model of the unconscious, by the disordered mismatched mess of the mind.

In the analytic treatment, the Rat Man's memories and symptoms begin to constellate around an elusive childhood episode, one that "evades any final elucidation," in part because it exists in several variations in unconscious fantasies, and has been subject to a complicated, ongoing process of remodeling.[87] Sometime between his third and fourth year—during the fatal illness of an older sister—the patient committed a misdeed. Freud suspects that the transgression was masturbation; the patient's mother recalled a biting incident. Punished with a beating, the boy flew into a terrible rage and "hurled abuse at his father even while he was under his blows."[88] This abuse, however, took a peculiar form; as he knew no insults, he called his father by the names of common objects, shouting: "You lamp! You towel! You plate." The episode made a "permanent impression" on both father and son: the former never beat the boy again; and the latter became a coward, "out of fear of the violence of his own rage."[89] Fixing suddenly on the objects close at hand, the young Rat Man divided his father, preserving the one he loved and turning the one he loathed into an inanimate object. The father he loved would always be with him; the one he hated was buried in the deepest depths of the mind, taking on the role of a violent super-ego punishing him with enigmatic obsessions.[90] The masturbation and castigation of the remote episode were substituted with rage (a second crime: that of wishing the father were dead) and fear (a second punishment, inflicted on himself).

The young Rat Man's sudden fixation on objects close at hand resembles the scene in which the Freudian fetish originates, that of a traumatic encounter with sexual difference, perceived as lack. The origin of the Freudian fetish in a sudden fixation evokes the synecdochic mode of reading elicited by texts like Dibdin's *Bibliomania* and the catalogs that drive Praz to the auction house.[91] The Rat Man case history anticipates Freud's elaboration of the specific form of negation associated with fetishism: *Verleugnung*, or disavowal.[92] Although "Fetishism" was not published until 1927, Freud presented a paper, titled "On the Genesis of Fetishism," at a meeting of the Vienna Psycho-Analytical Society in 1909, while he was writing *Notes*.[93] In "Fetishism," Freud describes a patient very much like the Rat Man who disavows—that is, at once denies and affirms—his father's death, and develops a moderately severe obsessional neurosis. According to Freud: "The patient oscillated in every situation in life between two assumptions: the one, that his father was still alive and was hindering his activities; the other, opposite one, that he was entitled to regard himself as his father's successor." The traumatic information consistent with the reality that the father is dead contrasts with the current of mental processes that accords with a wish: that the father is still alive. Freud describes the father in prohibitive terms; the assumption that corresponds with the wish that the father is still alive does not fill the young man with the joy but rather hinders him from action. Analogously, the traumatic reality disavowed through oscillation—that the father is dead—does not grieve him, but instead represents the happy fact of succession.[94]

The example of disavowal is doubly ambivalent: the disavowed traumatic reality coincides with a wish; the wish fulfilled is instead figured as a trauma. Freud does not specify any fetish object in this account of the young man who disavows his father's death—a notable omission, given that the subject of the essay is fetishism. What the Rat Man case history makes clear is that obsessions are like fetishes—fixations that represent, in a plastic form, opposing ideas. The indecision that defines the Rat Man's obsessive symptoms is articulated in *Notes* as resistance to narrative causality. The Rat Man cannot tell a story. Propelled by the obsessive idea that he owes money to Lieutenant A, the patient describes a series of exchanges, itineraries, and attachments that Freud cannot quite make sense of and certainly does not expect his reader to, even with the help of a map included in the text. When the Rat Man attempts to explain the terrible punishment, his speech devolves into a series of ellipses. Freud reads on the patient's face a "very strange, composite expression," which he interprets as "one *of horror at pleasure of his own of which he himself was unaware.*"[95] Unpacking the overdetermined expression as a causal sequence, Freud matches the conscious horror with the repressed pleasure that is its cause.

The British psychotherapist Adam Phillips discusses the way in which clutter itself achieves plasticity like that Freud sees in the composite expression in a 2001 essay about his treatment of a "mildly agoraphobic" painter in his mid-thirties.[96] The patient was raised in a "ramshackle but comfortable" bohemian household that contrasted with "more normal" orderly homes of childhood friends. As a teenager, he decided what to wear by using what he called the "mess-dress" method. He would empty the contents of his dresser and wardrobe onto the floor and wear whatever he happened to reach for. When the patient's mother objected to her son's messy room: "You can't find anything in this room!" he explained that that was indeed the point: "Our clothes should come find us." Similarly, when he began painting, the artist would fill up the canvas too quickly: "It was as though painting was too exciting, or too illicit, or too something, and he needed the clutter to stop what he thought of as the real painting happening"—a feeling he relates to an early fear of premature ejaculation. Though his own canvases were chaotic, the patient was influenced by the work of Francis Bacon, whose paintings he judged to be uncluttered and barren, but still "rather claustrophobic."[97] When he read of Bacon's technique of beginning new paintings by throwing paint at a blank canvas, "Everything fell into place."[98] Mess allowed the painter to rehearse a disavowed desire, providing a setting in which chance and intentionality coexist in undecidable suspense.

The cradle of psychoanalysis, Freud's office, was a shrine to such disorder. Implicit in the discussion of accidents in *The Psychopathology of Everyday Life* is the idea that clutter can act, in toto, in ways different from the sum of its parts, creating an inviting setting for deliberate accidents—a setting in which the workings of chance and desire are indistinguishable. The unconscious itself is a chaos that fosters the mismatched elements that motor obsessions and phobias in Freud's early writings. Without the intervention of an analytic interpretation, these forms of chaos resist narrative causality; they are like Elena Ferrante's *frantumaglia*, a "storehouse of time without the orderliness of history, a story."[99] The science of interpretation is rather the art of making order, of clearing out, or at least organizing such storehouses. Phillips writes: "Psychoanalytic theory—and indeed, its highly ritualized practice—has an aversion to clutter."[100] To make order—to match up ideas, feelings, actions, and objects to others with which they belong—is to elaborate a necessary sequence, or to tell a story.

The failure to elaborate a necessary sequence has become a defining feature of hoarding in recent psychological research. In their chapter on hoarding in a clinical handbook on obsessive-compulsive disorders, Frost and Steketee describe an "information-processing deficit" wherein obsessives "define category boundaries too narrowly," a feature they call "underinclusion."[101] Because every possession seems unique and irreplaceable to the hoarder, he is unable to settle upon a classificatory system adequate to encompass the glorious multitude of things. Underinclusion gives rise to a praxis of keeping characterized by distraction, indecision, anxiety, and avoidance:

> The hoarder begins to read a book but must stop to do something else. The book cannot be returned to the shelf because it is now in a different category—books being actively read. It is placed on the coffee table. Next, a cookbook is consulted for dinner and it too cannot be returned to the shelf because it is being used. It is deposited on the back of the couch. The dictionary used next cannot be re-shelved, lest the person forget the word he looked up. This process is repeated until there are books everywhere, none of which can be returned to its shelf because they are all different in their own category. Their new position in the room has meaning because each position represents a different category, and an idiosyncratic sort of organization exists, but the ultimate result is clutter and chaos.[102]

Frost and Steketee name the repetition of this process "churning" because the objects are constantly turned over within the same space: "This is repeated until the piles are so large and numerous that they begin merging (or collapsing) into one large pile. With each new attempt to organize and discard, everything in the pile is examined and moved to the new pile or repositioned in the old pile."[103] Churning replaces the thematic organization conventional in domestic interior spaces with a temporal one, that of objects organized by their being currently or recently in use, creating incongruous juxtapositions along the way: important documents piled with old newspapers, tchotchkes with treasures. The temporal organization is both subjective and unstable; things are arranged not according to the date of acquisition or manufacture but according to the most recent contact with the hoarder.

The reorganization (or disorganization) of objects according to temporal rather than thematic criteria can be restated as a privileging of displacement over condensation and of the linguistic axis of metonymy over metaphor. The linguistic analogy conjures a corpus of structuralist thought that, with Roman Jakobson's 1956 essay on the linguistic basis of two types of aphasiac disturbances, came to be associated with neurological differences.[104] Indeed, Michel Foucault's discussion of aphasia patients in *The Order of Things* is a picture of the same churning practices Frost and Steketee describe: "The aphasiac will create a multiplicity of tiny, fragmented regions in which nameless resemblances agglutinate things into unconnected islets." These unconnected islets soon bear a closer resemblance to boats in a harbor, with rafts and passengers moving between them: "In one corner, they will place the lightest-coloured skeins, in another the red ones, somewhere else those that are softest in texture, in yet another place the longest, or those that have a tinge of purple ... or those that have been wound up into a ball. But no sooner have they been adumbrated than all these groupings dissolve again."[105]

The possibility of a neurological basis of hoarding has conjured a curious case in the annals of medicine: that of Phineas Gage, a Vermont railway worker who survived an 1848 blast that drove a tamping rod through his skull and brain. Twenty years after the accident, the physician who treated had treated Gage, John Harlow, published an account of his patient's incredible recovery, as well as the personality changes that followed. A single sentence in the report has garnered the attention of neuropsychiatrists researching hoarding because it seems to suggest a link between hoarding behaviors and disturbances in the frontotemporal lobes: "He conceived a great fondness for pets and souvenirs, only exceeded by his attachment to his tamping iron, which was his constant companion during the remainder of his life."[106] Gage's new fondness for souvenirs, including the tamping iron, evokes hoarding practices. The case follows the semiotic pattern of underinclusion: a privileging of metonymy, continuity, displacement, and souvenir, over metaphor, similarity, condensation, collection.[107] With the examples of aphasia patients and the case of Gage, studies of hoarding return to the old idea of a material cause like degeneration or physiology, as in Nodier's call to phrenologists to "discover the collector's instinct . . . within the encasing of bone that houses our poor brain."[108]

Too stubborn an allegiance to binary structures of signifying systems distorts the meaning of underinclusion, which may look more simply like attention to what is at hand—myopia, yes, but also magnification, that is the proverbial failure to see the forest through the trees.[109] A 2001 *New Yorker* profile of the "polymath book and ephemera collector" Michael Zinman shows how underinclusion is often just indecision or even the resolution not to look for a forest until there are enough trees.[110] In "The Book Eater," Mark Singer describes the "critical-mess theory" developed by Zinman and his friend William Reese:

> "The most intriguing thing is how a collection like Michael's gets built," Reese said, by way of explaining the practical ramifications of the critical-mess theory. "When you start on something like this, you say, O.K., here is a genre, here is a field. And I'm just going to buy it, whatever it is that I'm collecting—signs from homeless people, imprints from before 1801. You don't start off with a big theory about what you're trying to do. You don't begin by saying, 'I'm trying to prove x.' You build a big pile. Once you get a big enough pile together—the critical mess—you're able to draw conclusions about it. You see patterns."[111]

Whereas Phillips's patient's mess-dress method entails delegating decision making to chance, Zinman's critical-mess theory is rooted in a positivist epistemology. Patterns emerge when a critical-mess has been reached: to be a collector, you must first be a hoarder. Yet some abstraction, some structural principle must intervene; no matter how much you churn cream, you will not get butter florets without a mold.

I churn, I stammer, I resort to cliché. The readymade linguistic units of cliché may help to tame a mess, to make it critical. More helpful, however, are the handy tools of Brown's thing theory, which distinguishes between objects, which unobtrusively lend themselves to use, and things, which confront us with their materiality. For Brown, modernism is the literary and artistic project of provoking encounters with matter that bring out the thingness latent in every object. The path for such a conception of modernism was cleared in part by the history charted in this chapter, which begins with d'Alembert's repudiation of bibliomania, because it entails relishing in the material form of a book rather than putting it to proper use by reading. Bibliomania was then reappropriated and celebrated by a rarified circle of book collectors in early nineteenth-century Britain. The most prolific bibliographer among these Romantic book collectors was Dibdin, whose *Bibliomania* and related works develop a literary style to match the subject matter. Dibdin's bibliographic writings prompt a mode of distracted reading that anticipates Freudian fetishism because it entails fixing upon some detail in place of the whole. Following Esquirol's introduction of monomania into the psychiatric lexicon, literary and medical treatments of bibliomania began borrowing from each other, and the mania for book collecting came to resemble other object-oriented manias. What these manias share with each other and with contemporary elaborations of hoarding is that they render the willful subject helpless before irrational attachments to things. Departing from the medical consensus that understood these attachments to result from degeneration or hormonal fluctuations, Freud proposed a psychodynamic model of obsessions, attributing them to a mismatching of elements in the mind. This disorder, Phillips shows in his case history, "Clutter," can be organized through the psychoanalytic reconstruction of a story that weaves cause and effect across expressive elements. The primary processes of condensation, displacement, and questions of representability, which translate unconscious material into symptoms and other expressive forms, cannot distinguish between wishes, memories, feelings, and thoughts and things.[112]

The Possessions of Others

Martin Hampton's *Possessed* ends with segments titled "Stasis" and "Abandon." Each features a support group member whose mother has recently died. Both homes are first

introduced in a sequence of three shots in the film's opening cred-
its. The first is of gloved hands scrubbing a plastic container in a
sink surrounded by clean dishes and empty plastic bottles. The
sounds of running water and aggressive scrubbing contrast with
the silence of the next shot, which is of used cotton rounds piled
in and over a cardboard box. The camera pans down slowly from
the peak of the cotton mountain to the base, which fills the screen.
The shot lasts more than twenty seconds—almost one-sixtieth of
the length of the entire film. Used at a rate of one or two a day, the
makeup-stained cotton rounds are an image of duration; the time
of accumulation—a year, perhaps—is like passing days scratched
on the wall of a prison cell. The movement of the camera emphasizes the magnitude of the heap but also suggests a futility that
extends to the medium itself; capable of reproducing motion, the
moving camera serves only to dramatize the stillness and stasis of
the cotton rounds. As the woman leads a tour of her home, the
camera focuses on "bizarre objects": traces of her body, like the
stained cotton rounds and a box of matted hair, as well as empty
containers of household products, clothes, papers, and plastic bags
with unknown contents.[113] Like the hoarder in "Submission," the
one in "Stasis" narrates ego-dystonic acts of acquisition, or in this
case, reacquisition; she describes waking up in the middle of the
night to find herself outside riffling through trash bins to rescue
objects she discarded during the day. Throwing things out only to
retrieve them from the trash, documenting stillness with a moving camera, the segment captures the static indecision that defines
fetishistic disavowal.

The third of the three shots in the opening sequence is of the
hoarder of the "Abandon" segment performing a series of futile
gestures. He bends down, sifting through a heap of clothing,
papers, and stuffed polypropylene bags, then shifts some papers

FIGURE 1.1
Martin Hampton, *Possessed* (2008).

to the top of the heap. He stands, the papers tumble back down. He starts to mumble something unintelligible. He takes the magazine he holds folded under his arm, refolds it, and puts it back under his arm. Motion in this shot and in the segment, "Abandon," is confined to such vain gestures, and to images of nullity—dust churned up as he riffles through piles of papers and clothes, his face twitching furiously. His rummaging also churns up a pornographic image: a photograph of a woman's body, from shoulders to knees, with her legs spread. The hoarder does not seem to notice the girlie magazine, though it occupies the center of the screen for almost six seconds.

Why does the film, otherwise so respectful of the struggles of the support group members, include such an egregious violation of the hoarder's privacy? True, the film is dedicated to its subjects' unusual, often obsessive patterns of acquiring and keeping, and of course, to the squalid chaos of their living spaces. In "Abandoned," stills of filth include the inside of a refrigerator, encrusted with ice and mold; decorative objects, cobwebs, and a bare lightbulb, all caked thickly in dust. But these images seem less prying—though in "Abandon" and the other segments, they serve to ironize the hoarder's monologue—because they are clearly relevant to the documentary's theme and to each individual's struggle. The shot of the girlie magazine seems an intrusion of a different order because the hoarder does not appear to consent to or even recognize the presence of the image in the film. But Hampton's inclusion of the image also, and more critically, thematizes the ethics of the documentary by evoking the primal scene of fetishism: that of the little boy's perception of sexual difference.

The difference that *Possessed* invites the viewer to confront is not sexual difference but mental illness. In Freud's account of fetishism, the perception of difference is terrifying because it arouses the threat of nondifference; if the woman has no penis, the little boy realizes, his own must be in danger. With this violation of the hoarder's privacy, Hampton invites the viewer to ask whether the terrifying picture of hoarding is actually an image of the viewer's own proximity to the object praxes the film documents. The sense, captured with the image of being precariously close to being possessed by objects, is what drives the history of the pathologization of acquiring and keeping charted in these pages. The image seems to dare viewers to look at the hoarder's suffering and turn away, disavowing their perilous vulnerability to possession.

2

Economies

THE FLEA MARKET

The forms of hoarding that have been pathologized in the twenty-first century result in accumulations that are, for the most part, of no direct consequence to the general economy.[1] These amassments are different from those elaborated in economic theories of hoarding, which focus on the accumulation of exchange value (bullion or representative money) or necessity goods (primarily grain). The hoarder's possessions often seem like junk to others: old newspapers and magazines, tattered plush animals, rusty tools, and auto parts are common examples. Hoarding looks like an investment of libidinal energy unmatched by economic value. Studies influenced by behavioral economics have described hoarding disorder as a failure of rational consumption, the result of poor decisions about resource allocation.[2] Some medical researchers—hoping to transform the pathologized hoarder into a *homo oeconomicus*—have even attempted to treat the disorder with economic instruction.[3] If only hoarders could properly assess value, the theory goes, they would be able to discard the objects that overwhelm their living spaces.

Given the contrast between rational investment in exchange value or necessity goods and irrational investment in broken-down matter, it may make sense to ask whether the two conceptions of hoarding—in economic theory and in popular culture—have any-thing more in common than a shared basis in accumulation. When grain spoils in siloes or sketches by old masters emerge from musty cellars, when whimsy fortune wreaks havoc on value with time, rational and irrational begin to look more similar. Both forms of hoarding are premised on the axiom that value changes over time. This truth—and its corollary that the moment of acquisition is decisive—is particularly evident at emporia like stock exchanges, auctions, pawnshops, popup stores, and those with which this chapter is concerned: flea markets.

Flea markets conjure hoards because they, too, are spaces defined by a multitude of objects, not piled up to the ceiling but spread across acres. Market merchandise comprises an array of postconsumer goods, in forms kitsch, counterfeit, or damaged; antique, authentic, or rare. As with hoards, the most striking aspect of flea markets for many who describe and document them is the variety of the merchandise and the odd juxtapositions that result. Flea market merchandise, like hoards, seems to elude classificatory schemes. But the similarities between flea markets and the pathologized object practices that define hoarding are more entrenched than mere physical resemblance. Flea markets enmesh political and psychic economies, modernity and obsolescence, intentionality and contingency, and art and abjection, anticipating structuring tensions and themes at the root of hoards. Here I trace a cultural history of flea markets, charting the narrative, rhetorical, and visual topoi that define them, as well as the characters that animate them. I show how flea markets become spaces in which openness to contingent meetings with undervalued objects becomes a defining feature of modern conceptions of the artist, poet, street photographer, and historian.

The first markets to gain the verminous epithet *marchés aux puces* (flea markets) were both produced by and excluded from the modernizing city of Paris. These markets developed in the Paris Zone, a *zona non aedificandi* established in the 1840s just outside the new Thiers Wall.[4] The prohibition of construction in the roughly 250-meter wide and 34-kilometer long area created a liminal space gradually given over to makeshift housing occupied by Roma, vagrants, ragpickers, and later, poor Parisians displaced by Baron Haussmann's renovation. The Zone also became the primary site for the processing and peddling of scavenged material.[5] There, *chiffonniers* (ragpickers) sorted and sold scavenged materials, including rags, bones, cardboard, nails and other scrap metal, shards of glass, and animal carcasses.[6] Gradually, these makeshift points of sale evolved from sites where waste is remade through labor, gaining market value in predictable ways, to places where chance seems to rule, and modernity seems distant. Guides to Turin and Milan occasioned by expositions convey a similarly antithetical relationship between the odds and ends at the market and the modernizing cities. By the interwar period in Italy, photographers and writers influenced by Eugène Atget's pictures of ragpickers and their dwellings and by André Breton's writings on surrealist objects found revolutionary potential in the markets.

The shifting economic underpinnings of the *puces* mirror the conceptual extension of hoarding from political economy to psychology, and across materials, from necessity goods and exchange value to enticing objects like the postconsumer bric-a-brac that ends up at the markets. Removed from their histories of production and possession, recovered by ragpickers, and ripe for reinvention, flea market objects substantiate subjective "marginalist" theories of value that developed contemporaneously with the first *puces*. Beginning in around 1870, political economists began to break from the classical theories of Adam Smith and David Ricardo, who understood cost as a function of labor.[7] Marginalism, instead, makes the price of a commodity dependent on expected satisfaction—that is, desire, or what Vilfredo Pareto called ophelimity, from the Greek *ópheleó* for useful, advantageous, or pleasurable.[8] In his 1973 study of the enmeshment of psychic and political economies, the French poststructuralist Jean-Joseph Goux argues that in the logic of marginalism, to produce desire is to create value, but also to produce the lack or scarcity that will intensify desire. In such calculations, labor and raw materials recede, becoming invisible or irrelevant. Marginalism explains what economists call the infinite elasticity of demand, which traps desire and scarcity in mutually reinforcing loops, creating bubbles—whether of tulips, rare books, or bundled subprime mortgages. Marginalism offers an illusory alternative to the "somber realism of labor value" by "dropping into the magnetic field of political economy (of market exchange-value) everything 'sacred' and 'transcendent' that might appear to escape it—including desire."[9]

As the raw materials of urban detritus and the labor of rag-pickers began to give way to the mysterious workings of chance, popular flea market anecdotes told of windfalls of exchange value, generally in the form of coins. These episodes imbued the markets with the logic of belatedness that defines gambling for Walter Benjamin: "The particular danger that threatens the gambler lies in the fateful category of arriving 'too late,' of having 'missed the opportunity.'"[10] This changed somewhat as the merchandise became more varied and less predictable; over time, the rule of chance came to function for the flea market flaneur in much the same way it did for Adam Phillips's agoraphobic patient.[11] Like the painter who begins a new work by splattering paint on the canvas and decides what to wear by grabbing garments at random, the flaneur finds at the flea market the possibility of chancing upon a unique object that answers to unforeseen desires. Because of the unpredictability of merchandise, every sale at the flea market is catalyzed by the fleeting time of an encounter—that is, by transience, which Freud defines as scarcity value in time.[12] Transience also characterizes the objects that seem to have outlasted their use and value. Accordingly, the flea markets often prompt nostalgic ruminations by writers—most famously, Breton—on the transient, the fleeting, the contingent—three terms Charles Baudelaire uses in *The Painter of Modern Life* to define modernity.[13] For Baudelaire, modernity is what will soon be gone. This, Theodor Adorno writes, is the "false promise" that makes the "idea of modernity": "everything modern, because of its never-changing core, has scarcely aged than it takes on a look of the archaic."[14]

In his allegorical reading of Paul Klee's 1920 *Angelus Novus*, Benjamin uses the modern production of the outmoded to illustrate the urgency of his historical method. He describes the angel in Klee's watercolor: "His eyes are wide, his mouth is open . . . his face is turned toward the past" and glosses: "This is how the angel of history must look."[15] He elaborates:

> Where a chain of events appears before *us*, *he* sees one single catastrophe, which keeps piling wreckage upon wreckage and hurls it at his feet. The angel would like to stay, awaken the dead, and make whole what has been smashed. But a storm is blowing from Paradise and has got caught in his wings; it is so strong that the angel can no longer close them. This storm drives him irresistibly into the future, to which his back is turned, while the pile of debris before him grows toward the sky. We call progress *this* storm.[16]

Scavenge work becomes the model of a historical method that takes up the urgent and unending project of resisting the devastating

FIGURE 2.1
Paul Klee, *Angelus Novus.* Israel Museum. HIP/Art Resource.

effects of the myth of progress.[17] Analogizing the past and present with dialectical images suggests not the work of mourning, but that of reviving and repairing; awakening the dead and making whole what has been smashed. Salvaging meaning and value from the debris that piles up in the name of progress is possible to imagine because of the way in which "the moderns"—those who consider themselves to be modern—understand themselves and their objects to exist at a point of temporal rupture so that what is past is irretrievably lost.[18]

Francesco Orlando considers the accumulation of obsolete objects in modern literature to be a return of what is repressed by a society driven by the functional imperative; flea markets might look similar to literature in this regard. In threadbare matter, furthermore, Orlando finds an image of the corroding, rather than ennobling effects of time, and in that, a way of understanding the obsolescence of the aristocracy. While Orlando focuses on the ways in which imaginary relationships to real conditions of existence are mediated by representations of objects affected by the passage of time, Michael Thompson's *Rubbish Theory* makes social status a determinant of the way in which time affects the value of objects. Thompson takes as a point of departure the axiom that possessable objects can be divided into two categories: transients and durables. The value of the former decreases until it reaches zero while that of the latter increases toward infinity.[19] He relates social status to the ownership of durables and marginality to transients, not so much because the wealthy can afford durables, but rather because the value of objects is made by social relations.

Unlike durables and transients, which gain and lose value in predictable ways, the alchemy of value, with regard to rubbish, is opaque. For Thompson, the creation of value, or the transformation of rubbish into durables, cannot be attributed to fortune, as in such windfalls as an original Renoir painting in a box of junk at a West Virginia flea market, or—a more quotidian example—a nice-looking table up for grabs by the curb.[20] The dumpster is, instead, a reflective surface; the value therein is a mirror of social relations so that what appears to be a spontaneous creation of value is produced by and contributes to the reproduction class-based society. The difference between a piece of junk and a valuable antique rests not in the objects but in social relations. Applications of Thompson's theory are everywhere in literary and visual texts dedicated to flea markets, which first focused on the ragpicker's stoic labor and then remade him as figure for the poet, artist, or street photographer. This metamorphosis creates the possibility for wild changes of value while obscuring the less dramatic profits made from the slower labor of repair—of slowing the deterioration of transients.

Thierry Bardini's playful and ambitious *Junkware* also obscures such labor by lending agency to apparently useless stuff: "Junk is junk. . . . You forget about it, and it somehow grows anarchically. Junk rusts, fades, decays. . . . Junk is its own cause."[21] Notwithstanding this agency, affective relationships of humans to junk are, for Bardini, determined by the social. To marvel at junk is a luxurious endeavor; nostalgia is a malady of the well-fed: "Junk . . . incarnates the sentimental scrap we choose to love tenderly in these parts of the world. It materializes the memories of consumption that we grew up idolizing. Junk, on the other hand, is a necessity for the starving."[22] The cultural history I trace in this chapter is one in which scavenged necessity gives way to sentimental scrap as chance comes to rule over the flea market.

The distinction David Trotter draws between forms of refuse brings into focus the stakes of the transformations of flea market merchandise. Mess, he writes, is "contingency's signature," an event with no author and no intention beyond chance.[23] Waste, by contrast, "is an effect which can be traced back to its cause. . . . However foul it may become, it still gleams with efficiency."[24] He explains: "Mess is waste that has not yet become, and may never become, either symptom or symbol. The difference between mess and waste is partly a difference of scale and point of view, and partly a difference in the imaginative uses to which they have consistently been put."[25] In other words, the distinction between waste and mess is not just ontological, but also aesthetic.

The Ragpicker Becomes an Artist

Charles Baudelaire's "Une Charogne" ("A Carcass") illustrates the aesthetic distinction between mess and waste by transforming the eponymous carcass from the former to the latter. The poet recalls to his beloved "that beautiful morning in June" when the two happened upon a carrion splayed across their path. From a mess— a shameless object "sweating out poisonous fumes," encountered by chance—the carcass becomes a memento mori laden with meaning for the lovers.[26] More important, its splendid putrefaction becomes a happy part of a cycle smiled upon by the sky. The carcass becomes waste: part of a system with ongoing, predictable results, including the worm-kissed decomposition of the beloved.

Ragpickers, especially those sorting and selling scavenged materials in the Paris Zone, were inspiration and allegory to modern writers and artists. In "Le Vin des chiffonniers" ("The Ragpickers' Wine"), Baudelaire likens the ragpicker to a poet, scavenging for beauty and meaning in the city's dross.[27] Benjamin describes Baudelaire's use of the ragpicker's labor as an extended metaphor for the poetic method: "Everything that the big city has thrown away, everything it has lost, everything it has scorned, everything it has crushed underfoot he catalogues and collects. . . . He sorts things out and selects judiciously: he collects like a miser guarding a treasure, refuse which will assume the shape of useful or gratifying objects."[28] In his 1869 *Chiffonnier*, Édouard Manet lends the ragpicker the stoic melancholy fitting for a "vital character in

FIGURE 2.2
Eugène Atget, *Chiffonnier*, 1899–1901. Courtesy of the Getty's Open
Content Program.

an urban drama," removing him from the streets of Paris to set him against a "featureless, peculiarly inappropriate, dissociative background."[29] In contrast to the stylized plainness of the background of Manet's *Chiffonnier*, the painter Jean-François Raffaëlli dedicated many canvases to ragpickers, usually depicted alone or accompanied by a dog, against the barren terrain of the outskirts, sometimes with factories billowing smoke visible on the horizon.[30] In his photograph of a ragpicker, taken between 1899 and 1901, Eugène Atget returns the doleful icon to the streets of Paris with a composition that is in dialogue with these painters. Looking apprehensively at the photographer, Atget's *chiffonnier* is immersed in the tedium of his work: he is dwarfed by the cart piled high with stuffed sacks of rags.

Like the carrion at the beginning of Baudelaire's poem, the objects and materials scavenged by ragpickers working in Paris are encountered by chance. According to Trotter's distinction, the refuse that ragpickers gather looks more like waste than mess because it is reproduced daily and scaled to the city's cycle of consumption. In an 1884 article in *L'Illustration*, Louis Paulian describes the important labor performed by ragpickers: "Household rubbish represents, in the city of Paris alone, an asset of 50,000–60,000 francs that is tossed into the street each day that would be lost to society if the ragpicker weren't there to gather it, transform it, and put it back into circulation."[31] The ragpickers' scavenging remakes the metropolis as an awe-inspiring system of producing and processing waste. Paulian concludes: "Thanks to the ragpicker, nothing is truly lost."[32]

Whereas these artists and writers represent ragpickers as solitary figures removed from or isolated within the city, gradually more attention was given to the spaces they occupied. Postcards depict ragpickers returning to the Zone in horse-drawn carts after their

FIGURE 2.3
Eugène Atget, *Villa d'un chiffonnier*, 1912. Courtesy of the Getty's Open
Content Program.

morning rounds.[33] In these images, the figures lack any detail of facial expression like those that distinguish the lone ragpickers of Manet, Raffaëlli, and Atget. In some images, ragpickers are absent save for the awe-inspiring traces left in the spaces they inhabit. In his 1912 *Villa d'un chiffonnier*, Atget captures the ornate exterior of a ragpicker's hovel, grandiose despite the humble origin of the building materials.[34] The "villa" is lavishly decorated with scavenged gargoyles: mangled dolls; pull toys of various sizes and species. A plush cat balances at the edge of the shingled roof, as if trying to catch the creature mounted just below; a poorly taxidermied bird of prey extends out from a wooden beam, as if ready to put its unpracticed wings to the test of flight; and two child-sized stuffed animals sit regally atop the roof like guardian lions. Anticipating the contemporary interest in the crowded dilapidation of hoarded homes, the picture becomes a portrait of the marvelous creativity or fascinating lunacy, rather than the resourcefulness, of the absent ragpicker.

A second photograph, taken the same year, depicts the interior of a ragpicker's workspace on the Boulevard Masséna. As in the *Villa*, the labor of the absent ragpicker, in the *Intérieur d'un chiffonnier*, enlivens the squalor with fascinating detail. The materials accumulated in the frame include a dozen or so baskets, a large drum, wooden beams, ladders, chairs, a wagon wheel, rope, as well as human forms: a graceful nude statuette, and the straddling legs of a broken doll. In place of the heavy bundles of unseen rags borne with weathered forbearance, both photographs display marvelous finds of absent ragpickers. The *Villa* makes the ragpicker's hovel a spectacular oeuvre; suggestive of some practice that lingers between resourceful labor, artistic genius, and mad compulsion. The *Intérior*, by contrast, delivers an inviting perspective for flea market shoppers in the debris punctuated with barely discernible and perhaps unrecognized treasures.

FIGURE 2.4
Eugène Atget, *Intérieur d'un chiffonnier: Boulevard Masséna*, 1912. Courtesy of the Bibliothèque nationale de France.

The changing picture of ragpickers' wares represented by these two photographs is, in part, the product of the increasing stratification of the profession. *Coureurs* or *piquers* worked by night with a lantern in one hand, a pick in the other, and a basket on the back. The slightly better-remunerated *placiers* scavenged in specific neighborhoods and transported their wares by cart. The *chineurs*, the highest earning among *chiffonniers*, dealt primarily in scavenged objects.[35] As the makeshift points of sale came to be officially designated markets—Montreuil-sous-bois in 1860 and Saint-Ouen in 1885—these *chineurs* began to predominate.[36]

Alongside the *chineur* was the *brocante,* defined in 1898 as a "dealer of old furniture, linens, clothing, jewelry, dishes, weapons, metals, and other objects and occasional goods."[37] The professionalization of ragpickers and the increasing proportion of *chineurs* and *brocantes* among those vending in the Zone resulted in a shifted emphasis; rather than a site for the processing of the city's waste, the markets came to be stocked with "objets et merchandises de hasard," and ruled by chance. This transformation is reflected in the shift from the portraits of ragpickers, alone and august—by Manet, Raffaëlli, and Atget—to the spaces where they keep the fascinating things cast off, lost, or forgotten by the modernizing city. With that shift, the fruit of scavenge work becomes increasingly invisible, even as the ragpicker retreats into an archaic world that seems to exist beyond the modern conception of time. The romanticized figure of the poet-artist who takes his place is not the vendor, but the shopper-flaneur.

Stories of Saint-Ouen

The beginning of the transformation of flea markets from points of sale for rags and bones to places where chance rules is reflected in the changing stuff of windfalls—first, luck strikes in the liquid form of exchange value; then in alluring objects, either valuable or strange. Two apocryphal accounts explain the origin of the term "marché aux puces." In the first, a guard looking out over the market from the heights of a watchtower along the Thiers Wall exclaims: "Why, it's a market of fleas!" The second, more probable explanation is that the term evolved from an old joke that the ragpickers sold clothes with everything—even the fleas—included.[38] In each case, the origin has to do with the filth and poverty of the markets; whether tiny indistinct laborers hopping about, or contagious bugs, the analogy was unlikely to attract shoppers like the well-heeled young women afflicted with *magasinitis* at the department stores.

Early uses of *marché aux puces* in the French press were consonant with the second anecdote. A note in the Paris crime report of June 24, 1891 in *La Lanterne* titled "Marché-aux-Puces" offers a primer on the Montreuil-sous-Bois market, presenting it as a picturesque urban secret.[39] "Few Parisians know about the 'Flea-Market,'" the note begins, then adds the description: "A mishmash of old ragged clothing, gibus hats collapsed into accordions, and shoes without soles, for sale alongside more or less fresh meat, the remnants of vegetables, and old crusts of bread."[40] The crime reported is a scuffle between two junk dealers over a shiny coin that rolled between their stalls. One ends up in the hospital with a broken leg, the other lands in jail. Introducing the aggressor, whose stall is decorated by a sign that reads "Michel knows rags and everything that comes with them," the note evokes the origin of the term "marché aux puces," adding: "So much meaning in that simple word '*everything!*'"[41] The glimpse of urban seediness, and of the shiny coin amid detritus, violence, and the suggestion of fleas made for a compelling vignette: the note captures themes that would remain vivid for decades in writing about flea markets. Art critic André Warnod writes, in 1914: "Despite the name, don't think that they sell fleas at the market. . . . Even if some fleas pass from seller to buyer, the prices stay the same."[42]

Just over a month later, *XIX Siècle* published a short note, "Surprises of the flea market," about Madame Pacaud, a widow who bought an old mattress to use for wool at the Montreuil-sous-Bois market.[43] She immediately cut open the mattress and began extracting its woolen innards, when out fell a heavy sack filled with 14,000 francs in gold coin. The note settles the nagging question of whether the widow would get to keep the gold: "The mattress had passed through so many hands, and through so many mansions that it would be impossible to locate the coin hoarder. The widow will therefore remain in possession of the hoard."[44] The note was reprinted that evening in *La Presse*. The anecdote marks the transformation of the market from a place where you can reliably go to find what you seek, to a place where you can stumble on something you never expected to see: the answer to your dreams.

These two news items from 1891 are representative of flea market narratives. Both are accounts of coins turning up unexpectedly. Scoffing at the scuffle over a couple cents, the first illustrates the poverty and desperation of the vendors. The second, by contrast, makes the flea market appear closer to bourgeois sensibilities. It is silent on the squalor of the market and offers no list of incongruous and broken-down wares. That a widow with a fixed abode would visit the market alone makes the advice offered in the monthly organ of the suburban landowners' association in 1897 seem alarmist: "Think of your safety and carry a gun when you walk through the Zone."[45] The two narratives are similar not only in sketching encounters with unanticipated riches but also in foregrounding uncertainty about the rightful owner of the riches. In these anecdotes, economic gain is granted by inconstant fortune; the windfalls come in the liquid form of specie, which cannot be traced to any individual and is therefore available to whoever is so lucky as to stumble upon it.

A third story—more widely reported than the previous two—suggests that unexpected flea market fortunes are contingent on this dangerous and alluring untraceability. In October 1895, the thirteen-year-old Henri Pouget purchased a box of old issues of *Le Voleur* at the Montreuil-sous-Bois flea market.[46] When he returned home, he began rifling through them and noticed some documents clipped to the pages. He showed the magazines to his father, who saw the name Mr. Haas printed on some pages, along with "Banque de France." Other pages were marked with phrases like "nominative share" and "bank voucher." The older Pouget did not know what to make of the documents, so he showed them to his friend, Mr. Cassagne. Once the two men realized that the documents were worth more than 150,000 francs, they hatched a plan to recover as much value as possible from them. They decided to go to Belgium, where they would not be recognized, and where no one would have heard of the recent death of the well-known miser, Charles Haas. There, they attempted to exchange the documents, but when they asked for a curiously low sum the bank teller tipped off the police, and the two were arrested.[47] The case was tried in February of the following year, and both Cassagne and Pouget were sentenced to four months in prison and a fine of fifty francs.

The *marché aux puces*, in these early anecdotes, is a place where humble fortunes can be reversed by an unexpected find: riches stitched into a bedbug-infested mattress or jailbait interleaved in mildewed magazine pages. Chance becomes the law of the market, though its rewards take a less liquid form; a form that is available only to those more cunning than poor Pouget and Cassagne or to those discerning enough to recognize its overtures. These anecdotes chart the transformations of flea markets—first associated with squalor, they next become places where luck might strike in the form of specie, and then places where fortune must be matched by some act of discernment. As chance prevails, flea markets gradually begin to attract the curious, idle, and nostalgic: flaneurs.[48]

Off-Modern Italian Markets

Like the Paris *puces*, miscellanea markets of the outskirts of Milan and Turin were spaces through and against which the idea of modernity was forged in Italy. In writings occasioned by two expositions—the 1881 National Exposition of Art and Industry in Milan and the 1884 Italian General Exposition in Turin—flea markets represent picturesque counterpoints to the modernizing city and essential stops on any visitor's itinerary. One of the most widely read of these exposition narratives is Edmondo De Amicis's *Torino 1880*, "the official portrait of the modern Italian metropolis."[49] Turin, De Amicis promised, would impress any visitor because of the stately elegance of its bright thoroughfares framed by mountains. But the Italian visitor, in particular, would be moved by the patriotic spirit that infuses the city's every stone, house, and portico: "There you can still feel the warmth of the great gust of patriotism that swept through the city, enflaming and overwhelming everything, like a hurricane made of fire. What Italian could arrive there and not feel moved?"[50] De Amicis reads perseverance, rectitude, and diligence on every visage, and democratic virtue in every building: "The architecture is democratic and egalitarian. The houses can address each other informally as citizens."[51]

In contrast to the sober grandeur of the city center boulevards, in De Amicis's account, is the raucous market, today called the Balòn.[52] Midway through his guide, De Amicis introduces the dramatic shift that will confront any visitor who ventures into the eastern part of the city center: "The nature of Turin's appearance morphs suddenly upon entering the part of the city that extends from via Santa Teresa to Piazza Emanuele Filiberto. Here, the city ages unexpectedly by several centuries, darkening, narrowing, winding, and becoming poor and depressed."[53] To wander from the modern Turin of Corso Francia to the area between Via Santa Teresa and Piazza Emanuele Filiberto is to travel back in time, to a place that "makes you want to deliver the breaking news of Italy's Unification."[54] The market, for De Amicis, is the core of this picturesque other Turin and requisite for any visitor. To see the city in its greatest complexity, he insists, one must visit on a Saturday morning in the winter when the market is in full swing. There, he writes, at once elevating his own project and the modernity of the city he lauds, a Zola from Turin could set a novel titled "Il ventre di Torino" (The belly of Turin).[55] "From one end to the other, the street is one enormous open-air junkshop, a great and pitiable display of misery such as would be impossible to imagine except by supposing that an entire neighborhood of Turin, invaded by some devastating fury, was turned upside down and emptied of every last article from each of its households, from the attics to the basements, and down to the last knickknack from the last cupboard."[56] The spectacle of the market is the scene that would result if every last piece of junk in every house in an entire neighborhood were tossed out the window and laid out neatly on the cement with scrupulous care. The merchandise is neither exotic nor valuable; it is the marvelous abundance of the everyday turned upside down and inside out.

The market De Amicis describes is distinguished by the variety of everyday wares: "It's a confusion of things and of remnants of things that would drive the poor wretch who had to inventory it mad."[57] Common to this miscellany is a threadbare, broken-down uselessness, which is conveyed—notwithstanding the mental health of the poor wretch—through the form of the list:

> The priest's chasuble, the misshapen infantry helmet, the broken marionette from the San Martiniano Theater, the torn silk

ballgown from the Scribe Theater, the 16th century lock, the unfin-
ished novel of Eugène Sue, the broken nail, the donkey saddle, the
oil painting, the feathered beret of the tenor, dentures, crushed
pins, pans without handles, helmets, globes, table legs, the spoils of
alcoves, living rooms, law offices, attics, workshops, taverns, moldy,
shredded, gnawed by mice, holey from moths, rotten from rain,
corroded by mud, consumed by rust, without color, without form,
without name, without price: everything cast off in the turbulent
waters of the human condition.[58]

De Amicis first names seventeen objects. The final item on the list,
spoils, is then divided into six types: spoils of alcoves, living rooms,
law offices, and so on. Two adjectives—moldy and tattered—
bespeak the deleterious effects of time. Five adjectival phrases then
reveal that the passage of time is accompanied by human use and
nonhuman abuse: the stuff is gnawed by rats, rotted by rain, and
consumed by rust. Next, four adjectival phrases attest to the properties the merchandise lacks: it is without color, form, name, or
price. The list eludes any single organizational principle beyond
the mere fact of presence; it seems to invite underinclusion. And as
with hoards, lists like the one above that expand in apparent defi-
ance of organizing principles direct a sense of marvel at the place
or being that brings together such disparate abundance.[59]

The coherence of De Amicis's list is not threatened by logical
impasses that develop from elements that work their way out of
the plane of denotation to distort the language that would contain
them, as in the "subversive" rhetorical figure of hypallage; rather,
it conforms to what Umberto Eco calls the "poetics of etcetera."[60]
Instead of (or in addition to) an overview of the multiplicity conveyed, "everything cast off in the turbulent waters of the human
condition," the poetics of etcetera involves the use of a catalog that
is ample, but that appears synecdochic; a metonym of even greater

multitudes.[61] Orlando's symptomatically monumental *Obsolete Objects* offers copious examples of the tendency of broken-down objects to accumulate in literature in the form of lists.[62] The uselessness of the objects listed, he argues, is accentuated by the structural properties of the list itself: the absence of any logical relationship between the objects beyond the simple fact of their presence.

In addition to an accumulation of broken-down objects, De Amicis's Turin market is a gathering place for people excluded from the economic life of the modernizing city. He writes:

> Work at the strange market begins in the dead of the night, by lantern light; the swarming crowds arrive at the break of dawn. The seamstress sneaks there to look for a cast-off shawl. The cash-strapped family man goes to buy oil for a lamp. The artist goes to find a dress for his model. The antiquarian, the bibliomaniac, the penniless actor, the Jewish junk-dealer, and a procession of collectors of baubles and all kinds of curiosities, are all eager to be among the first to fish in that great sea that might hide unknown treasures and small, unexpected fortunes. They ramble and rummage greedily until high day amidst the coming and going of peasants haggling over worn-out clothes, ambulant ragpickers loaded down with worn-out boots and cracked pots, porters, gleaners of cigarette-butts and papers, municipal guards, maids, shopkeepers, brokers, who float in two opposing currents between the farmers market and the great pandemonium of the nearby square.[63]

The human odds and ends come to resemble the objects they peruse in part through the shared aquatic metaphors. Like the wares, cast off in the rough waters, the market denizens "float in two opposite currents," all longing to fish first "in that great sea." The flow of shoppers in two currents recalls the avaricious and prodigal punished in the fourth circle of Dante's hell. There, the two groups of sinners crash against each other, "As does the wave, there over Charybdis, breaking itself against the wave it meets."[64] In hell, hoarders and squanderers calling to each other, "Why do you hoard?" and "Why do you squander?" are punished together because of their common abandon of measure and their attempts to trick fortune.[65] In De Amicis's market, the shoppers are both avaricious and spendthrift; they rummage greedily and squander their energy in search of fortune.

Like the assorted merchandise among which they wander, the people haunting the Turin market in De Amicis's account are odds and ends—their labor seems external to the general economy; they are more specimens than types. These characters contrast with those of Edgar Allan Poe's proto-detective story, "The Man of the Crowd."[66] The convalescent narrator of the 1840 story sits at the window of a London café, scrutinizing the changing physiognomy of the crowd outside. The procession of passersby is rationally matched to the hierarchical structure of the society. First to pass before the convalescent's gaze are the "noblemen, merchants, attorneys, tradesmen, stock-jobbers—the Eupatrids and the commonplaces of society—men of leisure and men actively engaged in affairs of their own—conducting business upon their own responsibility."[67] Next come the clerks, then, "descending in the scale of what is termed gentility," the pickpockets, gamblers, Jews, and beggars.

As darkness descends outside the café, the narrator is transfixed by the countenance of one passerby—"that of a decrepit old man, some sixty-five or seventy years of age." The visage "arrested and absorbed" the narrator's attention because of "the absolute idiosyncrasy of expression." That singular countenance conjures, "confusedly and paradoxically" within the narrator's mind, "the ideas of vast mental power, of caution, of penuriousness, of avarice, of coolness, of malice, of blood-thirstiness, of triumph, of merriment, of excessive terror, of intense—of supreme despair."[68] Poe scholar Paul Hurh offers an intriguing gloss: "What is idiosyncratic about the face is not any one feature, but the paradoxical synchronic manifestation of several common, *yet usually exclusive,* ones. . . . The stranger's is not just another face in the crowd; it is all of them."[69] The composite visage, a synchronic manifestation of disparate elements, resembles the market that contains all the everyday objects of the modern city.

With *Torino 1880,* De Amicis became the unofficial bard of the 1884 exposition and of Turin. The literary production associated with the 1881 Milan exposition bestowed no such laurels, though amid the prolific publicity the city acquired the enduring epithets of the "moral capital" and "the most *city* city" of Italy.[70] In addition to catalogs, the exhibition organizing committee commissioned two guides to the city: the four-volume *Mediolanum* and *Milano 1881.* Though they included contributions from prominent writers, the promotional style of these and other similar guides—their celebration of "an optimistic, Ambrosian [Milanese] efficiency"— ran counter to platforms of major intersecting literary circles in Milan: the *veristi,* the *scapigliati* (disheveled), and the *palombari* (divers).[71]

Although the Senigallia market is virtually absent in the exposition-sponsored guides, *palombari* and the *scapigliati* find rich material for their literary renderings of the city. Paolo Valera—one of the *palombari,* so named because they would "dive" into the world of the urban poor—makes brief mention of the Senigallia flea market in *Milano sconosciuta rinnovata* (*Unknown Milan Restored*), first serialized in the progressive journal he cofounded, *La plebe,* beginning in 1879. For Valera, the Senigallia market suggests not the transient, the fleeting, and the contingent, but rather the greed of modern capitalism. Valera contrasts this avariciousness with the generosity and warmth of Milan of yore. He laments the changed Sant'Ambrogio Fair, known as "Oh, bei! Oh, bei!" ("Goodie! Goodie!") because of the joyous cries of children who were given cotton candy and other sweets. Now, instead, he complains, people go to the "Oh, bei! Oh, bei!" the way they would go to the Senigallia market: "To see if they come across some outmoded tool among the old chestnuts. To look for shabby books cheap, to get themselves an iron or a fine suit stained by its last owner."[72]

The most significant guide to exposition-era Milan, from a literary perspective, is one that was published eight years after the event: *Il ventre di Milano: Fisiologia della capitale morale* (*The Belly of Milan: Physiology of the Moral Capital*), a collection of vignettes by a dozen-odd contributors edited by Cletto Arrighi (pseudonym of Carlo Righetti).[73] The work is organized around the idea of a banquet, with an introduction titled "Antipasto." The "Head Chef," Arrighi, presents the volume as a physiology of the city: "physiology in the strictest sense of the word—varied, extensive, yielding, breezy, palpitating—of this great city."[74] The literary ambition of the work is signaled by the title, which evokes Zola's *Le Ventre de Paris* (*The Belly of Paris*), as well as the Neapolitan writer Matilde Serao's *Il ventre di Napoli* (*The Belly of Naples*), published just four years earlier.[75] Arrighi is particularly vitriolic (and misogynistic) in his attack of Serao, whose *Ventre* he introduces as follows: "Instead of darning her husband's socks, Mr. Scarfoglio's wife put out a *Belly of Naples*."[76] In addition to neglect of her husband's socks, Arrighi objects to Serao's efforts to fundraise for her city:

> Poor Naples, how could you not be grateful to Mrs. Scarfoglio for her blessed belly? She presented you to Europe as an agonizing beggar, one who can do nothing but hold out a hand for alms. And, in the name of that beggar, the author turned to the government, to the

city hall, to the wealthy, to the benefactors—to all of them, imploring them to have mercy on those dying of starvation. Proud Parthenope is described by Mrs. Scarfoglio as the height of misery! If nothing else the Milanese can always be proud of never having exhausted their government and their neighbors with such whining.[77]

The vendors of Arrighi's Senigallia market, accordingly, are not greedy but aloof.

The short whimsical episodes in the section on the flea market in *The Belly of Milan* draw attention to the mangy and mismatched merchandise as well as the popular customs and vernacular. Arrighi does not list the objects for sale, in part because so many of them would be unidentifiable even to the vendors. What's more, "it would take at least ten dense pages to name all the objects displayed."[78] That, Arrighi explains, would create a farcical effect that might appeal only to "certain unrepentant ultra-realists." He therefore leaves out such a list for stylistic reasons: "I'll gladly renounce it, because objects named one by one don't seem to me to add any artistic value. It is only possible to find some expression of vulgar poetry or picturesque squalor in that exposition of misery if you consider it in its interminable entirety. Only then do contrasts jump out before your eyes and make you think or laugh or maybe even shudder."[79] These stylistic considerations also speak to the aesthetics of the hoard, according to which the whole becomes something more perplexing and pathological than the sum of its parts.

In lieu of a list, Arrighi presents the flea market through short vignettes, recording his conversations with vendors, noting their behaviors, and describing objects of particular interest. He begins by noting the mystery of the market's name: "that outdoor market, that the ragpickers and junk dealers of Milan hold every morning during the summer and that people call the *Fiera di Senigallia*. Don't ask me why it's called by that name." Arrighi notes that while ambulant rag-pickers in Milan wander the city calling out, "Rags for sale!" the stall-keepers at the Senigallia market are all "as mute as fish." He glosses their silence: "It's almost as though they want to ennoble their miserable wares by acting like serious dealers, or as though they are too proud of their merchandise to bother showing it off to passersby." Arrighi conveys the excitement of stumbling upon a delightfully outmoded and misshapen hat with the interjection: "How sublime!" A matchless right brodequin embodies the exasperating uselessness of so much of the merchandise. Asked about the left booty, an indifferent vendor shrugs: "There isn't one."[80]

As in De Amicis's Turin and Arrighi's Milan, in F. T. Marinetti's 1909 *Founding and Manifesto of Futurism*, the market—a figure for Italy itself—is the antithesis of modernity. Marinetti describes the nation teeming with the "fetid cancer of professors, archeologists, tour guides, and antiquarians."[81] "For much too long," he writes, "Italy has been a junk market."[82] Whether frequented by ragpickers digging through the debris of the past, or by aesthete collectors like the decadent poet and novelist Gabriele D'Annunzio, with his "profound passion for the past and mania for collecting," the market is a negation of the values celebrated by Italian futurists, even though the junk that accumulates there is a necessary by-product of the temporal the movement avows.[83] History itself, for Marinetti, belongs among the characters who frequent the market: "a miserable collector of stamps, medals, and counterfeit coins."[84]

Photographs and Found Objects

In futurist writings, as in De Amicis's modern and patriotic Turin and in Arrighi's quiet and proud Milan, the flea market is a picturesque milieu set apart from the modern city and nation. De

Amicis and Arrighi are not interested in stories of sudden riches but in the strangeness of the market—the merchandise and the people that frequent it, and its exteriority to the general economy. It is against the spectacle of abjection at the market that the modernity of the metropolis and the writer, reader, and touristic visitor of the markets can be established. The spectacle of so much curious stuff changes in the interwar period when flea markets become laboratories of surrealist thought. Where else might one expect to find a chance meeting of an umbrella and a sewing machine on a dissecting room table?[85] Breton roots his own artistic project in contingencies of *trouvailles* (found objects) and writes about the *puces* in his autobiographical novels *Nadja* (1928) and *L'Amour fou* (*Mad Love*; 1937).[86] Of the Saint-Ouen market, he writes: "I go there often, searching for objects that can be found nowhere else: old fashioned, broken, useless, almost incomprehensible, even perverse."[87]

Absent from Breton's accounts of the market are lists of knickknacks like those that clutter De Amicis's *Torino*. Instead, Breton focuses on the singular objects that attract his eye: "[An] irregular, white shellacked half-cylinder covered with reliefs and depressions that are meaningless to me, streaked with horizontal and vertical reds and greens, preciously nestled in a case under a legend in Italian." Neither Breton's description of the object, nor the accompanying photograph diminishes its dogged inscrutability: "After careful examination I have finally identified [it] as some kind of statistical device, operating three-dimensionally and recording the population of a city in such and such a year, although all this makes it no more comprehensible to me."[88]

What is the device? A representation of a historical dataset in the form of a phallic plaster sculpture? A meter that registers some invisible atmospheric quality, like humidity, temperature, or pollution? What could the air possibly say about the population in a certain area at distinct historical moments? Whether or not some measure exists that would make such a reading conceivable, the idea conjured is one of registering the traces of human presence that accumulate in the skies above like the odds and ends that pile up in the stalls below. That would make the statistical device similar to a camera, preserving an index of that-which-was-present-at-one-time. But the device would also preserve that-which-was-present-at-another-time; presumably, the traces would bear some indication of the duration of their presence so that a reading taken in 1880 would be able to measure the population in 1870 and 1860.[89] The device would thus index a presence that is intercalated by a "spacing" that reveals a multiplicity that undermines the illusion of "seamless integrity of the real."[90]

That is how Rosalind Krauss describes photography in a 1981 essay. She argues for the primacy of the medium for surrealism, not only because of specific works and artists but also and more important because its formal properties coincide so closely with the principles of the cultural movement. Surrealism engages and dismantles the most powerful illusion of photography: that it is the "capture of a moment" and the "seizure and freezing of presence." With heterogeneous techniques that range from the "absolutely banal" photographs by Boiffard that illustrate *Nadja* to multiple exposures, negative printing, and solarizations, surrealist photography conveys that "we are not looking at reality, but at the world infested by interpretation or signification, which is to say, reality distended by the gaps or blanks which are the formal preconditions of the sign."[91]

Susan Sontag presents the illusion of photography as that of chance reigning over artistic intentionality—that is, the rule of flea markets and found objects. She writes: "Photographs are, of course, artifacts. But their appeal is that they also seem, in a world littered with photographic relics, to have the status of found objects—unpremeditated slices of the world."[92] The similarities between ragpicking and flea market shopping, on the one hand, and photography, on the other, have been widely noted. This is in part because they are so vivid in the work of Atget, who first follows the footsteps of the ragpicker, with his early painterly portrait, and then follows in his footsteps, focusing on the fascinating objects of scavenge in *Villa d'un chiffonnier* and *Intérieur d'un chiffonnier*, as well as photographs of Paris junk shops with merchandise hanging from awnings and piled up along the sidewalks of empty streets.

Breton encounters a second significant object at the flea market in *Nadja*: "Our attention was simultaneously caught by a brand new copy of Rimbaud's *Œuvres Complètes* lost in a tiny, wretched bin of rags, yellowed nineteenth-century photographs, worthless books, and iron spoons."[93] The simultaneity of Breton's perception of the book and the statistical device delineates the spatial framing of an instant, suggesting photographic capture. The discovery of the *Œuvres Complètes* occasions a new friendship between Breton and the "extremely cultivated" stall-keeper, Fanny Beznos, who possesses "great revolutionary faith."[94] Between the pages of the volume, Breton finds a poem and some notes written by Beznos and discusses them with her at length.[95] The book seems to Breton to be an uncanny repetition of his chance meeting not long before with a girl who had asked for permission to recite Rimbaud's "The Sleeper in the Valley." The sense of simultaneity and chance is complicated by the accompanying photograph by J. A. Boiffard noted for its absolute banality. Ian Walker notes that the image is void of the encounters that animate the text: neither book nor statistical device is visible within the frame, Beznos is pictured with

FIGURE 2.5
Jacques-André Boiffard, *Marché aux puces*, 1928. Courtesy of the Archives
André Breton.

her back to the camera, and the merchandise—primarily fabrics
and furniture—is indistinct.[96]

The objects Breton finds at the flea market in *L'Amour fou*, like
those in *Nadja* are notable for their strangeness and their resonance

with the author. On an excursion to Saint-Ouen described in the novel, Breton and Alberto Giacometti first experience the place as a blur of indistinct objects creating a general impression of transience: "The objects that, between the lassitude of some and the desire of others, go off to dream at the antique fair had been just barely distinguishable from each other in the first half hour of our stroll. They flowed by, without accident, nourishing the meditation that this place arouses, like no other, concerning the precarious fate of so many little human constructions."[97] When particular objects emerge from this haze, they do so through grammatical formulations that lend them agency; they attract, draw in, and strike the flaneurs: "The first one of them that really attracted us, drawing us as something we had *never seen*, was a half-mask of metal striking in its rigidity as well as in its forceful adaptation to a necessity unknown to us."[98]

In such instances of "objective chance" in *L'Amour fou*, flea market objects are emissaries bearing the message of the recipient's desire, so that "finding of an object here serves exactly the same purpose as the dream."[99] A material unconscious, the flea market can only be a marginalist economy, one that "reconciles the laborious detours of the political economy with the subjective shortcut of the libidinal economy," obscuring the social relations and histories of the objects.[100] But objective chance does not short circuit desire in jouissance, producing desire only by satisfying it. Instead, objective chance presents desire in the enigmatic form of the surreal.

Squaring the Circle

Flea market photography influenced by the work of Atget as well as surrealist thought is particularly vivid in analogizing the labor of the ragpicker or junk-dealer and that of the street photographer.[101]

In André Kertész's 1929 *Paris Flea Market*, a vendor sits huddled under a cape or coat with a small rug draped over his lap—the border of the rug occupies the center of the frame. His wares include pictures and empty frames, a mirror, rags, a top hat, a helmet, assorted wicker baskets, and metal objects that might be identified as the stand for fireplace tools, the wheel of a baby carriage, the base of a folding card table. Though his eyes are veiled by the visor of his cap, the vendor looks resolute on surveilling his wares or keeping warm and unaware of or uninterested in the photographer. A top hat balanced on a tripod and a helmet balanced on the folding table rhyme visually with the vendor's cap, making him look like another peculiarly composite hatstand. A mirror next to the vendor reflects his profile and, with it, a fourth hat; if a rectangle were drawn connecting these four hats, they would frame nothing. An empty frame hanging on the wall behind the vendor misses the mark of a portrait. Nonetheless, it is positioned such that from a different angle the vendor's face would appear to be centered within it. The empty frame invites a comparison between the frame of the photograph and the arrangement of the merchandise by the vendor; the conflicting perspectives suggested by the two frames are aesthetic rather than economic. And the makeshift garments that keep the vendor warm attest to his poverty; his apparent indifference to the photographer seems to represent a repudiation of "somber realism of labor value" in favor of unpredictable flashes of chance, or desire.[102]

One of the first examples of Italian photography bearing traces of Atget's fascination with the outmoded is an uncredited picture that appeared in 1932 in *L'italiano. Periodico della rivoluzione fascista* (*Periodical of the Fascist Revolution*), a literary journal founded by Leo Longanesi.[103] The September issue included a still life of dispossessed domestic objects: a baby carriage, a trunk, a

FIGURE 2.6
André Kertész, *Marché aux puces*, 1929 © Estate of André Kertész /
Higher Pictures.

commode, a sewing mannequin, and assorted buckets and pans, all
arranged to face the camera and the empty road. The composition
is set against a sparse backdrop of scrawny trees, cement steps, and
an indistinct building.[104] No context explains the presence of the
objects by the side of the road; there is no indication of a nearby
market or of a move in progress. The objects appear to be of high
quality, and nothing is pictured—with the possible exception of
the sewing mannequin—that would not be found in a bourgeois
household. The sewing mannequin, though, is a simulacrum of
woman, making the scene a diorama of bourgeois life.[105] Unlike
still lifes of flowers and food, the photograph is a vivid reminder

FIGURE 2.7
Untitled photograph. Attributed to Leo Longanesi. Published in *L'italiano. Periodico della rivoluzione fascista* 7, no. 14 (September 1932): 195.

not of mortality but of the transience and emptiness of bourgeois domestic life.

Longanesi became a major figure in Italian publishing; he went on to start the first Italian illustrated news magazine, *Omnibus*, in 1937; it was closed two years later by the fascist Ministry of Popular Culture, known as Minculpop. Surrealism was an important influence for Longanesi, and a fascination with objective chance is evident in his collaborations with Cesare Barzacchi, who became his "photographic alter-ego" and may have taken the photograph above.[106] Barzacchi describes the frequent excursions the two would make to the flea market at Campo de' Fiori in Rome:

> Longanesi bought every sort of knickknack: crystal stars, blown-glass ornaments, cardboard prosthetic noses, carnival masks, a gypsy dress, an old tux and top hat, the angel from a Neapolitan nativity scene. And at the office he had accumulated a lot more stuff to use in his compositions: illustrated postcards, artificial flowers, gold cardboard letters and ribbons of various sizes—the ones used in funeral wreaths. Old military and diplomatic decorations, metals, empty boxes, women's shoes, lace doilies and linens. Glasses, Morandian bottles, armchairs, ottomans . . . In short, a strange and unusual universe that intrigues and excites Longanesi, suggesting crazy fantasies, absurd dreams, and unheard-of juxtapositions.[107]

Whether Longanesi would be a considered a hoarder today is entirely moot, but the sensibility of his creative projects is marked by what Ennery Taramelli describes as a "passion for collecting and accumulating traces and relics saved . . . the abysses of historical memory."[108]

Between 1937 and 1940, Alberto Lattuada, a young photographer who would go on to become a prolific film director, began taking pictures of the Senigallia market. His *Occhio quadrato* (*Square Eye*), a collection of twenty-six square Rolleiflex photographs of the Milanese periphery and its inhabitants, was published by Corrente in 1941. The volume is often considered a document of antifascism because it captures urban poverty censured by the fascist regime beginning in the mid-1920s.[109] The photographs also constitute an important contribution to the flourishing genre of documentary photography represented, in Europe, by the work of Bill Brandt and Henri Cartier-Bresson, and in the United States, by work funded by the Farm Security Administration. FSA-funded documentary photographers included Walker Evans, whose 1938 MoMA exhibition was reviewed by Giulia Veronesi in the journal *Corrente* in 1939.[110] Noting its resonance with photography outside of Italy, art critic Piero Berengo Gardin writes: "*Occhio quadrato* thus enters the history of photography as the title of a work, but also as an emblem of a particular aesthetic moment."[111] That aesthetic moment was one in which photographers took great interest in documenting poverty, which was conveyed visually in part by the objects with which the poor get by and make do.[112] Critical discussions of *Occhio quadrato* tend to focus on *La passeggiata della sera* (*The Evening Walk*), a photograph of an old man out for a stroll in the desolate environs of a hovel built from stones, tarps, and other found materials. The image captures a private, contemplative moment, conferring a dignity that is undermined by the angle of the photograph, shot from above.

Critics have focused less attention on pictures of vendors and wares at the Senigallia market, though more than one-third of the images of *Occhio quadrato* were taken there.[113] The seventeenth photograph, of wooden stands locked shut, captures a moment before the market opens. Lattuada explains: "One knows that at a certain point a thousand human voices will fill the air with the din of celebration and of the anxiety of selecting, of acquiring, of possessing for a coin that object . . . that dwells as a prisoner

FIGURE 2.8
Alberto Lattuada, *Fiera di Senigallia*, 1941. Alinari Archives, Florence.

now—at the moment of the photograph—locked in the inert stalls."[114] The following six images are also of the market; four are titled *Fiera di Senigallia*. The second of the photographs titled *Fiera di Senigallia* features a lamp and a vase, candelabra and irons, a trunk, a commode, and an electric fan. The most prominent human form of the composition is a female bust missing one arm. Her gown is loosely draped, leaving one breast exposed. She looks modestly down and to her left, beyond the frame. A vendor sits precariously—he seems to be floating—on a bedframe behind her: his gaze extends horizontally beyond the frame, never to intersect with hers. Five figures on the other side of a bicycle-cart stand with their backs to the camera, looking in at least three directions. What seems to predominate in the image is a sense of isolation; the sightlines of the vendor and bust do not intersect, a nondescript residential building looms over the scene, its windows blinded. But Lattuada also suggests serendipitous solidarity among the broken and maimed. The vendor rests his left hand on his right thigh; he is missing three fingers. As if in recompense, the bust's right arm reaches gracefully to her head, an unusually long and slender finger extends past the hair bun.

The next picture captures assorted merchandise: paintings, candelabra, dressers, mannequins, statues, plates, quilts, side tables, and frames. The frame is dominated by inanimate and animate human forms whose arrangement emphasizes both resemblances and communicative lapses. The top half of the frame is taken up with the residential building; the bottom half is dedicated to the flea market merchandise as well as the vendor, a cheery old man sitting on a stool. The human forms in the image can be used to imagine two diagonal lines. One line extends from the man to a sewing mannequin behind him, a standing lamp composed sturdy pedestal, a kitsch statue of a woman draped in a gold strapless mini dress that does not quite cover her breasts. She holds up a torch composed of three bulbs with three crenulated glass shades. Between the lamp and the vendor is a sewing mannequin. Another diagonal line can be formed from a framed oil portrait of an august man behind the vendor, to a figurine on the ground in front of him—paperweight, or bookend, or perhaps, judging the awkward angle of its recline, an ornamental element detached

FIGURE 2.9
Alberto Lattuada, *Fiera di Senigallia*, 1941. Alinari Archives, Florence.

from a façade. The vendor has a clubbed foot and only one shoe. As Arrighi marvels in *Il ventre di Milano*, shoes can be purchased at the market in units of one.

The final image bearing the title *Fiera di Senigallia* includes no human figures. The frame is entirely filled with objects, most of which are round: candelabras; oil lamps and lampshades; scales and weights; paintings and empty frames; clocks, grates, and goblets. The predominance of circular shapes within the square

FIGURE 2.10
Alberto Lattuada, *Fiera di Senigallia*, 1941. Alinari Archives, Florence.

frame, in a volume titled *Occhio quadrato*, brings to mind an idiom of futility: squaring the circle. The sale of such objects would be equally improbable. Like De Amicis's list of disparate wares at the Turinese flea market, the picture employs a poetics of etcetera, as objects extend beyond the frame, conjuring a larger space filled with more of the same. Disguised among this interminable sameness are two unexpected objects: a felt dog is nestled uncomfortably at halfway up on the right side of the picture.

More surprising is a second canine in the top right quadrant. A taxidermied dog's head extends up as if sniffing the air. It seems to be mounted on a plaque like a hunting trophy. Bringing a beloved pet back to life may be no less possible than squaring a circle. The taxidermied dog may once have been a warm reminder of a lost companion to the human who commissioned it. But upon the death of that person, the relic tests the boundaries between inert matter and forms of life.

Junk at the Gate of Eternity

In March 1940, Carlo Emilio Gadda published "Fiera a Milano" in *Panorama*, a short-lived biweekly illustrated news magazine that was shut down later that year by the Minculpop.[115] Gadda's essay appeared in the first issue of the magazine published under a new editor, the architect Giuseppe Pagano.[116] Under his direction, *Panorama* achieved a modernist sensibility different from the rationalist architecture for which Pagano is best known. The redesigned cover evokes Dadaist collage, with soldiers, planes, or ships cut into whimsical cloud shapes and pasted against a brightly colored background. The influence of surrealism and a tacit opposition to fascism are evident in the magazine in such features as an essay by Giulia Veronesi on anti-objectivist photography, one on the secret signs used by dissidents and medicants to communicate friendly participation in underground networks, and a photoessay on nudity in public art.[117]

Gadda's essay was accompanied by nine photographs by Pagano.[118] It is almost certain that the essay was commissioned to accompany the photographs since the objects enumerated in the text correspond closely to those pictured.[119] The title, "Fiera a Milano" (rather than "Fiera di Senigallia"), would have brought to mind a different sort of *fiera*: the expositions celebrating new technologies or fascist initiatives. The contrast between the glorification of the new, heralded by such expositions, and the worn-out junk of the Fiera di Senigallia would have seemed satirical, suggesting a restrained antifascism.[120] Pagano's photographs convey the arbitrary hodgepodge of the market thematically and through inconsistent cropping and layout. Four retain the square shape of the Rolleiflex negative; the others have been cut into rectangles of various dimensions.[121]

The first image shows two sets of coat-shrouded human legs and an advertising cutout of the shoulders and head of a smiling woman. All of Pagano's black and white photographs were shot with a Rolleiflex; the negative would have been square.[122] The uncropped image, which was included in a 2008 exhibition curated by Daria De Seta, shows a transaction-in-progress: one woman weighs out leather or cloth remnants. The version included in *Panorama* is cropped to the scale of the advertising cutout; the sacks of scraps in this version are inscrutable and the human legs, irrelevant. Sharing the page with the picture of the advertising cutout is one of a seated vendor with his back to the camera, poised as if to wait as long as it takes to make any improbable sale. A second old man, a shopper, is blurry across the expanse of unrecognizable merchandise laid out on the pavement. He holds the arm of his companion for support. The vendor and shopper here seem to mirror each other, each inhabiting a space and time beyond the bustle of the piazza, and, more broadly, the market economy.

The images on the next page highlight arbitrariness, both in the assortment of things depicted and in their layout in the magazine.

Fiera a Milano

Liberarsi da un vecchio arnese malato, da un aggeggio polveroso del bazar di nostra vita! uno sforzo psicologico che è peggio d'una malattia. Separarci da una cornice di mògano finto, inghirlandata di peperoncini d'oro, col ritratto della moglie di primo letto dello zio d'un cognato di nostro padre!

Divorziare dal busto in gesso di Garibaldi, dal cavatappi a cui s'è sdipanato un filetto, dal piccolo ordigno regolatore (in ottone) della vecchia lucerna a petrolio andata in briciole ad opera della Cesira, domestica dalle mani di fata!

Chi vende e chi còmpera le pere da cisterne del 1912, gli sgabelli spagliati, gli scaldini a carbone di legna, le trombe di grammofono in stile Liberty, ma senza il grammofono

re, del non mollare un bottone: comunque del non averci a perdere, dell'utilizzare in un qualunque modo e fino all'ultimo centesimo ri-

consentito dal mercato.

Mercato? Ma esiste un mercato dei turàccioli buchi, dei busti di Garibaldi, delle grattuggie usate, delle pi-

spagliati, gli scaldini a carbone di legna, le trombe di grammofono in stile Liberty, ma senza il grammofono, intendiamoci bene? C'è chi vende e chi compera tuttociò: esiste il mercato dell'impensabile. Tutto esiste a Milano. Milano è la scansia d'ogni possibilità, d'ogni idea che possa diventare industria o commercio. Non vi è industria, o commercio, che non sia rappresentata a Milano.

Anche l'istinto dell'ultimo profitto ha il suo mercato milanese; anche l'ultima possibile coincidenza fra il vecchio ritratto della zia Celestina e la cornice disoccupata di un ex-Giulio Càrcano o Filippo Càrcano (che ci sono stati l'uno e l'altro), di un ex-Zaccaria Bernasconi, ha luogo e tempo a verificarsi dentro la cerchia dell'onniprassi milanese.

Anche l'ultimo convegno d'amore fra l'ultima chiavetta smarrita e il rugginoso lucchetto che nessuno riesce più a disserrare. Tra il sellino che fu già di un coetaneo di Girardengo e il vigore novello del novello Ermenegildo, scapestrato garzone « ch'el fa el mekànik in del'Alfa Romeo ».

Questo convegno si chiama la fiera di Sinigallia, tenuta ogni sabato, di pomeriggio, « dalle parti di porta Ludovica ». Il mito di porta Ludovica — (che ci sia cia-

Tutto esiste a Milano. Milano è la scansia d'ogni possibilità, d'ogni idea che possa diventare industria o commercio. Non vi è industria e commercio, che non sia rappresentata

Più che una cagione di sentimento, si direbbe quell'altro motivo, costituzionale alla persona umana, anzi il fondamento dell'anima: (scusate la sincerità): quell'istinto del serbare, del prende-

cavabile, ciò che s'è acquisto, comperato, tirato in casa, goduto, magari per anni. L'idea che, dovendo alienare un turàcciolo, almeno se ne tragga il profitto ch'esso ci merita, il massimo profitto

pe con via il bocchino, dei sellini di biciclette sudati, delle chiavi di cui non si ricorda più l'uscio, dei clàkson senza la pera? Chi vende e chi còmpera le pere da cisterne del 1912, gli sgabelli

FIGURE 2.11

Giuseppe Pagano, "Fiera a Milano," *Panorama*, 1940.

FIGURE 2.12
Giuseppe Pagano, *Fiera di Senigallia,* 1940. Courtesy of Cesare de Seta, Archivio fotografico Giuseppe Pagano, Naples.

A picture of a pile of nuts, bolts, wrenches, and gears is cropped to an awkwardly long rectangle. The photograph of shoes is captioned with a line from Gadda's essay: "There you see slippers lined up, and shoes frayed and flattened by chaos like battalions of cockroaches."[123] The few pairs turned against the order of the battalions, and the intrusion of a basket and other unidentifiable

C'è un sogno di risparmio e di profitto, un tentativo di resurrezione in-extremis

scun lo dice, dove sia nessun lo sa) — pare proprio, sì... mi assicurano che è invece una cosa seria. Tutte le porte di Milano, del resto, si ha un bel fantasticare, ma han l'aria d'un mito: non fossero i granitici tempietti e gli archi Ferdinandei o Napoleonici superstiti ai vecchi dazi. Questa parentesi a proposito della Ludovica. Ma sull'esistenza della fiera di Sinigallia non ci sono dubbi: è stata addirittura fotografata. Il nome adriatico che ci ricorda Papa Mastai-Ferretti e l'irriverenza del Carducci, nonché l'estremo segno dei Galli nella penisola, nonché la jugulazione di Vitellozzo Vitelli e di Oliverotto Ufreducci ad opera del caro Valentino, per il buon popolo milanese, in sul naviglio alla dàrsena, o quasi, vuol dire nient'altro che « Vecchi pignattini d'alluminio, porta-ovi e cucchiai scompagnati, con manichi di padella in libertà, ghiere di ottone senza lucignolo, attaccapanni un po' sconnessi e bidets un po' zoppi ». E vi vedreste le allineate delle ciabatte: e scarpe sfatte ed appiattite da un marasma, come battaglioni di scarafaggi ottuagenari: e gavette, e viti d'ogni calibro, candelieri di zinco-lega, bomboniere, nel bric-à-brac un cane da

caccia di bronzo che «punta» contro le grattùge.

E anche un tavoletto per macchina da cucire, a cui però la macchina bisogna che ce l'attacchiate voi, beninteso se proprio volete anche quella; e una caffettiera di latta in figura di Carlo d'Angiò: un paniere per partite campestri in riva del Naviglio Grande: e dei manichini di sarta opportunamente decollati; delle biciclette, sia intere che a pezzi, delle forbici per le unghie, delle pinze da elettricista.

L'incredibile relitto s'è venuto ad arenare su questa spiaggia senza frangente come nei racconti dei naufraghi le scatole di biscotto zuppo approdano all'isola dei gabbiani. Non è un naufragio questo, ma il consunto costume degli umani: anche il costume, cioè l'«habitus» della nostra civiltà meccanica e incrottata viene a dimettersi, esausto, tra le braccia di questa rigattiera benigna, ma implacabile, che lo attende, in cima degli anni, « dalle parti di porta Ludovica ». Come il Petrarca sarà laureato poeta in Campidoglio, così il cavatappi, nel suo vecchio sàbato, assurgerà finalmente al collaudo della Ludovica: il pitale di ferro e smalto, il mozzo di bicicletta con via tre palle (biglie, sfere).

Oh! il vestito della civiltà umana è pur fatto di bagnarole e di pela-patate, di rotuline d'ottone e di orologi a cucù che fanno gra-gra, se pur lo fanno; di bullette a rosellina per i tacchi dei muratori e di coltella femmine

Rotelle, rotuline d'ottone, interruttori, chiavi inglesi...

Vi vedreste allineate delle ciabatte: e scarpe sfatte ed appiattite da un marasma, come battaglioni di scarafaggi

30

FIGURE 2.13

Giuseppe Pagano, "Fiera a Milano," *Panorama*, 1940.

objects in the upper left corner makes this seem like a particularly slovenly regiment of cockroaches.

Many of the recognizable objects—human forms, picture frames, a basket—are cut off, and the framing highlights the absence of logical connections between the objects pictured. In the photograph with sewing mannequins, a finger points from the shoppers' side of the makeshift stall. The three mannequins seem to mimic the shoppers; they too are without heads. What's more, it seems like they are the ones looking out over their wares. Indeed, after the first two pictures the images on the remaining four pages do not feature living people, with the exception of the legs of shoppers and the pointing finger.

FIGURE 2.14
Giuseppe Pagano, "Fiera a Milano," *Panorama*, 1940.

The studied artlessness of the page layout contrasts with Gadda's notably wrought language and accentuates the arbitrariness of the flea market merchandise. Gadda surveys the bric-a-brac that comes forth from the attics and basements of Milan on Saturdays—rusted keys, bent coat hangers, terracotta figurines, lopsided bidets, mismatched tableware. These and other worn-out, broken-down, and obsolete objects convene on the squalid pavement to await improbable moments of sale at the Senigallia market. Gadda focuses on the motivation of the vendors, sketching the conflicting theories of value that circulate amid the eclectic wares. The essay opens with three exclamations of the difficulty of discarding, each beginning with a verb that aggrandizes the act, naming it a "liberation," "separation," and "divorce." Ironic descriptions thicken the objects, detailing their broken-down uselessness and inscribing them within family bonds, class relations, and national lore. A fake mahogany frame wreathed with golden chili peppers, for example, holds a portrait of the first wife of the uncle of a collective "our" father's ex-brother-in-law. A little brass knob for sale at the market is what remains of an old petroleum lantern shattered by Cesira, the housekeeper with a light touch. Garibaldi is commemorated at the market with a chipped plaster bust. The goods are tattered traces of a disappearing world of deceased relatives and national heroes.

Though the incipit emphasizes the sentimental value of the objects for the vendors, the essay goes on to claim that it is not sentiments that motivate the vendors, but economics. Gadda even makes the urge to save appear both rational and universal:

> Rather than sentimental reasons, we might say some other reason, constitutional of the human person, or better, the foundation of the human soul: (excuse the sincerity): that instinct to stash away,

to retain, to never let go of a button: in any case never to take a loss, to utilize in whatever way possible, and down to the very last cent salvageable, that which is acquired, bought, lugged home, enjoyed– perhaps even for years. The idea that having to divest yourself of a cork, you might at least extract the profit it merits, the maximum profit allowed by the market.[124]

The "instinct to stash away," here constitutive of the "human person" is a drive to extract—from even the most improbable of objects— as much profit or use as the market allows. However peculiar the determination to stash away even disintegrating corks, the locus of wonder—and parody—in the essay is not the vendors' instinct, but the metropolitan marketplace that matches even such dregs as these with buyers: "Market? But can there be a market of holey corks, busts of Garibaldi, used graters, pipes with mouthpieces missing, mangled bicycle seats, keys to who knows what door, bike horns without squeezers? . . . There are those who buy and those who sell all of that: there exists a market of the unthinkable. Everything exists in Milan."[125] The marvelous Milanese market- place renders the instinct to stash things away a rational behavior; this is a dramatic (and satirical) departure from earlier flea mar- ket writings like those of De Amicis, Arrighi, and Breton. Gadda's *fiera* is not in direct dialogue with the unconscious, or antithetical to the modernizing city—it is a perfectly efficient market, where every last trinket can be matched with a buyer. Whether a vendor is a *homo oeconomicus* or a hoarder depends on the fortunes of his wares at the market; at the Fiera di Senigallia, all wares fare well, albeit because of the "combinatorial certainty" that points to the remotest future.

Gadda emphasizes the timelessness of the market, imagining the objects washing up at Porta Ludovica like shipwrecks: "The incred- ible relic comes to graze upon this surfless shore, like in stories of shipwrecks when tins of soaked cookies wash up on the island of Melancholy. This is not a *shipwreck*, but the consumed customs of humans: even the costumes—that is, the '*habitus*' of our mechanical and bandaged up civilization, resigns itself, exhausted, at the end of its years, to the arms of the junk dealer."[126] The knickknacks that come to graze on the pastures of the market are like shipwrecked objects, but Gadda specifies that they are not actually lost to the abyss of history.

To arrive at the Fiera di Senigallia is the crowning achievement in the life of an object: a testament to its having been passed down through generations, to its having almost outlived any use or exchange value. Unlike shipwrecked objects, which would loll about the shore in obscurity, the junk at the *fiera* could yet be transformed by a redemptive moment of sale; designated, in Gadda's essay, with the dialect locution, a literary analog to the indexical quality of the photographic image: "el moment bon!" Because of such moments, the market becomes a wondrous site of economic efficiency, as customers emerge from all corners of the city to transform the odds and ends, sometimes after years: "There's a dream of savings and profit, an attempt at resurrection *in extremis*; . . . but also an economy and a combinatorial certainty—of managing to smash together the frayed with the useful, the part with the whole, and infinite patience with perfect timing: "el moment bon!" that in which the tuning peg of a broken violin will be resold for nineteen cents, after eighteen years on display, to the fiddling mendicant from via Mac-Mahon, who just broke one in his hand three days ago."[127] The "dream of savings and profit," unthinkable or unlikely as it may seem given the utter ruin of the merchandise, could be realized with "el moment bon!" that would transform a hoard into an investment, remunerating (and rendering rational) the eighteen-year wait.

Gadda draws attention to other popular idioms related to the market, capturing dialect locutions in direct quotations in a way that parallels the indexical quality of the photographic image. He writes: "This convocation is called the Senigallia Market; it's held every Saturday, in the afternoon, 'Out around Porta Ludovica.'" Gadda explains the vague directions: "The myth of Porta Ludovica," which he repeats: "Everyone knows it exists; nobody knows where."[128] The 1905 urban renewal involved the demolition of Porta Ludovica so that what remained of the renaissance city gate was popular memory and myth. Three years after the publication of "Fiera a Milano" in *Panorama*, Gadda changed the title of his essay to "Carabattole a Porta Ludovica" ("Knickknacks at Porta Ludovica").[129] The new title is suggestive; because much of the essay is dedicated to listing the *carabattole*, the Porta Ludovica of the title seems at once the imaginary urban space, the essay itself and, more broadly, the literary text.

Like the Fiera di Senigallia, where long-awaited encounters result in improbable moments of sale, the essay concludes with an abrupt change of course, in the form of a consideration of the mechanics of the essay itself: "At the end of every poem of manners, every portrait of the times, there is, perhaps, a perfunctory device [*buggerata meccànica*], just as in the depths of every home you love there is a well-known trap, the spring-loaded sort, with a piece of dry cheese, to catch the unreachable mouse that would otherwise go drown himself in the demijohn of oil. Life is a fight, and you've got to fight with traps, with old junk."[130]

The perfunctory device of the essay—Gadda's poem of manners—consists in the introduction of the essayist into the fiera as a market flaneur who, after the tedium of a strange day, would happily open a bottle of Barbaresco: "But good grief, how can that be done? You need the corkscrew, the corkscrew! But where is this rascal of a corkscrew! It was in the drawer on the left, at the stall on the right. But what if it's not there anymore? No, it's not there! Don't despair! At the Fiera di Senigallia there's a cork, and a corkscrew."[131] The serendipitous encounter between the weary essayist and a corkscrew for sale at the market works as a prose mousetrap. With this perfunctory device, Gadda signals his own participation in the cruel optimism of "el moment bon," which inspires the vendors to show up, day after day, week after week, and year after year with their broken violin strings and their fake mahogany frames. With the direct quotations—the exclamation "el moment bon!" and the vague "out around Porta Ludovica"—Gadda situates the literary text between the mimesis of the essay and the indexicality of the photographs; between representation and trace. Orlando argues that the useless objects of modern literature convey anxieties about the usefulness of literature itself while embodying the uselessness repressed by the functional imperative and the myth of progress. But in Gadda's essay, such uselessness cannot exist because for every object there is an eventual flea market shopper prepared to pay what it is worth.

With the serendipitous mousetrap, the essay analogizes the relationship between the photographs and prose to that between vendor and shopper; the reality of value is produced somewhere in between. After explaining the myth of Porta Ludovica, Gadda writes: "But of the existence of the Fiera di Senigallia there can be no doubt: It's even been photographed."[132] That the objects accumulate at a place that does not exist except in popular memory and in the essay substantiates Orlando's conception of the literary text as a repository of repressed uselessness. The photographs enact a transformation analogous to "el moment bon" that returns the objects lulling about on the shores of oblivion to economic legibility and ontological certainty. The Fiera di Senigallia is where the frayed meets the useful, the part meets the whole, and infinite patience meets perfect timing, as in "el moment bon" that transforms the merchandise into a sale. It is a place where the free market is realized in the most improbable of ways, as even an old violin string and an eighteen-year wait earn the nineteen cents they are due.

The Senigallia market of the *Panorama* feature encompasses economic rationality and grotesque uselessness; the documentary claims of street photography and the wrought language of the archiveaholic; the modern city of Milan and the *lieu de mémoire* of Porta Ludovica. Gadda's essay and Pagano's photographs condense the cultural history of flea markets traced in this chapter. First points of sale for scavenged materials, the flea markets of the Paris Zone evolved into emporia for *objets d'hasard*—from places where waste is processed in predictable ways by labor, they become places where chance rules. The contingent meetings with undervalued objects that results become a defining feature of modern conceptions of the artist, poet, street photographer, and historian. That hoarding continues to be animated by these hallowed heroes of modernity helps to explain its tenacity and ambivalence.

The threatening obscurity of market and metropolis come together in the episode discussed of young Henri Pouget's discovery of registered stock shares and bank vouchers attached to the pages of old magazines purchased at the flea market. The provenance of the flea market treasure Pouget finds is not in question; the financial documents are traceable to one Mr. Haas, a recently deceased miser whose wealth was the stuff of local legend. The reinvention engendered by the market's anonymity is instead one of identity: Henri's father and his accomplice, Cassagne, attempt to redeem the vouchers under a false name in Brussels. Their severe punishment—four months in prison and a fine of fifty francs—attests to the danger perceived in such anonymity. An even stronger testament to this sense of danger is the success of the literary genre I investigate in the next chapter: detective fiction.

3

Epistemologies

THE CRIME SCENE

It is no accident, Walter Benjamin writes in his 1931 essay on photography, that Eugène Atget's pictures look like crime scenes.[1] The strange compositions of furniture set out before alleyway *brocantes* and the curious objects concealed amid rotting wood and scrap metal exist in spaces where confidence tricks and fleas might meet the intuition of the detective or the taste of the connoisseur. The enigmatic provenance of flea market merchandise, moreover, is matched by the veil of anonymity offered by the city for the "type and genius of deep crime" that lurks within the crowd.[2] Benjamin asks, "But isn't every square inch of our cities a crime scene? Every passerby a culprit? Isn't the task of the photographer—descendent of the augurs and haruspices—to reveal guilt and point out the guilty in his pictures?"[3] Like the ragpicker and street photographer, the detective of modern fiction finds a likeness in the hoarder of contemporary psychiatry, not because of accumulated possessions. Rather, both detective and hoarder are distinguished by their acute perception of marginal details—though only the former transforms them by putting them to interpretive use, as does Sherlock Holmes: "[piecing] them together, and . . . [devising] some common thread upon which they might all hang."[4]

In *Stuff*, Randy Frost and Gail Steketee describe hoarders as bad orators whose speech is characterized by excessive detail: "People who hoard often speak in overly elaborate ways, including far too many details."[5] Their voice messages, Frost and Steketee observe, are "long, rambling, almost incoherent, [and] filled with irrelevant details."[6] In his family history, *The Force of Things*, Alexander Stille describes a similar lack of structure in the conversational style of his aunt Lally, a hoarder: "In some ways, the state of her apartment was a bit like her conversation. In the piles of stuff, her most precious things were mingled hopelessly with junk of no possible interest, just as in her conversation, remarks of genuine interest were lost amid streams of trivial chatter."[7] This linguistic peculiarity seems to develop from what Frost and Steketee describe as a heightened capacity to appreciate things overlooked by others: "For hoarders, every object is rich with detail. We disregard the color and hue of a magazine cover as we search for the article inside. But if we paid attention, we might notice the soothing effects of the colors, and the meaning of the object would expand in the process. In this way, the physical world of hoarders is different and much more expansive than that of the rest of us."[8] Details transform the magazine from something to be read into a wondrously textured, colorful entity. The magazine is removed from an invisible totality that enables object-use and everyday functioning to become, in the language of Bill Brown's thing theory, a thing. The vibrant saturation of the hoarder's physical world, however, presents itself in anticipation of an interpretation that would lend some structure to the jumble of detail, transforming it with causal logic. As one subject of *Stuff*, Irene, explains to Frost and Steketee: "I'm a detail person, not a big-picture person, but I've been saving details for so long, I need to put them together."[9] The details—along with (and inseparable from) the things set aside for future use—exist for the hoarder in a temporality defined by the anticipation of retrospection, though the moment of retrospection never arrives.

In a seminal 1979 essay, Carlo Ginzburg isolates an epistemological paradigm rooted in the transformation of marginal details. He dates the method to prehistoric times when hunters interpreted small signs—tracks, scat, broken branches—to construct a sequence of events that had not been experienced directly, some variation of "someone passed this way."[10] The rhetorical figures through which this sequence is elaborated—part for whole, effect for cause—are rooted in the narrative axis of metonymy, "with the rigorous exclusion of metaphor."[11] Ginzburg compares the method to a carpet, with threads running vertically through historical periods, diagonally across cultures, and horizontally across disciplines. The multiple disciplinary threads lend the paradigm several names: evidential, divinatory, venatic, conjectural, and semiotic. Hoarding, I propose, is something like a nonslip pad for the elegant tapestry Ginzburg weaves; a coarse and unbecoming double from which the evidential paradigm nonetheless derives function and form.

Although the vertical threads begin in prehistoric hunting cultures, their density increases dramatically in the 1870s and 1880s, when the evidential paradigm establishes itself in a new method of art attribution, a new science of interpretation, and a new literary genre—those introduced by art historian Giovanni Morelli, Freud, and Arthur Conan Doyle, respectively. Their methods share an interpretive attention to apparently negligible details. Ginzburg explains: "In each case, infinitesimal traces permit the comprehension of a deeper, otherwise unattainable reality: traces—more precisely, symptoms (in the case of Freud), clues (in the case of Holmes), pictorial marks (in the case of Morelli)."[12] In each discipline, the paradigm entails an abstraction of some detail from the context—the plane of signification—in which it is found. The psychoanalyst extracts a symptom—a slip of the tongue, perhaps—from the patient's speech and uses it to put together a causal sequence that orders the mismatched stuff of the mind. The art connoisseur isolates a detail from the artwork—the shape of an earlobe, for example—and interprets it along a different plane of signification: the circumstances of production and the identity of the artist. The detective, finally, uses some detail from the scene of the crime to reconstruct the story of what happened and whodunit.

In each case, marginal details are used as cairns marking a specific hermeneutic path, a causal sequence. The details, clues, or symptoms act as hinges between layers of narration or planes of signification. Gerard Genette calls this movement "narrative metalepsis": "the transition from one narrative level to another [by] introducing into one situation, by means of a discourse, the knowledge of another."[13] It is the redoubled structure of the detective story—its division into the story of a crime and the story of an investigation—that prompts Tzvetan Todorov to claim that the genre resembles the basic structure of a work of fiction in which "what really happened" (the *fabula*) can be distinguished from the telling of it (the *sjužet*).[14] Even more broadly, the redoubled structure of both detective story and work of fiction exemplifies "the originary doubleness of the metaphysical concept of signifying."[15] As Giorgio Agamben puts it: "Only because presence is divided and unglued is some thing like 'signifying' possible."[16]

A noted example of the way in which the division of presence and absence makes signification possible is the Fort!/Da! game, which Freud first describes in *The Interpretation of Dreams* and returns to in *Beyond the Pleasure Principle*. The game is simple: a child throws a spool of thread and cries, "o-o-o-o" (go away!). He then pulls the spool back, joyfully exclaiming, "da!" (here it is!). "This, then, was the complete game—disappearance and return."[17] Freud interprets Fort!/Da! as a way for the child to gain mastery over the pain of his mother's absences. Lacan, by contrast, uses the game to illustrate the moment that "gives birth to the symbol," when a child is "born into language."[18] Through the repeated gesture, the child "raises his desire to a second power" so that "Fort!" and "Da!" signify beyond the context of their utterance and the object becomes irrelevant.[19] The exclamations "Fort!" and "Da!" bear meaning in relation to each other rather than the object. It is only by letting go of an object (if only to summon it back) that signification beyond the spool becomes possible. However glaringly literal the comparison to hoarding, the game, and Lacan's gloss on it, is an apt allegory of the need to gain distance from the materiality of a thing—in the idiom of thing theory—in order to find its meaning as an object.[20]

In detective stories that thematize hoarding—from the conventional (e.g., Arthur Conan Doyle's "The Musgrave Ritual" [1893]), to the neo avant-garde (e.g., Luigi Malerba's *Il serpente* [*The Serpent*; 1966]), to television forensic dramas (e.g., 2010 episodes of *Bones* and *CSI: Las Vegas*)—hoarding and detection maintain a tension inherent to realism. The hoarder, overwhelmed by the onslaught of detail and unwilling to dismiss any perception as irrelevant or unimportant, represents one extreme. The detective, by contrast, zeroes in on some apparently useless, marginal detail and uses it as a hinge that connects the investigation to another layer of narrative or signifying plane.

The analogy between the labor of the literary critic and that of the detective is well known; Roland Barthes's "The Reality Effect" (1968) can help to parse its implications. Barthes argues that apparently useless details function in fiction like symptoms and clues.[21] He proposes that insignificant notation—the detail "apparently detached from the narrative's semiotic structure"— serves the significant function of creating the "referential illusion": the appearance of reality.[22] As an example, Barthes quotes a description of Mme. Aubain's parlor in Flaubert's "A Simple Heart": "An old piano, standing beneath a barometer, was covered with a pyramid of old books and boxes."[23] Barthes reads the piano as a testament to Aubain's bourgeois standing and the clutter as an indication of decline. He considers the barometer to be an extraneous detail that seems to serve no function, but in so seeming actually serves the important function of attesting to the reality of the scene described: Why would the detail be included, the logic goes, if the barometer weren't *actually* there, in a different plane of signification, that of real life? "The Reality Effect" effectively makes uselessness impracticable within the plotted space of literature, for what appears useless—the empty signifier—is actually filled with new meaning and made useful as a testament to "reality."

It is not surprising many have taken issue with Barthes's argument, since—to paraphrase an axiom of hoarding—one man's insignificant notation is another's interpretive crux. In *The Material Unconscious*, Brown counters Barthes's example of apparently insignificant notation by pointing out that the popularity of the aneroid barometer, invented in 1844, would have made the ornately decorated oak-pedimented sort atop the piano in Aubain's parlor appear outmoded. The barometer could hardly be considered insignificant within the story's setting and symbolic system.[24] Brown also addresses the conceptual significance of the barometer itself: an object that denies any schism between "science" and "culture," and that indexes an "absent presence" by gauging atmospheric pressure.[25] As Naomi Schor writes, summing up many critical responses to Barthes's essay: "There are no inessential details, just inadequate readers."[26] This would be the case in Barthes's reading as well, except that his method for excising uselessness is not to interpret it within the diegetic world but to make it a hinge to another layer of narrative or plane of signification. Regardless of what is made of the barometer, Barthes essay conjures a textual economy that is without waste. No detail is wasted, nothing is *truly* extraneous.[27] He asks: "What would any method be worth which did not account for the totality of its object, i.e., in this case, the entire surface of the narrative fabric?"[28]

Despite the contrast between the perception of details described in *Stuff* and the epistemological uses to which they are put to create the effect of reality or according to the evidential paradigm, the specter of hoarding has long haunted the figure of the detective. This is, in part, because of the idiosyncrasies of Arthur Conan Doyle's Holmes. In his *Oxford Handbook* chapter "Hoarding in History," Fred Penzel ventures that the eccentric detective "might have been somewhat of a compulsive hoarder."[29] As evidence, Penzel cites Watson's description of the cluttered Baker Street apartment he shares with Holmes in "The Adventure of the Musgrave Ritual." The story, which is dedicated to a case involving the mysterious disappearance of an ambitious butler and a lovesick maid, is also an account of the perspicacious neglect of irrelevant detail that results in a triumph of the epistemology of detection over the cumbersome presence of old stuff. The story begins with an excursus on a scene of clutter as Watson reflects on the "personal habits" of his roommate: "One of the most untidy men that ever drove a fellow-lodger to distraction."[30] He elaborates: "Our chambers were always full of chemicals and criminal relics, which had a way of wandering into unlikely positions, and of turning up in the butter-dish or in even less desirable places. But his papers were my great crux. He had a horror of destroying documents . . . thus month after month his papers accumulated, until every corner of the room was stacked with bundles of manuscript which were on no account to be burned, and which could not be put away save by their owner."[31] Watson's description foregrounds the abundance of the material, the incongruous sites of accumulation, and the idiosyncratic organization.

The action begins one winter night when Watson suggests that Holmes tidy up a bit to make their apartment "a little more habitable." Holmes responds by luring Watson into a complicit fascination with the clutter; he withdraws to his bedroom then returns with objects nestled, like the mystery he will relate, within an elaborate series of frames. He brings back a large tin chest, from which he extracts first several bundles of paper, and then a small wooden box full of strange and apparently useless objects: "a crumbled piece of paper, an old-fashioned brass key, a peg of wood with a ball of string attached to it, and three rusty old disks of metal."[32] The remainder of the story is dedicated to a sort of metaphysical clean out; the apparently useless odds and ends are resignified as material traces of a mystery of utmost historical significance. The way to clean out a hoard, the story suggests, is not to throw things out, but to lend them new meaning through narrative.

Watson's story of the material disorder of a winter night recedes as Holmes explains the provenance of the mysterious objects by relating Reginald Musgrave's presentation of "strange doings" at his estate, Hurlstone. Musgrave responds to Holmes's invocation, "Pray, let me have the details," with an account that, like his estate, is "rambling," and crowded with extraneous detail: one Thursday night he could not sleep; he had taken black coffee after dinner; he struggled to sleep until two and then decided to read; his book was in the billiard room; he put on a dressing gown and went to get the book; to reach the billiard room, he had to walk past the library. Though he includes all this irrelevant information, Musgrave denies the importance of certain details and, in doing, signals their significance. When he walks past the library, Musgrave catches his butler, Brunton, studying a piece of paper—"nothing of any importance at all," "a thing of private interest . . . but of no practical use whatever."[33]

Three days after Brunton is caught snooping, he disappears. And three days after the butler's disappearance, his spurned lover, the maid Rachel Howells, also goes missing, leaving a trail of footprints that lead to a small lake on the estate. Draining the lake turns up no corpse, but rather a linen bag containing "a mass of old rusted and discolored metal and several dull-colored pieces of pebble or glass."[34] At Holmes's insistence, Musgrave produces the document Brunton had been studying in the library— the same one that ends up crumpled in the box that prompts Holmes's account to Watson. The paper has moved metaleptically, as clues do, across layers of narrative: from the library to Musgrave's account to Holmes, to Holmes's to Watson, to Watson's to the reader.

The paper contains what Musgrave calls a "rather an absurd business": the eponymous ritual that consists of seven questions and answers—the "strange catechism to which each Musgrave had to submit." Like the stuff in the Baker Street apartment, the ritual appears to be useless—though it does symbolize the antiquity of the family, substantiating Francesco Orlando's argument that the timeworn objects in modern literature express changing attitudes about aristocracy. Musgrave is a model of obsolescent aristocracy. He is an outsider among the bourgeois students at the college where he and Holmes first meet, in part because "something of his place of birth seemed to cling to the man." He is a metonym for his estate, the "venerable wreckage of a feudal keep."[35]

In his reading of "The Musgrave Ritual" as an allegory for plot—in its multiple meanings, as "the interpretive activity elicited by the distinction between *sjužet* and *fabula*," as a secret plan, and as a small piece of land marked out for a purpose—Peter Brooks explains that the resolution of the mystery consists in the unpacking of the metaphor of the ritual as a metonymy, a sequence of events bound by cause and effect.[36] The seven questions and answers plot the location of a treasure buried on the estate: the crown of Charles I, which had been entrusted to Sir Ralph Musgrave, the "prominent Cavalier and the right-hand man of Charles the Second." The mass of old rusted and discolored metal contained in the linen bag is this crown. The crumpled paper, brass key, wooden peg, and rusty disks that Holmes keeps are souvenirs of the case. The objects either helped Holmes locate the crown (the peg, the crumpled paper) or were contained in the box (the key, the rusty coins) where the crown lay for years before Brunton handed it up to Howells from the small underground chamber where he would be buried alive. The story Holmes tells lends significance and value to the objects that clutter the Baker Street apartment, just as his interpretation of the details Musgrave provides transforms the rusty metal in the linen bag into a relic "of great intrinsic value, but of even greater importance as an historical curiosity."[37]

At the outset of the story, Watson contrasts Holmes' disordered housekeeping with his meticulous intellection: "in his methods of thought he was the neatest and most methodical of mankind."[38] In the twenty-first century popular accounts of hoarding, which presume that there is a continuity between domestic and mental spaces, such "anomalies of character" would not be possible. The analogy between the mind and physical space recurs in Doyle, beginning in his first novel, *A Study in Scarlet* (1887). Holmes explains his image of the brain to Watson:

> I consider that a man's brain originally is like a little empty attic, and you have to stock it with such furniture as you choose. A fool takes in all the lumber of every sort that he comes across, so that the knowledge which might be useful to him gets crowded out, or at best is jumbled up with a lot of other things, so that he has a difficulty in laying his hands upon it. Now the skillful workman is very careful indeed as to what he takes into his brain-attic. He will have nothing but the tools which may help him in doing his work, but of these he has a large assortment, and all in the most perfect order.[39]

The space of the mind is governed by the laws of physics that dictate that multiple things cannot exist at the same time in the same place: "It is a mistake to think that that little room has elastic walls and can distend to any extent. Depend upon it there comes a time when for every addition of knowledge you forget something that you knew before. It is of the highest importance, therefore, not to have useless facts elbowing out the useful ones."[40] Once the brain is full, nothing new can be added unless some old thing is cast off to oblivion.

"The Five Orange Pips" (1891) sees some modification of this theory, as Holmes allows books to serve as extra storage space for the rarely-used information that would otherwise clutter the mind: "A man should keep his little brain attic stocked with all the furniture that he is likely to use, and the rest he can put away in the lumber-room of his library, where he can get it if he wants it."[41] Whereas the industry of professional organizing (and much of contemporary hoarding discourse) presumes that home and mind mirror each other so that the organization of one brings order to the other; for Holmes, the mind is an orderly functional space that can dwell in a cluttered apartment and be supplemented by a well-ordered library.

The content and organization of such lumber-room libraries was a daunting concern for late nineteenth-century criminologists. The flourishing of detective fiction in these years, Ginzburg and others have emphasized, corresponds to the consolidation of bourgeois notions of private property and laws designed to protect it through a detention-based system of punishment. This system, coupled with the anonymity afforded by urbanization and increasing mobility, required new methods of gathering, organizing, and storing an unruly hoard of photographic, anthropometric, and historical information in order to identify suspects and recidivists.[42] Agents and institutions charged with collecting, verifying, storing, and organizing data were overwhelmed by the accumulation of detail. "The fundamental problem of the archive," writes Allan Sekula, is the "problem of volume."[43] In an essay on the convergence of photography and statistical methods in the development of early technologies of criminal identification, he argues that "the central artifact of this system is not the camera but the filing cabinet."[44] This is also true of other indexes like the skulls, measurements, tattoos, drawings, and writings of criminals gathered by positivist criminologist Cesare Lombroso, whose daughter described him as a "born collector" who noticed things overlooked by others.[45]

Lombroso's pursuit of the "born criminal" and other abnormal or unworthy types that he believed to be at least in part biologically determined—prostitutes, female offenders, geniuses, the mentally ill—was the basis of an oeuvre of more than thirty books and a thousand articles, as well as the magnum opus, *L'uomo delinquente* (*Criminal Man*), which grew from 255 pages when it was first published in 1876, to more than seven times that size in the

1896–97 edition.[46] Detective fiction disavows the prosaic labor of cataloging such lumber-room libraries as Lombroso's expanding collection of relics—organization is replaced with intuition; the abundance of the archive is circumvented by a good story, like the one that Holmes relates to Watson about the contents of the small wooden box. The triumph of intuition over organization is also one of metonymy over metaphor, as when the Musgrave ritual is unpacked first as the plotting of a map leading to buried treasure, and then as the result of a plot to safeguard the crown for the king's successor. Malerba's *Il serpente* also thematizes hoarding and detection but adopts a structural logic of the former to undermine the latter. Before turning to the novel, I chart the clashing epistemologies as they are conveyed through intemperate perception and interpretation in two texts that pose similar challenges to the redoubled structure of realism.

Problems of Volume

A short story by Jorge Luis Borges, "Funes the Memorious" (1942), is an exploration of the signifying implications of an immediacy of detail like that which troubles the speech of Lally in *The Force of Things* and disrupts the everyday lives of the hoarders in *Stuff*.[47] Borges's narrator relates a conversation that took place years earlier with Ireneo Funes, who had been paralyzed in a horse riding accident that also left him with an extraordinary capacity to perceive so much detail as to render the physical world "almost intolerable in its richness and sharpness." The narrator repeatedly contrasts Funes's exceptional ability with his own faulty memory and dull discernment, implicitly calling into question the account he gives. He begins, for example: "I remember him (I have no right to utter this sacred verb, only one man on earth had that right and he is dead)."[48]

Funes, the narrator explains, could perceive every detail: "at one glance, all the leaves and tendrils and fruit that make up a grape vine" and remember every perception: "The dog at three fourteen (seen from the side)," as well as "the dog at three fifteen (seen from the front)." In a direct quotation that belies the narrator's disavowal, "I shall not attempt to reproduce his words, now irrecoverable," Funes explains: "My memory, sir, is like a garbage heap." His memory is like garbage not because of any willful act of jettison, but rather because nothing is discarded by forgetting. Unlike the narrator, whose story can take shape only because of its elision of detail—its inexact replication of experience—Funes is unable to produce a meaningful rendering of his perception or memory. The narrator concludes: "To think is to forget a difference, to generalize, to make abstractions. In the teeming world of Funes there were only details, almost immediate in their presence."[49]

The detailed immediacy of Funes's world seems to preclude even language. He is unable to perform the abstraction that would allow the dog at three fourteen and the dog at three fifteen to be named by the same word, "dog." He thereby inverts the linguistic turn of post-structuralist theory: his perception is indistinguishable from language not because it is made by language, but because it allows no space for language.[50] Adriana Cavarero differentiates between Funes's perception and recollection but notes that the products of these capacities are identical. Both amount to a detailed replication of a reality unmediated by language—that is, a presence without the space for the absence that makes signification possible. Although the hoarders of *Stuff* demonstrate no such powers of recollection, their deluging perceptions seem like a less extreme version of those of Funes. Funes's memory is a replication of the world, but hoarders entrust nothing to memory; possession is instead a material anamnesis.[51]

For Funes, seen through the disabling gaze of the narrator, every perception remains distinct, unintegrated; the dog at three fourteen and the dog at three fifteen cannot come together as iterations of a dog, or even of a dog in the afternoon. Wildly different from the excruciating immediacy of Funes's perception but no less disruptive to the "the originary doubleness of the metaphysical concept of signifying" that structures detective stories and realist fiction is the epistemological delirium of Carlo Emilio Gadda's best-known novel, *Quer pasticciaccio brutto de' via Merulana* (*That Awful Mess on the Via Merulana*; first serialized between 1946 and 1947, then published in a revised and expanded form in 1957). Set in fascist Rome in 1927, *Quer pasticciaccio* is the story of the investigation of two crimes—apparently unrelated—at the same arriviste residential building in Rome. The first crime is a burglary at the home of the countess Menegazzi, a Venetian widow whose jewels and bird-brained carelessness were fabled throughout the city—she once left a topaz ring at a public bathhouse. Three days later a pious housewife, Liliana Balducci, is murdered in her home. Her handsome younger cousin discovers her body in a pool of blood, her throat "all sawed up," her face "worn, emaciated by the atrocious suction of Death."[52] Liliana's longing for a child and her husband's philandering brought a revolving cast of maids and "nieces" into their home; girls who came from the outskirts of Rome and stayed until they went off to get married, or got caught stealing, or, in one case, seduced husband and wife "in two unconnected directions."[53]

The investigation also veers off in two directions: the municipal police—including detective Francesco Ingravallo—begin working on the two cases, but carabinieri take over to follow up on clues that lead outside of the city, and then to the jewels stolen from Menegazzi. The second crime, the gruesome murder, remains unresolved, though Gadda said in a 1968 interview that the novel, which famously ends with the word "quasi" (almost) was "literarily concluded": "The officer realizes who the killer is, and that's enough."[54] The "tragic incompleteness" often attributed to the novel is telegraphed by the tangling multiplicities of Ingravallo's philosophy: "He sustained, among other things, that unforeseen catastrophes are never the consequence or the effect, if you prefer, of a single motive, of *a* cause singular; but they are rather like a whirlpool, a cyclonic point of depression in the consciousness of the world, towards which a whole multitude of converging causes have contributed. He also used words like knot or tangle [*groviglio*], or muddle [*garbuglio*], or *gnommero*, which in Roman dialect means skein."[55] Gadda's posthumous philosophical treatise, *Meditazione milanese* (Milanese Reflection), elaborates a similar model of a complex tangle: "The hypotyposis of the causal chain should be amended and remade ... as a mesh or a net: but not a two-dimensional mesh (a surface) or a three-dimensional one (... a spatial chain, a chain in three dimensions), but rather a mesh or net that is infinitely dimensioned, so that each link or node or tangle of relations is bound by infinite filaments to infinite clots or knots."[56] Gadda's and Ingravallo's philosophies bear out the idea of the "butterfly effect," which the former adapts: "If a dragonfly takes flight in Tokyo, it triggers a chain of reactions that reaches me."[57]

In keeping with the philosophy of an infinitely dimensioned mesh, the textual universe of *Quer pasticciaccio* seems to be one from which no detail or clue could be subtracted. As Robert Rushing writes, "A 'proper' citation from Gadda would necessarily require dozens if not hundreds of pages, as every scene is always enmeshed, situated within a sub-digression of a digression from what appeared to be a principal plot."[58] Objects, too, are caught in this great mesh; Gian Carlo Roscioni glosses, "Objects are points from which infinite rays depart [or rather, at which they converge] and they don't have, they can't have, 'boundaries.'"[59]

This boundlessness is illustrated in the breathtakingly baroque description of the Menegazzi jewels, recovered by two carabinieri from a hovel in Lazio. The gems sparkle through time and space, metaphor and metonymy. The passage foretells the near future, when the stones will be identified "by the jeweler with the hooked nose, on the counter, after theft and recovery," and the remotest past: "Jewels they were . . . incubated and born in the originative millennia of the world."[60] The jewels are likened to "frightened animals" or "ladybirds who fold their wings." They are unmasked lies, mysteriosophic candy, fabulous caramels. One is like a "poor little egg between pale-blue and milk-white like the gland of a dead pigeon, to be thrown in the refuse," another "tiny bauble, like a little ball of methylene bluing to get the yellow out of the wash." Rubies and garnets are like "twin cherries amid the twinned stems of their sisterly couples" and a "red pomegranate seed that a chicken might peck." This list of metaphors, however, is misleading, since the descriptions expand defiantly, mixing metaphors, confounding signifying planes. For example, an ancient ring, "A gold-bound cylinder which had circled the thumb of Ahenobarbus or the big toe of Heliogabalus" boasts a metamorphosizing gem: "a big caramel orange-green then a moment later, lemon-color: pierced by all the rays, slightly, of the equinoctial morning as the tender flesh of the martyr by his hundred and ninety arrows: perfused by pale-green lights, like the sea at dawn, to the brightness of flint: which made the two men dream at once, spellbound, of a mint syrup with soda in Piazza Garibaldi at noon."[61] From the big toe of a promiscuous young emperor, to the present of the fictional setting, the ring is pierced like the Christian martyr and rouses minty daydreams.

The gemstones are made by God and science, undoing of the separation between nature and culture to which the moderns lay claim: "Noble in [their] structural accepting of the crystallographic suggestion of God: memory, every gem, and individual opus within the remote memory and within the labours of God: true sesquioxide Al_2O_3 truly spaced in the ditrigonal scalenohedral modes of its class, premediated by God." The jewels even conjure old enigmas of prepositions and typographical errors. One of the carabinieri, Guerrino Pestalozzi, reads the list of stolen jewelry: "ring 'of' ruby with two pearls, brooch with small black pearl and two emeralds, pendant 'of' sapphire, as one might say of a pastry, 'surrounded' with brilliants, *carcanet* typed as *carcanot*, then corrected as *carcano*."[62] The words even begin to mime to the clues, as if caught in the atrocious suction of converging causes: the "o" of the letters are likened to holes punched in a railroad ticket found at the scene of the burglary.

These jewels are not hinges between the investigation and the crime, *fabula* and *sjužet*, but rather nodes in a countlessly dimensioned mesh or tangle. Because of this density of causal relations Italo Calvino uses *Quer pasticciaccio* to illustrate one inflection of the aesthetic principle of multiplicity to which he dedicates the fifth (and last) of his *Lezioni americane* (*Six Memos for the Next Millennium*; 1988): "In its eagerness to contain the whole of the possible, [the text] fails to give itself a shape or define its own limits, and . . . remains incomplete thanks to the very mission that brought it into being."[63]

Words and Things

Though they inundate the hoarders of *Stuff* and Funes, marginal details are the crux of detective work and literary realism. Zeroing in on details unobserved by others, detectives like Holmes move between layers of narrative—that is, between the scene of the investigation and that of the crime. Gadda's *Quer pasticciaccio* disrupts this redoubled structure with its dizzying multiplication of causality. Malerba, a founding member of the short-lived and loosely knit Gruppo 63, a literary movement named after the year it was formed, challenges conventions of detection by exploring the paradoxes that result from the equation of words and things. The critic Angelo Guglielmi (also a founding member of the Gruppo 63) has characterized the cultural context of the early 1960s as one in which "Every bridge between word and thing has crumbled."[64] Experimentalist writers of the Gruppo 63 confronted this semiotic context with expressive forms that thematize or traverse the gulf between word and thing, however quixotically. Malerba's first book, *La scoperta dell'alfabeto* (The Discovery of the Alphabet; 1963), a collection of short stories set in rural Emilio Romagna, begins with the eponymous story of a peasant who learns the alphabet and a few words but soon suspends his studies, announcing to his teacher— the eleven-year-old son of a landowner: "Now that's enough for me, at my age."[65] The comfort of his learning remains material: "He would look for words he knew on old newspapers, and when he found them he was happy, as though he had met an old friend."[66]

Marilyn Schneider describes the physicality of words in Malerba's work: "Words are wondrous not only for the wily meanings they conjure, like a witches' brew, but also to be gazed upon, 'held' and 'sniffed' by all the senses, like a precious object."[67] In critical writings and interviews, Malerba describes literature as a parallel world, with "no connection to reality."[68] He proposes a "concrete approach" to literature, which he contrasts with "the escape into symbols," which in turn looks like facile Freudian analysis that would allow no cigar to be just a cigar.[69] Barring a semiological bond between literature and reality, Malerba proposes something like a tautological mode of signification based upon the immediacy of objects. Guido Almansi explains the way in which the equation of words and things produces a textual world free of figuration: "This ametaphorical world exists literally, as if the ancient fracture between words and things had never been invented; and its inhabitants are often terrified victims of this literalness."[70]

This understanding of literature as a parallel world in which signifier and signified are felicitously united but bear no relation to reality underpins Malerba's first novel, *Il serpente*, a crime story without a crime related by a narrator who repudiates his own narrative. The text undoes itself on the level of plot, like (not coincidentally) a serpent swallowing its tail. The novel thus employs the narrative strategy Brian Richardson calls "denarration," which emphasizes the extent to which the fictional world comes into being only through its articulation."[71] By confounding or repudiating its own propositions, the denarrated text undermines any claim to a referential relationship to reality, suggesting instead an alternate space in which logical contradictions can occur unchecked: people and things can both exist and not exist; events can happen and not happen.

The narrator of *Il serpente* is an unnamed thirty-three-year-old stamp dealer with a shop on via Arenula in Rome. His life is saturated with extensive readings of magazines, newspapers and various trade journals—though the words he reads, like the stamps that surround him, accumulate without amassing narrative momentum: "It's hard to explain, I read the words but I wasn't connecting them, I would read the advertising, the stock market quotations, and I wouldn't understand anything."[72] In addition to the accumulation of words and stamps, the narrator's days are consumed by his hateful relationship with his wife, who, he later reveals, is a fiction: "To tell the truth I was lying when I said I was married. I've never had a wife or anything of the sort."[73] The narrator joins an amateur choir where he meets a young woman, Miriam, who becomes his lover. He begins to suspect his friend and fellow philatelist, Baldasseroni, of having an affair with her. Increasingly jealous, he brings his reluctant girlfriend to the well-known radiologist, Occhiodoro (Goldeneye), hoping that the specialist will be able to use X-rays to detect

traces of infidelity. When Miriam leaves him after being subjected to the medical molestation, the narrator uses telepathy to
lure her back to his shop, where he poisons and cannibalizes her.
The narrator continues to suspect Baldasseroni—now of working
for an international philatelic crime ring. Convinced that Baldasseroni's conspiracy must be stopped, he turns to the police. The narrator confesses to Miriam's murder, but when the police commissioner
searches the store, he finds no trace of the crime. The commissioner,
apparently amused by the narrator's prodigious inventions, encour-
ages him to write a report—an account that mirrors *Il serpente* and
its undoing. As this summary suggests, the novel concomitantly com-
pels the reader to sleuth for "what really happened" and reveals the
preposterousness of such a search. Since the entirety of the novel—
with the possible exception of fourteen italicized passages that separate the chapters—is related from the point of view of the narrator,
to try to tease out layers of reality within the fiction would be futile.
Yet the reader of the novel, like the commissioner who proposes that
the narrator write a confession, is left hunting for clues to establish
the narrator's guilt or innocence.

Denarrated texts in general and *Il serpente* in particular foreground
the problem of separating story or *fabula* from *sjužet*—and accordingly preclude the movement between layers of narrative that neither
Funes nor the hoarders overwhelmed by detail in *Stuff* are able to make.
Because of the inaccessibility of "what really happened," the reader's
focus is directed not to the story but to its telling: the narrating voice
becomes the locus of interpretation. The first-person denarrated text,
Richardson writes, "invites more possible interpretive positions concerning the subjectivity of the narrator, as the reader wonders whether
the narrator is incompetent, disoriented, devious, or insane."[74] Such
texts elicit interpretations that are investigatory and individualizing,
but also pathologizing. The reader comes to understand the discourse

as issuing from the contortions of a troubled mind, and thus locates some "reality" in the narrated fiction: that of mental disorder.

In *Il serpente*, this mental disorder takes the form of a relationship to things that is recognizable as hoarding. The material disorder of the narrator's shop and apartment seems to increase in direct proportion to his disengagement from reality. As he severs his already limited social bonds and becomes "possessed" by obsessions, the spaces the narrator occupies become increasingly squalid and disorganized. The unventilated shop begins to smell of mildew and mold: "The humidity had released an odor from the walls of the shop, from the floor, from the old wooden shelves, from the papers and piled-up stamps, an odor of mold and rotten apples."[75] More critically, the narrator's attempts to clean the shop do not result in any coherent organizational system, but rather the stasis-in-motion that resembles the "churning" described in contemporary psychiatry:

> The shop was all in disorder, several days before I had started counting the envelopes of stamps on the shelves and then the stamps inside the envelopes, marking everything down in a notebook by nationality. I had also begun creating some order among the albums of rare items I keep mixed up with the others to fool thieves. Perhaps I would be wise to remove them and put them in the safe with the other more valuable rarities, along with the stamps of the German Inflation. But what is this rage for order? I said to myself. Are you making an inventory perhaps? What you're doing resembles a will more than an inventory. So I had left everything in disorder, the envelopes on the floor, piles of albums all over the place, on the table, on the Olivetti filing cabinet.[76]

The narrator begins by counting the stamps and listing them by nationality, then considers arranging the rare stamps in albums, but ultimately resigns himself to the disorder. This churning replaces thematic organization with a temporal one, arranging objects according to their most recent contact with the hoarder. The reorganization (or disorganization) of objects according to temporal rather than thematic criteria can be restated as a privileging of displacement over condensation and of the linguistic axis of metonymy over metaphor.

The mess of the shop takes the place of any specific incriminating detail and as such stalls the engine of detection. When police search the narrator's shop, they find no clues: "Only stamps, catalogues, nougat bars." Similarly, a search of the narrator's house turns up nothing: "No trace of Miriam, not a photograph not a letter a stocking a garter, nothing. Not a lipstick stain a hairpin, not even a strand of woman's hair, nothing."[77] These passages occupy a privileged status in the text because they conjure the evidential paradigm: the absence of material traces suggests the absence of a crime. The novel poses a more entrenched challenge to the epistemological paradigm Ginzburg identifies through its structural collecting.

At the outset of the novel, the narrator sets out two distinct models of collecting. It is an irrational uncontainable drive, like the object-oriented manias of nineteenth-century psychiatry: "It's a bad habit, a mania, like all forms of collecting, and it serves to protect the collector from other bad habits or to hide them, but he never achieves happiness through his collection." Philately may ward off or dissimulate other vices, but it is not a means to achieve satisfaction: "If a man has a hundred stamps, he wishes he had a thousand, if he has a thousand he wishes he had a hundred thousand. The number of stamps is finite, and yet if a collector managed to collect all the stamps in existence he wouldn't be happy, I'm sure of that."[78] Collecting, for the narrator, is rooted in a desire not to possess all stamps but rather to possess ever more. Though a collector could never possess infinite stamps—or even all extant stamps—his passion is articulated in a formula that is asymptotic.[79]

In a second elaboration, collecting more closely resembles economic theories of hoarding insofar as it is presented as a rational investment strategy. When Miriam asks about the principles that guide the appraisal of stamps, the narrator explains: "Stamps are valuable if they are old and if they are rare, as a stamp gradually becomes old it also becomes more rare because many copies are lost, but there are rare stamps that aren't old like the San Marino issue where they printed a robin with a parrot's tail, or else stamps that are old but aren't rare like the first English One Penny issues."[80] Though age may add to rarity, rarity does necessarily imply age, as the San Marino misprint demonstrates. Age and rarity, however, converge asymptotically; time will eventually bring both. The investment strategy the narrator garners from these principles, accordingly, is to wait: "The secret would be to keep them there and wait while they become old and rare at the same time." He shrugs off the trouble fundamental to this method—that time spares no one age: "But in the meanwhile you become old too, Miriam said, and she was right about this, but a person becomes old in any case."[81] With the articulation of collecting as an investment strategy guided by the principle that value is related to rarity, which increases over time, the wager of space against time (a formula for hoarding) becomes one of people against things.

The novel's structural collecting is performed by the italicized passages that separate the chapters. These passages resemble a collection as they form a sequence of discrete entities that do not participate directly in the narrative development. Each italicized passage explores a logical paradox that engages obliquely with the themes of the novel. More important, the novel performs hoarding by detaching objects from their original functions and grouping them by some shared quality. In the first instance of such a resignifying process, yellow objects are grouped together. Given that, in Italian, *giallo* denotes both the color yellow and the genre of crime fiction, there is a coincidence of the resignifying practice and the locus of its effects: that which makes the novel falter as a *giallo* is performed using the word "giallo."[82]

The signification and resignification of yellow begins in the first chapter of the novel, the only chapter that is not set in contemporary Rome. The chapter consists of the narrator's childhood memories of Parma during the period of economic autarky in fascist Italy, then of the biting cold of the Eastern Front, and finally of his return, changed, to the changed city.[83] The narrator distinguishes between the gelato of Parma's Caffè Tanara, which was made from real eggs (egg yolk—*tuorlo d'uovo*, also called *rosso d'uovo*—is considered red, not yellow in Italian), and gelato made with yellow egg powder imported from China. The narrator then transfers the national origin of the yellow egg powder to everything else yellow: "You often hear them talking about this yellow powder that comes from China. Everything that's yellow comes from China, including those little yellow balls an old man sells under the arcades of City Hall."[84] Because of the extraneous setting of the first chapter, the episode suggests a sort of primal scene that might provide the sleuthing reader with insight into the disordered mind of the narrator.[85] The chapter emphasizes not the specificity of the narrator's life, but the shared experience of fascist imperialism, from a child's perspective: parades, songs, and radio broadcasts.[86] A typewritten draft of the novel corroborates this historical specificity. A crossed-out sentence—left out of the published novel—situates the historical moment more explicitly: "I wander around the city, one hears a lot of talk about autarky, we must be moderate in everything."[87] Autarky, here, represents for the narrator a vaguely understood mandate of moderation in the context of scarcity.

In addition to the scarcity that defines autarky, the articulation of boundary offsets the structural and thematic collecting of the text through the frequent use of the rhetorical figure of antimetabole. A subset of the chiasmus, antimetabole entails the repetition of the same words in reverse order. The first paragraph of the novel alone, which describes a parade, contains three such inverted structures: "cork heads, heads stuffed with cork, cork helmets on their heads"; "What are they doing? Where are they going? What are they going to do?"; "when [the radio] stopped singing it talked, it went on talking, and then it started singing again, it never stopped."[88] The remainder of the novel employs the figure with similar frequency. The catchiest antimetaboles—"Never kiss a fool or be fooled by a kiss"—emphasize the importance of word order, since the same words, rearranged, emerge with vastly different meanings. In the antimetaboles of *Il serpente*, the rearrangement of word order creates negligible semantic changes.

The irrelevance of word order mirrors the changing and changeable relationships between objects in a collection. That unfixing resembles Jean Laplanche and Jean-Bertrand Pontalis's understanding of the subject of fantasy: "In fantasy the subject does not pursue the object or its sign: he appears caught up himself in the sequence of images. He forms no representation of the desired objects but is himself represented as participating in the scene although, in the earliest forms of fantasy, he cannot be assigned any fixed place in it."[89] In the first chapter, the narrator inserts himself into the logic of collecting by describing how, upon returning home from Caffè Tanara, he would recount what he saw there to a boy from his neighborhood, who would, in turn, pass the story on to other boys: "I talk about ice cream with a boy who lives in my street, a very poor boy with scabs all over his knees, I also talk to him about the merry-go-round, the boy listens to my tales and then repeats them all to the other boys even poorer and with more scabs." In this economy, the narrative develops out of material deprivation and participates in the production of a hierarchy, the gaps of which are bridged with anecdotes. The narrative binds together boys who are grouped based on their shared qualities: poverty and scabs. Like collections, the concatenation of poor scabby boys is ever expanding: "It's incredible how there's always a boy poorer and scabbier than the poorest and scabbiest boy you know. And the scale keeps going down, there's no telling where it ends."[90] The narrating ensemble, like the collection, expands ad infinitum, with the position of each poor scabby boy constantly changing with respect to the others.

Kinship structures, for the narrator, are guided by the same asymptotic logic as the chain of scabby, narrating boys. Baldasseroni's stamp collection, composed solely of stamps featuring royalty, leads the narrator to a consideration of kinship: "It's incredible how many people are relatives of other people, relationships run in a horizontal direction as well as vertical and even diagonal, they involve present and past, they stretch out in space and in time, as is well known. If you go back we're all related to everybody." The stories the narrator reads in newspapers similarly undermine the fixing of subject positions: "Often another thing happened, when I assumed the role of a man, I imagined the girl or wife as Miriam. When instead I was the wife or the girl, I pictured the man as Baldasseroni."[91]

The ostensible crime of the would-be *giallo*—the murder and cannibalization of Miriam—temporarily halts the ever-expanding chain of interchangeable subject positions. The narrator first insists on the rarity of the crime: "I had become a downright rarity." This rarity is then promptly undermined by a lengthy discussion of various cannibalistic practices throughout the world. The narrator concludes by establishing Europe as an exception: "And yet in

Africa characters like you are not so rare, I said to myself. Also in Oceania, in Asia, in South America. Instead in Europe you're the only one, I said to myself, and this was a thing that made a profound impression on me." Cannibalistic practices in Europe surface shortly thereafter, though they are distanced by time—a familiar topos of Orientalist and Africanist discourse: "In Europe these things don't happen, in Europe there's only me, except for the very rare cases that happen during the war, among shipwrecked men or during sieges in ancient times. During certain sieges in the Middle Ages men ate one another also in Europe, for instance during the famous siege of Paris."[92] Though the text devotes considerable attention to determining the extent of the crime's singularity, failure of individuation is already inscribed in the novel's thematic and structural use of collecting. The property of being yellow, scabby, poor, or royal—like cannibalism—is guided by an asymptotic logic; people, like things, are subject to a constant process of churning.

The Story of the Space

Churning is also integral to the investigative itineraries of twenty-first-century heirs to the detective story: television forensic dramas. Both the season 5 finale of Fox's *Bones*, "The Beginning in the End," and an episode from season 11 of CBS's *CSI: Las Vegas*, "House of Hoarders," begin with a dead body discovered in a hoard. In each episode, "churning"—or some distortion of it—is used by detectives to locate the story in the hoard. The shows elicit horror with abrupt dissonant clangs and ghoulish images: a skull crawling with maggots, a skeleton whose pelvic bone is nest to a "scorpion and her babies," a corpse slimy after a week of decomposition.[93] In each episode, the spectacle of fascinating abjection gives way to an investigation that uses a divulgation of contemporary medical research to locate clues within the overcrowded, squalid spaces teeming with life (and death).

"The Beginning in the End" begins with a scene of domestic elation: a young boy jumps on his bed. As plaster dust begins to fall from the ceiling, he calls to his mother, "Mom, it's snowing!" She arrives just in time to call her son to her side before the ceiling comes crashing down. The two stand in the doorway and watch the gruesome cascade of debris that includes a skeleton and its detached, maggot-infested skull, which rolls onto the floor, wobbling in ghastly close-up. The skull turns out to be that of the upstairs neighbor, Tim Murphy, who had died a month earlier. Coincident with the investigation into Murphy's death is the discovery, in the Maluku Islands, of "a full set of interspecies hominid remains" that the forensic anthropologist Temperance "Bones" Brennan (Emily Deschanel)—who hopes to go work with the research team there—believes "could be a crucial link in the evolutionary chain."

In contrast to the overseas research opportunity, the mystery of Murphy's death holds no such promise: "Upstairs can't really shed light on the interspecies similarities of human evolution." The irrelevance of the hoarder's death to the science of evolution poses a decisive question not only for Brennon as she considers her next career move, but for the series, dedicated to the investigation, each week, of a new murder. Brennon muses: "The murders will never stop, but this find has real, finite value. I'd be able to answer questions about our origin, evolutionary track. It has implications for history, science." Ginzburg's contrast between the divinatory, venatic, conjectural, semiotic, and evidential paradigms, on the one hand, and the epistemological bases of the natural sciences, on the other, is analogous: "The quantitative and anti-anthropocentric orientation of natural sciences from Galileo on forced an unpleasant, dilemma on the humane sciences: either assume a lax scientific system in order to attain noteworthy results, or assume a meticulous, scientific one to achieve results of scant significance."[94] "The Beginning in the End" will have to unpack the hoard as a single sequence of events that explains Murphy's death, and then repack it as some general truth that bears significance for "science, history," or at least for the psychology of the major characters.

The individuating narrative to explain Murphy's death begins with the most obvious suspect: the landlord, who cannot legally evict Murphy and makes no effort to hide his eagerness to clean out the apartment and rent it at market rate. Two other suspects are questioned after experts analyze digital photographs and recognize two areas of interest in the hoard: one where objects were most recently moved, another where objects of greater sentimental value are kept. (The explanation of how this works is a union of vague evocations of cutting-edge digital imaging, forensic science, and psychiatric accounts of underinclusion.) Back at the Jeffersonian Institute for Forensic Anthropology, the forensic artist Angela Montenegro (Michaela Conlin) explains: "Hodgins is dating each pile of junk according to insect larvae, rat droppings, and the yellowing of the paper. Apparently [Murphy has] been hoarding stuff for about four years. The oldest stuff is where he fell through the ceiling." Brennan adds: "Hoarders often organize their holdings by category and value, much like one would find in a museum." Though her assessment is at odds with psychiatric discussions of underinclusion, it is indebted to their conclusion, that there is a logic to the spatial arrangement of the possessions.

Searching the location of recent movement in the hoard, investigators find unhatched silverfish eggs. Back at the lab, they identify the agent that prevented the eggs from hatching to be uranium oxide, which was used in the glaze of a rare Fiestaware Christmas gnome—a collector's item valued at $50,000. Some sleuthing reveals that Murphy had purchased one such gnome at a flea market for a mere $12. This information leads investigators to the second suspect, Rocky DeKnight (Reginald Ballard), who had telephoned several times and visited Murphy around the time of his death. DeKnight, it turns out, did not kill Murphy, though the two argued. DeKnight then pushed Murphy and left with the gnome.

The final suspect is located thanks to the identification of the area where Murphy kept the objects he valued most highly: a collection of travel guides, one of which contained a picture of a former colleague, Elaine Akusta. The two had been in love and had hoped to travel together, but Murphy refused to leave his apartment. Lance Sweets (John Francis Daley) explains that "A level five disposophobic might also be an agoraphobic, which would uh, limit his relationships in the outside world."[95] When Akusta visited Murphy to discuss their plans, they argued. She pushed him and left without realizing that he had fallen and, unable to move, would die of starvation amid the hungry vermin in the hoard. This was no murder, we learn, but rather the sad story of a man who shut out the world and put his things before his relationships with humans. Therein lies the "scientific, historical," interest of the case. The hoarder becomes a foil for the main characters of the series who, at the season's close, face major decisions about the next phase of their relationships and careers. In *Bones*, Murphy is the victim not of murder, but of his own stasis. His death inspires the characters to think about the relationships and experiences that matter to them, and answer the call of duty, research opportunity, and love.

The *CSI: Las Vegas* episode is more precise in its use of churning to locate clues within the hoarded space. Like the *Bones* episode, "House of Hoarders" draws on idioms of horror with images of abjection and evokes the word with the near homophony of the title. The episode begins as Marta Santiago (Bertila Damas) has been issued a cleanout order by the county because of the public safety risks posed by her home. After neighbors complain about the smell, investigators find the decomposing corpse of Marta's older daughter, who had come to visit a week earlier to try to help her mother with the cleanout. In a scuffle prompted by an attempt to discard books and magazines, the daughter had suffered a serious injury and died amid the hoard.

Dr. Priscilla Prescott (Annie Wersching), a social worker who had been working with Santiago for two years, offers a non-sequitur in place of explanation to the investigator Raymond Langston (Lawrence Fishburne): "She's a hoarder, not a killer. . . . She's well groomed, she has a job, works as a librarian, supports herself. She's quite high functioning." The etiology of hoarding in the *CSI: Las Vegas* episode is not rooted in the capacity to perceive marginal details, like that of Lally in *The Force of Things*, hoarders of *Stuff* and Funes. It is "clutter blindness," that enables Marta to remain unfazed by her daughter's corpse. Prescott explains: "Every hoarder experiences something called 'clutter blindness.' For a level one hoarder it could mean ignoring a stack of newspapers piling up in a room."[96] The lesson imparted through the investigation, however, ultimately has little to do with the medical research. Marta suffers from caring too much: she wants her children and just about everything else— an old pen, the tissues she uses—to remain by her side.

Expert intervention comes in the form of an explanation of churning, and the way it reorganizes objects in a space according to the most recent contact with the hoarders. Using that principle, the investigators are able to locate key objects. Soon after the discovery of the corpse of Marta's daughter, investigators find a second body in the house, and then a small burial ground in the back yard. With the exception of Marta's daughter, the victims were killed by arsenic poisoning, their wrists were bound with red ribbons. Dating the most recent death by arsenic poisoning to six months earlier, and using the psychiatric account of churning, investigators locate the ribbon and arsenic in the hoard. Prescott offers an explanation taken almost verbatim from Frost and Steketee, who write: "Most of us live our lives categorically—at least the part of our lives dealing with objects. Tools are kept in the toolbox; bills to be paid are kept in a special place in the office area and then filed after payment; kitchen utensils go in a drawer. But Irene organized her world visually and spatially, not by category."[97]

Prescott modifies the contents of the drawer—from kitchen utensils to underwear—for salacious effect: "If you're asking if a hoarder like Marta has some sort of system, then that answer is yes. Most of us live our lives categorically. Pots and pans go in the kitchen, tools go in the toolbox, *underwear* goes in the drawer. But Marta organizes her world visually, and spatially by stacking." Conflated with the spatial organization that results from churning is that of time capsules—like the more than 600 made by Andy Warhol.[98] Prescott offers an explanation that begins with an amalgam of noun and verb, plural and singular: "These look like time capsules. Time capsule is a compulsive act by a hoarder to throw away groups of items into a single container at a single moment of time. However, the intention is to deal with these items later. All those items belong to [her younger daughter] Elisa." The concept of time capsules here, however, is a "regression," the bins are not the product of a chance sweeping off of the desk at a given moment but rather a meticulous chronology. Langston explains: "This is like we're going back in time. It's a regression. Like she's putting her back into the womb." The womb, it turns out, is a closet, where Santiago's younger daughter is restrained in handcuffs. The expert gloss conflates churning with archeology; the personal chronology of the hoarder's chance encounter with the material coincides with the shared time of calendar and clock. The shackled teenager is responsible for all the arsenic poisonings; her mother kept her chained up at home in the hope of extinguishing her daughter's compulsion to kill. The culprit is not the hoarder, but the young woman who responded to domestic dysfunction by becoming a serial killer, and who was unable to recognize her mother's devotion through the piles of debris. Stokes remains baffled by the hoarding until Langston explains: "The philosopher Erich Fromm, he forecast a society that was obsessed with possessions. . . . Unfortunately Fromm also predicted that a culture driven by commercialism like the one we live in today is doomed to the 'having' orientation, which leads to dissatisfaction and emptiness. When you consider that in 1960 there was no such thing as public storage in America; today there's over two billion square feet dedicated to it. Makes you think he had a point." Stokes seems to learn something; in the final scene, he cleans up his cluttered office. Stokes—and more broadly, the *CSI* franchise—may be the heir to Holmes, but his cluttered office signifies only as analogy; he sees something of himself and something universal in the house of hoarders.

In a schematic sense, detective stories—beginning with that of Oedipus—are redoubled narrative itineraries: the conventional story of detection has the investigator following the tracks of the criminal and piecing together the story of what happened. Marginal details—often thing details—in the form of clues, allow the detective to switch from one layer of narrative to another: from the scene of investigation to that of the crime. Nothing could be more detrimental to the epistemological work of detection than the acute attunement to detail—the indiscriminate perception of every marginal detail. The discord of the detective and the hoarder recapitulates the larger problem of the realist novel: that it can never be identical to reality: it can never reproduce the world. The detective and the hoarder—modernity's hero and its outcast, its genius and its madman—are part of the same story. Where the hoarder anticipates retrospection, the detective finds story in the space of the hoard.

4

Ecologies

AN *OIKOS* FOR EVERYTHING

Since the dire warnings of Malthus, fears of global scarcity have been waxing, waning, and transforming.[1] The great promise of modernity—that humanity would use inventive genius to triumph over scarce matter—began to look like a lie in the second half of the twentieth century when the irreversible damage caused by industrial capitalism and military technologies became apparent.[2] Rather than population growth, scarcity is now better understood to result from the late capitalist mode of production that pollutes ocean, land, and atmosphere with microplastics, oil spills, municipal and industrial waste, and carbon dioxide emissions. Hoarding often obscures such considerations; no matter what waste is or how it could be avoided, the hoarder eschews collective action and takes it upon himself. Hoarding narratives make wastefulness seem like a personal failure rather than structural necessity and economic strategy of the capitalist mode of production.[3]

The Hoarding Handbook: A Guide for Human Service Professionals (2011) contains an assessment interview that includes the following question: "Are you afraid of wasting a potentially useful object when you try to discard something? That is, are you concerned about being wasteful because the object could eventually be put to good use?" Interviewees are invited to respond with a number from zero, for "Never," to eight, for "Nearly always." A second iteration of the question reframes the aversion to wasting not as a reluctance to discard but as a propensity to acquire: "Do you acquire things because you are afraid of wasting a potentially useful object if you don't get it?"[4] Implicit in both questions is the idea that wasting can be avoided not only through use but also through the recognition of the possibility for use. To waste, the questions suggest, is to foreclose that potential. Whether by acquiring objects from dumping grounds or by refusing to throw out what appears to others to be void of use or exchange value, hoarding entails a rejection of the apparently definitive temporal endpoint marked by discarding an object—that is, by *making* waste. Hoarding imposes a different boundary—the property—creating a sanctuary space of protected disuse, where things can be, without being waste.

That spatial distribution of property and waste coincides with the way the former is conceived in the Roman origins. As the political philosopher Roberto Esposito articulates: "Property was always created by occupying an empty space or by taking possession of an object that had no owner."[5] That unoccupied space, that ownerless object is the definition of waste; in Latin, *vastus* refers to an area that is vacant, devastated, or immense. There is no a priori ontology of waste; it is made by an interpretive act.[6] It is an effect that can be traced to its cause; its materiality cannot be separated from its history. Comprising sacred and profane, use and disuse, scarcity and abundance, waste can be counted among the "primal words" that combine antithetical meanings.[7] Antithetically conjoined to wasting, hoarding encompasses an analogous semantic sweep.

Use and disuse, as well as scarcity and abundance, are also structuring binaries of economic inquiry, which is concerned with the allocation of limited resources to alternate ends. The binaries remain sturdy when the *oikos*—the Greek word for home and the root of the prefix "eco"—is situated in the environment rather than the market, in ecology rather than economy. Though "ecology" first referred to the study of organisms in their physical surroundings, contemporary usage conveys the urgency of the scarcity of the planet's resources and the aim of conservation, and as such invests both hoarding and wasting with new significance.[8] Wastefulness, a misuse of limited resources, is both bad economy and bad ecology; it is irrational and immoral. Waste is as protean as the finitude that makes it possible; hoarding transforms the boundaries—spatial or temporal, physical or conceptual—that make waste. Hoarders are certainly not the only ones who are committed to avoiding waste, but whatever it means to avoid wasting, the hoarder, by definition, does it differently.

Implicit in any understanding of waste are claims about where scarcity is located, what causes it, and how it can be reduced. In one narrative, scarcity is situated in the past but remains vivid in the memory of those who have survived traumas like war, economic hardship, or forced migration.[9] However economically irrelevant an attic full of dusty boxes or a staircase piled with books and papers may seem to overcoming scarcity, hoarding acquires a veneer of rationality through such narratives. Set against a here and now sustained by shared fantasies of plenty, the frugal resourcefulness of hoarders may appear inappropriate. Out of place or out of time—to evoke influential formulas for dirt—it is no wonder that the hoarder is often figured as a sort of "human detritus."[10] Another narrative, which situates scarcity in a future when fossil fuels and potable waters are depleted, imagines remedy in the resourceful avoidance of waste. The hoarder of this narrative may seem heroic, an embodiment of quiet dissent who resists the harrowing pace of planned obsolescence by refusing to waste.

The binaries of scarcity and abundance and use and disuse that structure economies and ecologies and that mark the spaces in which hoarding and wasting are possible are also essential to the *oikos* of aesthetic objects. Literary and visual texts constitute their own economies and ecosystems within and beyond which use and disuse, scarcity and abundance take a range of forms. This chapter studies the antithetical relationships between hoarding and wasting as they reverse and refract in representative texts from Nikolai Gogol's *Dead Souls* (1842), which features one of the first and most memorable hoarders of modern literature, Stepan Pliushkin, to the first episode of A&E's *Hoarders.*[11]

Once a paragon of resourceful household management, the miserly landowner of Gogol's novel withdraws from all social bonds and, rather than avoiding waste, he seems to become it. In a passage that makes the reception of writers a function of the loftiness of their subject matter, Gogol links the fate of his own work to the Pliushkin episode. I argue that a short story by Carlo Emilio Gadda, "L'Adalgisa" (1940), responds to Gogol's desolation by developing the antithetical relationship between making art and making waste. Building on my discussion of these two texts, the chapter concludes by turning to twenty-first-century visual texts—an installation and a documentary film—that present the hoarder as a tragic hero and transform the objects amassed in the name of avoiding waste into art by arranging them in a gallery space or by documenting them in film. The hoarders in this chapter avoid waste not by making use of things, but by suspending them in a bounded space of potential. The property becomes a sanctuary of protected disuse, where matter awaits a redemptive moment of economic, epistemological, or aesthetic transformation (like a sale at the flea market, or narrative at the crime scene). The relationality that defines hoarding—a clash in perspectives about value—becomes the basis of the aesthetic transformation of waste within and between these texts.

A Lemon and a Pearl

The fame of the miserly landowner Pliushkin in Russia rivals that of the Collyer brothers in the United States, and "Pliushkin syndrome" is one of many popular synonyms of hoarding disorder.[12] Gogol's merciless comic description of Pliushkin's village, manor, and person captures features of hoarding that are as relevant to postwar New York as to feudal Russia. Like the Collyer brothers, Pliushkin dresses in beggarly tatters despite his considerable wealth. He owns more than a thousand serfs and has more stored grain than any other landowner in the province. His warehouses are so full of baskets, buckets, jugs, bowls, barrels, and other household goods that they look like a Moscow market, albeit one without customers and with objects that see neither circulation nor use: "A whole lifetime would not suffice to use them, even given two estates the size of his." He is the lord of a village that brims with ruination in glorious and grotesque detail, like a dried-up lemon "no bigger than a hazelnut" and a discolored toothpick that looks as if it had been used "perhaps before the French invaded Moscow."[13]

Like Langley Collyer and other notorious hoarders, Pliushkin goes out wandering every day, combing through the alleys in search of still more stuff.[14] The role of chance is essential to such excursions; Pliushkin acquires whatever detritus he happens upon. The narrator quips that there is no need for street sweepers after Pliushkin passes through the village since he carries home any detritus whatsoever that catches his eye: "the sole of an old boot, a woman's rag, an iron nail, a shard of pottery." When peasants see the old miser in the village, they call out: "Look, the fisherman's out fishing!"[15] Pliushkin's "fishing" expeditions consist of taking possession not of what has no exchange or use value, but of what is un-owned or unused. The dilapidated plenitude of the village is the result not only of these fishing expeditions but also of his attempt to avoid wasting by repudiating use. Pliushkin's thrifty household management once earned him the respect of friends and neighbors until a series of tragedies left him embittered and alone. His wife died, his older daughter eloped with a spendthrift military officer, his son entered civil service and took to gambling, his younger daughter died. Following these losses, the widower severed his remaining social bonds and became "locked in a maniacal relationship with objects."[16]

The behaviors that started as thrift when Pliushkin's familial and social bonds extended into a future beyond his lifetime are now unattached to any idea of economy or rational utility.[17] Every year more windows of his manor were boarded up; buyers stopped coming for the products of his estate, and the unused crops went to waste. The hay and corn rotted and turned into compost, the flour became as hard as a rock, and the canvas and cloth disintegrated into dust. Because Pliushkin was too miserly to use the products of his manor or to provide for his exploited serfs, everything around him turns to waste, and "the owner himself turned into human detritus."[18] It is not only disuse that ravages Pliushkin and all he owns; it is the modern conception of time as something irreversible and unrepeatable. The conflicting perspectives about value that define hoarding are, in the Pliushkin episode, rooted in the miserly landowner's disavowal of this conception of time.[19] The village is a sanctuary of disuse, a liminal space where objects and people await an endpoint defined by making waste, by making use, or by a different moment, the one that everyone else seems to think is already overdue: Pliushkin's death. Only death could end such futile desuetude so that the humanity worn out and unrecognizable in his features of old age could at least be marked by an epitaph. Gogol writes: "The grave is more merciful than old age, at least we have a grave that carries the inscription: HERE A HUMAN BEING IS BURIED, but there is nothing to read in the frigid, unfeeling features of inhuman old age."[20] Everything in Pliushkin's village, even the old miser himself, seems to have reached the end of its use-time, though it continues to exist.

Pliushkin is the fifth landowner visited by the novel's protagonist, Pavel Ivanovic Chichikov, a disgraced mid-level government official who attempts to reinvent himself in a provincial capital by claiming to be a landowner on private business. Chichikov gains acceptance among the local gentry and sets out to buy up serfs, or "souls," (as they were recorded in official registers), who had died since the most recent census. Although dead serfs could not work the land, their names were indistinguishable, on paper, from those of the living. As Chichikov understands, the souls could therefore provide testament to private wealth sufficient to secure a loan, and landowners would be happy to sell the souls for trifling sums in order to be rid of the tax burden. Chichikov, then, traffics in immaterial signs, signifiers of wealth that are not subject to decay, though they can be transformed into material wealth. It is no coincidence that so notable a hoarder as Pliushkin—like those who have become a cultural fixation in the twenty-first century—emerges at a crossroads between embodied forms of value and semiotic alchemy.[21]

In two excurses that frame the episode of Chichikov's visit to Pliushkin's village, Gogol shows that what is at stake in the contrast between the forms of value accumulated by each is the relationship between material reality and literary realism. In the first excursus, Gogol describes Pliushkin's village as an intrusive material reality that cannot but strike the visitor. The excursus begins as the narrator recalls the joy of youth when nothing escaped his notice, and everything held fascination. To grow old, it seems, is to filter out the distractions of the material world, to abandon one's sense of curiosity. As an adult, instead, the narrator is unmoved by the world he encounters: "What would in former years have aroused vivacious facial expressions, laughter and a torrent of words, now passes me by, and my immobile lips preserve a bored silence."[22] That indifference is shattered by the physical intrusion of Pliushkin's village. Though he trades in immaterial signs, Chichikov is jolted out of his thoughts by the deteriorating road through the village. The reader is similarly struck with an analogously loud metaphor that has the rotting logs of the road moving up and down under Chichikov's carriage like keys of a piano. The excursus establishes the village as a reality that disrupts not only the thoughts of the conman who traffics in signs (Chichikov), but also the narrator who works with linguistic signs, and even the irreversible progression of time. Just as Pliushkin fails to recognize the irremediable decay all around him—his own, that of the shrunken lemon, the rotting hay and corn, or the hardened flour—his village disrupts the disinterest that accompanies aging in Chichikov and the narrator.

A second excursus begins by contrasting the lucky traveler whose wife and children eagerly await his return with the poor bachelor who is weary and alone after a long voyage. Family man and bachelor are likened, respectively, to exalted and reviled writers. The difference between the two sorts of authors rests in the way each treats the world he encounters. Gogol explains: "Happy is the writer who transcends dreary, loathsome characters that strike one with their wretched reality." Such a writer flatters his readers by concealing the miseries of life and devoting himself to "exalted images divorced from the earth." Just as Chichikov hopes to do, these writers gain prominence and wealth by manipulating signs without regard for reality. By contrast, the writer who resembles the bachelor is "without communion, response, or sympathy." Like Gogol, the reviled writer takes up the base and the everyday, "everything that is constantly in front of our noses and which is invisible to indifferent eyes, all the frightful, shocking swamp of trivia that traps our lives, all the depths inhabited by frigid, fragmented, squalid creatures which swarm over our earth." The unsuccessful writer uses "his great strength," as well as "his intransigent sculptor's tools," to render his subject lifelike, in full relief. The realist writer does not indiscriminately appropriate all he encounters, as Pliushkin does, but uses art and science, chisel and magnifying glass to render the world vivid: "Today's judges do not admit that the magnifying glasses which survey suns are equaled by those that show the movements of insects too small to see with the naked eye; they deny that a great spiritual depth is needed to illuminate a picture taken from base life and exalt it into a pearl of creation."[23] The reviled realist writer neither adds to nor falsifies the world he encounters but renders it more vivid with tools of art and science. The work of exalted and reviled writers can be distinguished on the basis of how each confronts reality: the latter works directly on the material at hand, like Gogol's narrator, and, as I will show, like Carlo, the collector and amateur entomologist of Gadda's "L'Adalgisa."

The Tools of Art and Science

Gogol's excursus on the loneliness of the unappreciated writer who remakes even what is frightful and squalid functions as a call to future readers who may be more generous in their assessment of his work. Gadda answers that call with "L'Adalgisa." The short story offers an indirect response to Gogol, redressing the erroneous judgments of his contemporaries. The excursus on the loneliness of the bachelor and the mistreatment of the realist writer must have made an impression on Gadda; he includes Gogol in a list of genius bachelors, along with Catullus, Beethoven, Michelangelo, Tasso, Descartes, Leopardi, and implicitly, Gadda himself, or at least the bachelor character Angeloni.[24] Scholars have overlooked Gogol's influence on Gadda, even though the personal library of the latter attests to the enduring interest amply borne out in "L'Adalgisa."[25] "L'Adalgisa" takes up Gogol's challenge to illuminate a picture taken from base life and exalt it into a pearl of creation, and in so doing seems a gesture of solidarity from a fellow bachelor and writer fearful of remaining without laurels. When it was published in 1940, Gadda wrote to his cousin Piero Gadda Conti, "I wrote a story, 'L'Adalgisa,' of twenty-five pages (or more) for *Tesoretto*. No one takes me seriously, though; I'm broke, I'm old—or rather, I'm in an advanced state of putrefaction."[26]

The story was published for the second time as the last of ten included in a volume, also titled *L'Adalgisa*, published in December 1943 (though it bore the date of 1944).[27] *L'Adalgisa* was "matter in the wrong time" not only because of this trifling bibliographical inaccuracy but because the historical satire seemed inappropriate in a time of war.[28] Claudio Vela calls the collection "an extraordinary fruit that ripened out of season," and Gadda's letters convey his shame at the inauspicious release.[29] The publication was delayed by the slowness of Gadda's revisions, which included the addition of extensive footnotes—a sort of formal waste because of their relationship of extraneousness to the prose they gloss. Internal correspondence at Le Monnier describes the challenges of printing *L'Adalgisa* given the slowed pace of production as specialized workers were conscripted. When *L'Adalgisa* was republished in 1945, the notes and three stories were left out because of a shortage of paper.[30]

The story takes place in a public garden, where the widow Adalgisa is out for a stroll with her two rowdy sons—who run off to admire another boy's toy gun—and her sister-in-law, to whom she recalls her career as an opera singer and her marriage to the accountant Carlo Biandronni, a character modeled after Gadda's uncle and namesake.[31] In a letter to his friend, the philologist Gianfranco Contini, Gadda writes, "This uncle of mine, named Carlo, is pretty much Carlo of 'L'Adalgisa'—I altered his hair color and gave him the mustache that he never had."[32] He adds, using French to convey his uncle's cosmopolitan pretensions: "A bit of a boozer, sure, but quite cultivated and alert *dans le domaine de la littérature e[t] de la science*." The two Carlos also share a "collecting mania" (*mania collezionistica*) rooted in a positivist worldview and a dilettantish interest in science (minerology, entomology), and history (philately).[33]

In "L'Adalgisa," stamps, insects, and minerals spilled through the house, filling its drawers, shelves, and closets. Adalgisa remembers: "With 'just minerals alone,' he had filled more than one closet in the home, an old credenza from the grandparents, and the drawers of a desk, and the mantle of a chimney-less fireplace, and the two side-tables in the '*sala de ricéf*' [front hall]—the big one and the small one." The collections seem to have expanded through some agency that inverts functionality: "Paperweights (of calcite or sulfite) flowed through the house, and consequently, papers." After Carlo's death, the collections are unsentimentally removed and ungracefully discarded: "The tragic removal was a sort of cataclysm. The tornado of bad luck tore through the house, sweeping toward the dark, and forcing [Adalgisa] to dispose of four quintals of rocks, to say nothing of the reefs and seashells and the few long pieces of calcium carbonate—stalks of stalagmite, like dripping candles. And for no profit, not even a cent! . . . It might as well been *me* paying *them* to take it away!"[34] Treasures to Carlo during his lifetime, the collections become waste after his death.

Among Adalgisa's fond memories of her learned husband is one that revolves around another sort of waste: a pellet of excrement pushed through the sands of Viareggio by a Scarabaeus sacer, a dung beetle. Adalgisa recalls her husband's "famous capture" of the Atheucus (as they are also called), one of the most dramatic scenes in the story.[35] She proudly introduces the capture as a triumph of modern scientific knowledge: "Even the kings of Egypt— think a bit about what a superstitious age it was then, compared to the science of today—worshipped [the Atheucus] like a sacred animal, like a peacock."[36] Adalgisa's awe of her husband's scientific learning illustrates the ambivalent break that, for Bruno Latour, subtends the "constitution" of the moderns. Unlike the superstitious Egyptians of yore, who worshipped dung beetles, scientists like Carlo access truths about the natural world. Gadda ironizes Adalgisa's confidence in the victory of modern knowledge over ancient belief when the widow compares the dung beetle to a peacock, reproducing the superstition of the Egyptians.

Adalgisa's operatic account of the famous capture also confounds the distinction between art and science. Carlo's scientific inquiry, in her telling, is a heroic tale that draws on religious and mythical themes. She describes how Carlo watched as the scarab rolled a perfectly spherical mass of dung across mountains and valleys of sand, attempting to reach the residence of his lady-beetle, "who waited, anxiously, on behalf of the little one, the imminent larva, for that providential nourishment." The beetle undertakes the short journey with "the tenacity of Sisyphus," crossing "the ridges of sand; to us nothing, enormous bastions to him." With heart pounding and tweezers poised, Carlo captures the scarab, ending its odyssey in the prison of a small jar. A boy—one of several gathered to watch the epic hero—grabs the treasure left behind on the sand, "eager to claim his share of the fortune." When the round pellet squishes between the boy's fingers, his friends screech, "It's just a turd and you're a moron!"[37] Separated from the epic journey of the scarab, the pellet transforms from a home and feast for future pupae to a turd. Like Carlo's collections after his death, it becomes waste.

As part of Carlo's collection of insects, the beetle becomes illustrative of the marvels of the natural world. The narrator—who comes out in the course of the story as a participant in the setting of belle epoque Milan—recalls how Carlo would hold forth on philosophy and science, illustrating the marvels of the natural world with objects from his collections.[38] With proud eloquence, surrounded by members of the Milanese bourgeoisie and by his insects, minerals, stamps, and "portraits of landscapes of Libya," Carlo confirmed the extraordinary find: "It was indeed the Atheucus Sacer Linnaei."[39] Had Carlo not put a premature end to the sandy journey, the scarab's lady would have deposited her eggs in the perfect sphere made up of "the stuff that those kids called . . . by its name."[40] For Carlo, the saga is not abject but regal; the little larvae would have been born with a banquet before them and would have dined like princes on the dung. He concludes by offering his entranced audience a bit of schmaltzy wisdom: "Every generation paves the way for the next generation."[41]

Gadda creates a literary analogue to the realia of Carlo's salons with a footnote—the longest in *L'Adalgisa*, itself the most extensively footnoted of Gadda's works. The approximately 2,000-word note is offered as a gloss on the following sentence: "Because in short poor Carlo (8) was also an entomologist, which is why

certain ladies I knew—among the most cultured of our coterie—
called him a professor of etymology." Placed mid-sentence and
mid-clause, between the subject and the verb, the note comments
on an epithet, "poor Carlo," that has already appeared five times in
the story. The note is itself a form of waste, out of place not only
because it is excluded from the body of the text, but also because it
is belated as a gloss on the epithet. The note begins, "'Poor Carlo'
was rooted and raised in the 'positivistic' age" and concludes,
"Every age has its wisdom." The list sandwiched between, the bulk
of the note, thus functions in toto as a sketch of the positivistic
age. This portrait of the person, "poor Carlo," takes the form of
a catalog of the elements of age—one that is risibly replete. The
list names libraries, insurance cooperatives, and credit unions; billiard rooms, public pools, and hiking clubs; geologists, crystallog-
raphers, and the minerals named after them (sellaite, dolomite);
Austrian and German beers—light and dark, with corresponding
connoisseurs—the first Italian beers (and related controversies),
French liquors and wines; carriages, steam locomotives, and coal
smoke; asparagus servers, citrus juicers, and spoons for scraping
marrow from a bone; hats, hairstyles, shoes, and corsets; as well
as standards of health and hygiene. This is a most positivistic presentation of the positivistic age: to understand "poor Carlo," you
need to know about his bathing suit, his facial hair, and the tubes
that penetrate his intestinal depths, his "most remote bum bum."[42]

Gadda uses the rhetorical figure associated with uselessness to
map civil society and explain the emergence of the Milanese bourgeoisie. A paragraph that begins by listing forms of transportation
continues, asyndetically, to name derivative phenomena like the
colloquialisms that result: "The presence and efficiency of horse-
drawn carriages and horse-drawn carriers with little canopies
(called 'gardeners')." He notes the changed streetscape engendered

by old and new forms of transportation: heaps of horse dung and puddles of urine that became part of everyday life. Without straying from the list form, Gadda includes a network of causal relations: "Locomotive smoke: relics of the aforementioned in auriculae, hair, eyebrows, and nostrils." Trains belch out coal dust, which gets in everyone's eyes, producing a new ailment, "carbon in the eye," and a new praxis, that of removing coal dust from the eyes with the corner of a handkerchief. With fashions—lace-up booties, for example—come sexual and literary obsessions: "Psychopaths (two or three of them in Europe) enamored of used booties, or rather, used *borzacchino* (the 'brodequin' of Baudelaire): which became a bit of a fetish for everyone." With new pastimes come new nuisances: "Picnics in the park, precautions against green grass stains on clothing (bum bums, skirts, knees)."[43]

Although the property of the Scarabaeus sacer is its excrement, and the collections of Carlo become discards, neither the scarab nor Carlo resembles Pliushkin, since both use their treasures. The ball of dung may be a turd in the hands of the boy on the beach, but had the beetle completed his odyssey across the Viareggio sands, it would have become home and banquet for his pupa. Similarly, Carlo's minerals, insects, and stamps are brought to life in his salons as illustrations of his philosophy and learning. It is only after Carlo's death that the collections turn to waste, becoming as useless as hail cannons, and as extraneous to the bourgeois interior as the eighth footnote is to the story. With the scarab's dung and the collections of Carlo, who delights in nature's abject marvels, Gadda answers Gogol's call to elevate base matter—the "squalid creatures which swarm over our earth," into a pearl of creation. But Gadda's reading of Gogol's lament consists not only in making exalted images of squalid stuff but also in emplotting its transformations to reveal the instability of abjection, the capriciousness of today's judges—and those so unforgiving to Gogol's reviled writer.

In *Dead Souls*, Pliushkin's commitment to avoiding waste consists in salvaging objects that have been discarded or abandoned and in refusing to impose a temporal endpoint on what has already expired—such things as the dried-out lemon, an ancient toothpick, rotten grain, and hardened flour. In "L'Adalgisa," Gadda relates a series of events of making waste through expropriation. Both writers draw more or less explicit parallels between acts of salvaging and keeping and their own aesthetic projects. Pliushkin's hoarding is defined by acute attention to the material—to anything whatsoever that has been abandoned in the alleys of his village. That tendency to be struck by even what is squalid or trivial in the material world is contagious; Pliushkin's dilapidated village seizes the attention of Chichikov and of the narrator and becomes a defining feature of works by reviled realist writers like Gogol. Gadda incorporates an overwhelming collection of obsolescence—objects, ideas, institutions—into a textual storehouse in the form of the eighth footnote of "L'Adalgisa." Like the pellet of dung left behind on the sand after the scarab's capture or the quintals of minerals removed from the Biandronni home after Carlo's death, the footnote becomes waste; a lumber-room of the positivistic age and of the story from which it is excluded. The relationship developed in "L'Adalgisa" between making literature and making waste is apparent not only in Gadda's lament of his own putrefying state but also in the advice Adalgisa delivers to her sister-in-law at the start of the story: "'Be happy, enjoy life while you still have time. Don't think about it, don't be so sad. It's all poetry, nothing but poetry, believe me.' She said 'poetry' like she would have said feces or other putrefying matter."[44] Indeed, it is all poetry, in the hands of a Gadda or a Gogol, but it is a poetry that, each writer (mistakenly) feared, would remain unrecognized by contemporary arbiters of value, like pearls of dung and jars of dead bugs.

Future Unused

Similar poetry is captured in contemporary texts dedicated to hoarding: the television series, *Hoarders*; Song Dong's installation, *Waste Not*; and Martin Hampton's short documentary film, *The Collector*.[45] These twenty-first-century visual texts thematize hoarding in its antithetical symbiosis with wasting, presenting clashing perspectives about value in dramas of making, refusing to make, or unmaking waste. *Hoarders* aired on August 17, 2009, to become A&E's most popular series; it remains a central text in contemporary cultural studies of hoarding.[46] Each of the more than one hundred episodes features two households whose inhabitants—hoarders and their exasperated families—face an imminent crisis like the intervention of governmental agencies like child protective services or public safety because of the condition of their home. Junk removal and cleaning services, professional organizers, social workers, and psychologists descend upon the hoards, laboring against indignant protests. The subjects of *Hoarders* keep all sorts of objects—old newspapers and magazines, expired food, tattered dolls and stuffed animals, rusted tools and auto parts are common examples. The dramatic conflict in each episode is built around clashing perspectives about value, as professionals urge hoarders to consign cherished possessions to the dumpster.

Jill, a sixty-year-old engineer and Milwaukee resident featured on the first episode of *Hoarders*, has become emblematic of the show, in part because her segment is discussed in several academic studies of hoarding in popular culture.[47] Her episode—set during the housing crisis in one of the country's hardest-hit urban areas—deflects attention from infrastructure to make poverty and homelessness appear to result from poor housekeeping.[48] The crisis that demands the speedy clean out funded by the television program is the threat of eviction, a particularly terrifying prospect for Jill, who had recently lost her job and been diagnosed with a serious health problem.

The segment is introduced with a montage calibrated to evoke disgust; the sequence includes the door of a brimming freezer slowly opening, fly-tape encrusted with death, and a rotting mush of pumpkin, images accompanied by a voice-over of the psychiatrist David Tolin: "The smell is the first thing that hits you when you walk in that house. It's like a blast in your face." Jill's hoarding takes the form of a refusal to discard expired food items; by her account, however, she seems a righteous paladin opposing a culture of food waste. She describes her aversion to wasting food by evoking two familiar narratives about hoarding. One narrative is moral: "I feel guilty about wasting something that somebody could be using," and one is personal: "I've had periods of poverty where I haven't had a choice about what I could eat." She disdains the bacteria-phobic consumers unwilling to trust their own senses over the hard law of sell-by dates. Mocking such credulity, she holds up a foreboding container of sour cream, and asks, "What's gonna go wrong with that? What is it gonna go sour?" Unlike other consumers who place blind faith in sell-by dates, Jill describes the positivist principles that guide her choices about what to keep: "I look at things rather scientifically. I don't intend to eat anything that is going to make me ill. I'm not going to dogmatically follow the dates that are on something. I'm going to use my mind. Because I've got a mind." For Jill, to discard food in accordance with the mandates of sell-by dates amounts to blind faith in the system of industrial food production. The squalor of Jill's kitchen is a testament to her campaign of resistance; it is no wonder that viewers have recognized something heroic in her plight.

The clean out process unfolds through a series of negotiations between Jill and the professionals and family members who insist that she discard food items. Remarkably, what they ask of her is faith. She explains her rationale for keeping an aseptically sealed box of broth: "It's not puffy; it's expensive; I don't have the money to replace it; and it is something that I can eat on my diet." Tolin counters these perfectly good reasons by insisting that she abandon her positivistic approach and believe—if not in the sell-by dates—then in the medical expertise he offers: "My thought is that you have a blind spot here. My thought is that you're falling into one of your hoarding habits." Only by giving herself over to a faith in expert knowledge at odds with her experience of the world and her training as an engineer will she be cured. Tolin insists: "You have to recognize that you are ill."

The positivist principles Jill uses to justify keeping the broth are set aside in other scenes of negotiation like the memorable pumpkin scene, when Tolin attempts to appeal to her inductive reasoning: "You know sometimes when you get a strong smell and a lot of flies buzzing around it means that there is something rotting." Jill swears that, though there are some rotting apples in the kitchen, there is no rotten food in the living room. The camera follows Tolin's conspicuous glance across the room and zooms in on a rotting pumpkin. Jill concedes: "Oh, I'm sorry, the pumpkin! It was a very nice pumpkin when it was fresh!" Jill's attachment to the decaying pumpkin despite its state flattens time. Where Tolin sees only the abjection of the present, Jill remembers the time when the pumpkin was nice and imagines a future that it potentially still holds; its seeds could grow into more pumpkins, the overripe fruit could be used to make pie.[49]

An update episode, which aired the following year, includes a follow-up visit to Jill's still somewhat clean house. The tour culminates in a close-up of one gourd that survived the clean out nearly two years earlier and now occupies a regal position on her coffee table. "The remaining pumpkin is still here—the reigning pumpkin," she says of the proud, faded squash. "I'm hoping that it'll hold its color, and that it'll look as pretty as it does now. I love the filigree pattern on it." The professional organizer concedes, "You know, some people want two-year-old pumpkins in their houses, and some people don't." His assessment signals the success of the treatment: her housekeeping choices are no longer symptoms of mental illness but expressions of taste. Only once the pumpkin is transformed into an aesthetic object that can be enjoyed in the present does it stop being a symptom.[50]

The hoarders of popular media keep things for the same reasons as everyone else: they find some sentimental, intrinsic, or instrumental value in them.[51] Though it may entail a gross oversimplification, these can be aligned with distinct temporalities; the sentimental value is generally rooted in an object's past, the aesthetic value in its present, the instrumental value in its future. Critical to distinguishing the hoarder's forward-looking appreciation of instrumental value from the investor's wager of space against time is that for the former, the redemptive moment when, for example, the seeds are planted does not arrive. Delay is dangerous. In his widely anthologized essay "On Dumpster Diving," Lars Eighner issues a warning to that effect, imparting a fundamental rule for scavengers: take only what is of immediate use.[52] To do otherwise is to be overwhelmed by the extraordinary plenitude of so many good things abandoned in dumpsters.

Marie Kondo's trademarked Konmari Method is rooted in a similar injunction to the present tense: to get rid of any possessions that do not "spark joy."

Like Jill, the hoarders of Song's *Waste Not* and Hampton's *The Collector* are defined by their unwavering commitment to avoiding waste. The television presentation of Jill's expired food invites disgust, whereas the accumulations of *Waste Not* and *The Collector* inspire something more like awe. The hoarders in these texts are presented as tragic figures, bearing some resemblance to the "Assistants" Giorgio Agamben describes: "More intelligent and gifted than our other friends, always intent on notions and projects for which they seem to have all the necessary virtues, they still do not succeed in finishing anything and are generally idle [*senz'opera*]."[53] Though they may not know it, their disavowal of death—or waste—holds open the door to the future, a gate through which the Messiah, or at least some artist who might transform their plight—might pass. These brilliant friends, helpless parents, and eccentric roommates are the ones we leave behind: "They give us help, even though we can't quite tell what sort of help it is. It could consist precisely in the fact that they cannot be helped, or in their stubborn insistence that 'there is nothing to be done for us.' For that very reason, we know, in the end, that we have somehow betrayed them."[54] Presenting their subjects as such, Song and Hampton both deny and aver their own artistry.

Song's 2005 *Waste Not* answers the call for future use issued by a hoard of instrumental value: the stuff accumulated by the artist's mother, Zhao Xiangyuan, over the course of her lifetime. The installation consists of the contents of her modest home— more than 10,000 household objects amassed over decades of avoiding waste—which Song moves into the Beijing Tokyo Arts Projects (BTAP) Gallery in Beijing.[55] The work contemplates the intersection of resourceful and pathologized refusals to waste. The display of threadbare redundancy fills some 3,000 square feet of gallery space with domestic objects—apparel and accessories; furniture; kitchenware of every kind, food packaging, and other alimentary ephemera; dolls, plush animals, and other toys—all sorted and arranged around and within the bare wood frame of Zhao's home. The orderly disposition of the objects and the skeletal remains of the humble dwelling invite viewers to marvel at the improbable geometry: all that was in there.

The magnitude of the display—the meticulous arrangement of so much postconsumer stuff—engenders awe, an emotion that psychologists describe as a combination of perceived vastness and accommodation; in other words, the adjustment of mental structures to assimilate what resists comprehension.[56] Awe shares features with disgust; both fix boundaries between feeling subject and affecting object. The perception of immensity that distinguishes awe achieves a similar effect of distancing: "This object is different from me and greater than me," thinks the subject-in-awe. *Waste Not* embodies immensity in the form of so much detritus; the viewer's awe is directed at the magnitude of the display, and by implication, Zhao's dogged—or even sacred—commitment to its preservation.

The installation remakes the hoarded objects as a monument to an ethic of conservation that is shared by a generation. Song writes: "'*Wu jin qi yong*' ['waste not, want not'] is the guideline of my mother's life, but it is also the portrayal of a whole generation of *Chinese* people," the one that lived through the Cultural Revolution.[57] In addition to the shared historical context of the refusal to discard, the catalog offers a different etiology of Zhao's hoarding by presenting her biography as a series of sudden changes in fortune, lending her commitment to a familiar narrative. Zhao's

Figure 4.1
Song Dong, *Waste Not*. Installation view of the exhibition, "Projects 90: Song Dong," June 24, 2009 through September 7, 2009. The Museum of Modern Art, New York. Photographer: John Wronn. Digital Image © The Museum of Modern Art / Licensed by SCALA / Art Resource, New York.

formidable resolve is presented in *Waste Not* as a historical relic, now out of place in a time of plenty. Song explains: "In times when goods were abundant, the habit of 'waste not' became a burden." The curator, Wu Hung, also emphasizes the presence of the past in the exhibition: "[*Waste Not*] does not *transform* the material world into a different representational medium, but only *transports* the past to the here and now."[58] The glosses of Wu and Song temporalize the chasm crossed by the affect of awe; awe-inspiring vastness takes the form of a pastness present in the objects and in Zhao's custodianship.

Zhao was present for much of the BTAP installation, discussing the work with gallery patrons and rearranging the objects in the collection. Wu explains: "Song Dong's idea was to transform his mother into an artist—an active participant in the art project he was designing." Zhao is credited as a coartist of the BTAP installation, and the catalog includes her writings—edited and arranged thematically by Song into sections—"Clothes," "Eat," "Live," "Use." Song describes the installation as a homage to his mother's ethic and an answer to the call for future use issued implicitly by the stuff she so devoutly set aside, "the majority of which would be considered garbage in any other situation." The transformation of objects, for Song, is a way to "[make] her collection finally 'useful'" and thus to heed her adherence to the doctrine of "Waste not, want not." The exhibition honors her resolve and treats her hoarding not by cleaning out her home and making waste of her possessions, but by realizing her dream of future use and turning the domestic objects into art. "In this way, he hoped, her pathological attachment to the past might be cured, and she would be free from the specter of memories to enjoy her life again."[59] Despite the shared artist credit, Zhao's contribution is framed as material to be transformed—or transported—and loss (of her husband) to be mourned, and madness to be cured.

The narrative of *Waste Not* affirms this is a time of plenty. Avoiding waste seems like an archaic practice of a past generation: "Now that the standard of living has improved, this particular way of thinking creates a generation gap—mother not only prevented herself from discarding this stuff, she also prevented us from doing so. As such, our living space was occupied by things waiting to be used and thus 'not wasted.'"[60] Transformed into intrinsic objects on display in a gallery space, Zhao's household effects—like Jill's coffee table pumpkin—are no longer caught in a time of suspense, awaiting some future use. Jill's hoard was sacrificed to normative ideas of hygiene and economy; the choices she saw embodied in expired food have all been made; what remains is the episode, a lot of waste, and one proud decorative gourd. Although Song's mother is given credit as a coartist in the BTAP installation and figures prominently in the exhibit catalog, it is Song's intervention that transforms the accumulated material into art. Zhao's hoard, like Carlo's collections in "L'Adalgisa," "loses its meaning as it loses its personal owner"; however, as art, at BTAP, it gains value.[61]

The Collector also remakes a hoard as art, capturing the tireless labor of Christian Guienne, whose scavenging in the small French town of Buis-les-Baronnies earned him the nickname "the Diogenes of Baronnies."[62] Guienne sets out to counter the culture of waste by remaking the temporal boundaries that define waste as spatial ones. In place of objects that have outlasted their use-time, waste becomes, for Guienne, the space beyond his property: the *vastus*. The film's title invites the viewer to interpret the awe-inspiring assortment of broken-down consumer goods that fill Guienne's house and sprawl across his property as a purposeful—even artful—aggregation, though it is the result of decades of scavenging through the dumpsters:

> There are certain people who say, there is enormous wastefulness. It's terrible. For thirty or forty years I have watched people throwing stuff away. There is great wastefulness. They throw away millions and millions of clothes. They throw away millions and millions of things. They even throw away new things. They chuck out things that work! Radios that work! Coffee machines that work! Machines that still work. Even washing machines that still work. Fridges that work! I have a fridge that I found a year ago that still works.

Guienne conducts a tour of his home and property, proudly urging the camera operator to capture a room full of bread which, he insists, cannot go bad because it is dried out, and a stretch of lawn covered with dozens of refrigerators that double as shoe-racks, and a heap of four or five hundred bicycle tires. Like Jill and Zhao, who consider their possessions to have instrumental value and keep things with the idea of their potential use, Guienne imagines that his acres of junk will serve improbable "clients"—whoever might find himself in need of, for example, a broken refrigerator filled with shoes or, for that matter, ten. He explains that the people who sometimes come to rummage through his de facto junkyard are welcome to take anything; occasionally, he even makes sales. Guienne's lifetime of salvage work creates a space where objects are suspended in time. Although he patiently awaits clients who would return objects to use; the period of suspense is closed by Hampton's film, on the one hand, and by the clean out ordered by the town of Baronnies, on the other. In 2009, Hampton made a short epilogue, *The Collector, Part II,* which relates the unhappy final year of Guienne's life after the town seized his possessions and placed him in an elder care facility. In *Part II,* all the enthusiasm Guienne displayed in *The Collector* is gone, his decades of rescuing waste from the dumpsters of Baronnies have become wasted time. Like so many other hoarders subjected to forced clean outs, Guienne falls into a deep depression and dies soon after, in the barren space of an elder care facility.[63] The film transforms Guienne into a martyr to the resourceful avoidance of waste. Hampton describes his subject as an archivist and artist: "This enormous collection of fridges, televisions, toys, shoes, books etc. . . . represents a remarkable material history of the town's consumer habits, and I consider it to be an outstanding artwork."[64] Though it may be transformed into an outstanding work of documentary film, or a monument to Guienne's work, the sprawling, unfocused junkyard is unlikely to be useful as a material history of consumerism.

In a 2008 Editor's Column in *PMLA*, Patricia Yaeger considers the emergence of a canon of contemporary art and literature dedicated to salvaging and savoring postconsumer debris. She argues that the schism between nature and culture that for Bruno Latour underpins the modern constitution is transformed, in this developing corpus, into a rift between waste and culture.[65] The idea of nature as something external to culture and untouched by human intervention—something "considered from afar, through the shelter of bay windows"—now takes the form of what has been used up, worn out, or cast off, and carries the potential once associated with "Nature."[66] Though Yaeger does not address the reemergence of the hoarder, her survey of contemporary artists and writers who act as custodians of rubbish helps to explain the extent to which hoarders resemble artists or martyrs in contemporary works—at least for viewers more moved by Jill's commitment to avoiding waste than repulsed by the waste that surrounds her.

Hoarders of modern literary and visual texts see the potential in waste, but they cannot manage to transform it through use or art, and stuff just piles up. Nonetheless, just as the aim of preservation is implicit in the term ecology, for Yaeger rubbish ecologies are marked by a commitment to the notion that there is something worth saving in postconsumer debris and other discards. But even as hoarders act as proprietors of a rubbish ecology, their stuff remains rubbish until it is transformed through use or art. Pliushkin's accumulation—his failure of household management—becomes Gogol's pearl of creation. Gadda's "L'Adalgisa" subjects matter to further transformations. The mineralogical and entomological specimens that Carlo uses to illustrate platitudes for rapt audiences at his salons become junk after his death, only to be transformed again into art. It is no wonder that when she says, "it's all poetry, nothing but poetry," Adalgisa says "poetry" as she would "feces" or other putrefying matter. In the junkyard of Guienne and the home of Zhao, the material accumulations are so great that they can only be used as art. If hoarders are tragic figures—failures in household management, positivistic inquiry, and artistic production—it is because they take on the impossible task of avoiding waste.

Conclusion

ARCHIVE FAILURES

The hoards described in this book have included things wondrous and strange: Avon bottles, samovars, and a shriveled lemon. The clean out of the Collyer home yielded a two-headed fetus preserved in formaldehyde, an old X-ray machine, fourteen pianos, a rowboat, grandfather clocks, and a model T. But the real weight of the hoard was in the paper: "Newspapers—thousands and thousands of newspapers—were everywhere: stuffed under the furniture, stacked in unsteady piles against the walls."[1] Paper is heavy and flammable; it makes hoards dense and more dangerous.[2] It was the paper that buried Langley alive; his body was discovered under a suitcase, three metal breadboxes, and bales of newspapers.

Newspapers had been piling up in hoards since well before the Collyer brothers met their macabre fate. In his 1890 *Principles of Psychology*, William James writes of an unnamed miser who was found dead in Massachusetts under similar circumstances; he collected "wrapping-paper, incapacitated umbrellas, canes, pieces of common wire, cast-off clothing, empty barrels, pieces of iron, old bones, battered tin-ware, fractured pots, and bushels of such miscellany as is to be found only at the city 'dump.'"[3] But mostly, his hoard was composed of newspapers that filled "all the rooms of his good-sized house, from floor to ceiling [so] that his living-space was restricted to a few narrow channels between them."[4]

Ubiquitous in hoards, newspapers are at once collections of reproducible text and paper things. Like eighteenth-century critiques of bibliomania that focused on the failure to use books by reading them, the pathologization of hoarding newspapers avers a fissure between paper, a material surface, and the reproducible text impressed on it. This rift is but one inflection of that "original doubleness of the metaphysical conception of signifying," expressed in the oppositions between signifier and signified, matter and spirit, female and male.[5] In *Paper Machine*, Derrida addresses their manifestation in paper and text. Paper, he acknowledges, has material, technological, symbolic, and linguistic histories that complicate the idea that it is a mere substratum for text. Nonetheless, Derrida adds that while books may hold value for readers and bibliophiles as literary texts and as physical objects, newspapers are paradigmatic ephemera, in word and in thing. Out-of-date newspaper bears negligible (or negative) exchange value; ink smears, paper decomposes; "we know in advance that it can deteriorate into wrapping paper or toilet paper."[6] There is little reason to keep newspapers; municipal recycling programs mitigate the guilt associated with discarding, and there is no economic reason to hold on to them—though obviously economic irrationality does not stop anyone from hoarding.[7] Even the immaterial text of newspaper is transient; "yesterday's news" is an idiom for uselessness.

The prevalence of newspapers in hoards can help to explain the vigor of hoarding discourse in the twenty-first century, as print culture goes digital. The glow of screens may not shed light on the reasons that people save newspapers, but it contributes to the sense—among those who do not—that the practice is pathological. And insofar as the hoard is produced by clashing perspectives about value, that sense—that saving newspapers is pathological—is constitutive. The "persistent difficulty discarding or parting with possessions, regardless of their actual value" that defines hoarding disorder remains unchanged when the possessions in question are newspapers, rather than, say, books, dolls, or musical instruments; though newspapers are more manifestly impersonal, ephemeral, worthless, and dirty.

A 2011 BBC special about hoarding features Richard Wallace of Westcott in Surrey who lives amid papers piled up so high that rather than squeeze through narrow "goat paths," he has to slither through the clearing between the ceiling and the stacks to move between rooms in his house. In his memoir, Barry Yourgrau describes his visit with Wallace. The "extreme hoarder" explains to Yourgrau that he would discard the tons of decomposing newspapers and magazines he had accumulated over the course of decades, but only after sorting and scanning them.[8] The project is an afterthought. Although the papers were accumulated over the course of decades, Wallace's ambitious plan to catalog and preserve them in a digital format develops later—a Scheherazadian ruse to stave off the threat of separation.[9] Wallace—like the hoarders discussed in chapter 4—keeps the newspapers suspended in time, creating a protected space of disuse. He is unlikely to ever begin and certain to never complete the archive project. The mildewing decomposition of the newspapers is just one of the many obvious obstacles to its execution. More important, the digital archive Wallace envisions would impose a break between the immaterial text and its material form, diminishing the power of the hoard that is their fusion.

Hoarded newspapers make time visible and material. They pile up predictably, at regular intervals. A stack of newspapers transforms time into space, literalizing one formula for hoarding: a bad wager of space against time. The text printed on the decomposing pages is just as unpredictably accessible as memories; it is all there, though it may not all be intelligible. The architecture of a digital archive would make the text accessible, transforming the exhilarating potential into a "mild boredom of order," as Walter Benjamin describes books in their places on shelves.[10] Like the generative mess that was essential to the creative process of Adam Phillips's agoraphobic patient in "Clutter: A Case History," discussed in chapter 1, or the chance encounters at flea markets in chapter 2, the opaque meaning of the decomposing papers is essential to their intrigue. In *Stuff*, Randy Frost and Gail Steketee describe one patient, Irene, whose hoard was thickened by piles and piles of newspapers, magazines, and assorted clippings. Irene explains the appeal they hold: "Look at all those newspapers and magazines. Somewhere in the midst of all that there may be a piece of information that could change my life; that could make me into the person I want to be."[11] For Irene, all matter is equally and essentially worth keeping. Her reluctance to foreclose wonderful potential necessitates disorganization incompatible with hegemonic ideas of interior decoration, cleanliness, and even value; photographs of family members mixed in with old newspapers; envelopes of cash nestled between pages of magazines. The jumble of meaning and value that ends up in such paper hoards results in a "flat epistemology" that, like the "flat ontologies" that have marked the posthuman turn in the humanities and social sciences, eschews hierarchies and organizational principles in favor of polyvalent connections between elements. It is in part such flatness—as I argue in chapter 3—that distinguishes the hoarder from the detective who is able to separate layers of narrative, moving between the signifying planes of investigation and crime.

A similarly debilitating commitment to all paper—one that also results in a collapsing of signifying planes—is the theme of Moscow Conceptualist Ilya Kabakov's *The Man Who Never Threw Anything Away* and *The Garbage Man*, part of his "total installations" *Ten Characters* (1988) and *The Great Archive* (1993), respectively.[12] A short text written around 1977, incorporated into the *Ten Characters* installation, and first published in English in 1989, describes the flat epistemology that governs the accumulation of paper for the character, the Man Who Never Threw Anything Away and, more broadly, the Soviet subject so deeply connected to "each thing—paper, feather, nail" that "to discard them would mean to discard and ruin this life."[13] The text describes the interior—part of the installation—of a state-owned apartment inhabited by a plumber, absent save for a breathtaking hoard of paper: "There was no plumber in the room. . . . All those who had entered with Uncle Misha couldn't regain their wits for a long time and stood still, transfixed, looking around in amazement." What awes the intruders is the magnitude of the accumulation: "The entire room, from floor to ceiling, was filled with heaps of different types of garbage," but also the cleanliness and order: "this wasn't a disgusting, stinking junkyard, but rather a storehouse of the most varied things, arranged in a special, one might say carefully maintained order."[14] The catalog of organized eclecta concludes with paper— "piles of paper, manuscripts" not yet labeled and organized. Uncle Misha reads one page, an article titled "Garbage," apparently written by the absent resident.

"Garbage" begins by asserting that papers just tend to pile up: "Usually everybody has heaps of accumulated piles of paper." The tendency, the resident continues, is so extreme that "our home literally stands under a paper rain: magazines, letters, addresses, receipts, notes, envelopes, invitations, catalogues, programmes, telegrams, wrapping paper, and so forth." The article explains that the "streams, waterfalls of paper" require the inhabitant to periodically separate out important papers, divide them into categories—different for every individual—and throw out the rest. Without "these sortings, these purges," the "flow" of paper engulfs the inhabitant. This happens when a person does not know which are important and which are not, what principle of selection to use, or what distinguishes necessary papers from garbage. When this happens—as it has for the plumber—"a different correlation arises in his consciousness": everything, without exception, must be considered to be valuable or to be garbage.[15] Choice is too agonizing; every document is associated with some memory, and every memory is connected to all others: "All points of our recollections are tied to one another."[16] Every document is, as detective Ingravallo from Carlo Emilio Gadda's *Quer pasticciaccio* might put it, a cyclonic point of depression in the consciousness of the world. Why, the article asks, should the common sense that makes the papers seem like garbage to others be given more weight than one's own memories? Instead, the plumber saves everything, assembling and organizing all the loose papers into folders and binders that "comprise the single uninterrupted fabric of an entire life." The resulting "Garbage Novel" does not represent a life, but indexes it: "the way it was in the past and the way it is now."[17] To make waste is to impose a hierarchy, to give texture to an otherwise flat epistemology—to do what the narrator in Luigi Malerba's *The Serpent*, discussed in chapter 3, is unable to do.

E. L. Doctorow makes newspapers a key conceit in his 2009 fictionalization of the life of the Collyer brothers, *Homer and Langley*. In the novel, the newspapers are essential to Langley's ongoing research to test his "theory of replacements"—Doctorow's invention. The narrator, Homer, explains the theory as follows:

"Everything in life gets replaced. We are our parents' replacements just as they were replacements of the previous generation."[18] The theory underpins Langley's collections throughout the novel, which take the form of the pursuit of an ideal, spawning multiple versions of everything that comes into the Fifth Avenue townhouse. Hoarding, in Doctorow's novel, is propelled by a quest for perfection, rather than, as for Irene of *Stuff* or the plumber of Kabakov's total installation, by an indecision that results in a flat epistemology, a valorization of everything. Although most of the objects Doctorow introduces in the novel are emblematic of specific episodes in the brothers' lives, the newspapers pile up throughout in connection with an ambitious editorial project Langley devises to corroborate his theory of replacements. Doctorow's fictional Langley aims to create a single edition that would be timeless and accurate, "sufficient to any day." The "eternally current dateless newspaper," Doctorow's Homer explains, would be "the only newspaper anyone would ever need."[19] The idea of a perfectly representative edition, with stories that balance description and narration, specific and universal, begins to look like a theory of the novel.

It is no coincidence that Doctorow's novel makes the newspapers such an essential component of the hoard, given its publication at the end of the first decade of the twenty-first century when print circulation was being superseded by digital editions and smartphone applications. A menacing immateriality is implicit in the discussion about the technology section of the eternally current dateless newspaper. When Homer asks what technological achievement could possibly stand for them all, Langley responds: "Ah my brother, don't you see? The ultimate technological achievement will be escaping from the mess we've made. There will be none after that because we will reproduce everything that we did on earth, we'll go through the whole sequence all over again, somewhere else, and people will read my paper as prophecy, and know that having gotten off one planet, they will be able to destroy another with confidence."[20] The greatest technological achievement would be not to speed things up or to fix what is broken but to make space. For Doctorow's Langley, making space would not entail creating more paper on which to print more stories but rather making a new planet that would be a referent of a representation of this one.[21] That is the achievement that Malerba playfully thwarts in *Il serpente*, allowing no part of the fictional world to appear distinct from its telling; it is an achievement that would be impossible for Jorge Luis Borges's Funes, discussed in chapter 3.

In a short 1924 paper, Freud asks whether such clearing out or making space is at the origin of the concept of time. "A Note upon the 'Mystic Writing-Pad'" begins by introducing the problem of finitude. Like money, which embodies the contradiction between quantitative limitation and qualitative boundlessness, paper sets the finite space of any surface against the endless possibilities of language, and the posterity of the written word. Freud describes the simple technology of the mystic writing pad, magic slate, or *Wunderblock* as a resolution to the riddle of scarcity and as a metaphor for the mind.[22] The pad is made of a dark-colored block of resin or wax covered by a layer of thin waxed paper and a transparent sheet of celluloid; the three layers are joined along one side but remain detached on the others. Writing on the celluloid with a stylus leaves no mark on the transparent surface, but presses the waxed paper into the slab, making the writing visible. The page can be erased by raising the two-ply covering and severing the close contact between the resin and the paper that makes the writing visible. Though the surface writing is cleared, Freud explains the basis of his comparison: "It is easy to discover that the permanent trace of what was written is retained upon the wax slab itself and is legible in suitable lights."[23] Freud ultimately deems the metaphor insufficient. The resin may preserve traces of all the writing that has been impressed upon it, but it cannot send traces back to the surface: "It is true, too, that, once the writing has been erased, the Mystic Pad cannot 'reproduce' it from within; it would be a mystic pad indeed if, like our memory, it could accomplish that."[24]

A better approximation of the unconscious, in this sense, may be the hoard, which—unlike the resin—can act on its surfaces, with unforeseen (and sometimes tragic) effects: ink fades and smears, paper obelisks wobble and fall. But the analogy is also insufficient because the hoard is composed not only of traces but of praxes, relationalities, and aesthetics. The Clutter Image Rating developed by Frost and Steketee as an assessment tool, for example, models the aesthetic criteria that constitute the "objective reality" of a hoard. The mise-en-scènes photographed, however, are hollowed of the subjective temporalities and architectures produced by the hoarder's churning.

San Francisco-based Carey Lin illustrates the elusiveness of this objective reality with her series *Hardly Nothing to Live Without* (2011), paintings of Google image search results for "compulsive hoarding." *Untitled (Screen shot 2009-10-19 at 1.20.48)* is a representation of a digital index of the artist's life—that is, the late October night when she turned to Google for images of "compulsive hoarding." And that digital index of her life, in turn, is an index of some other time and space—unknowable, irrelevant to the painting—when the "objective reality" of a hoard was captured in a photograph.

Some debris of the material landscape of contemporary consumer culture is recognizable in the painting: an old mattress, cardboard boxes, garbage bags, and the back wheels of a tricycle

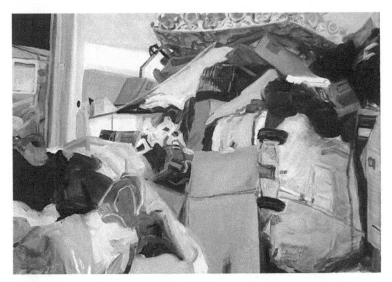

FIGURE 5.1
Carey Lin, *Untitled (Screen shot 2009-10-19 at 1.20.48)*, 2011, Oil on canvas,
15 in. × 22 in. from the series *Hardly Nothing to Do Without.*

or a mechanical lawnmower. Much of the frame, however, is filled
with abstraction; blue, white, and black forms that could be
clothes, plastic bags, and papers become indistinct artifacts from
the rubbish ecology of the Anthropocene. *Untitled (Screen shot
2009-10-19 at 1.20.48)* introduces a hoard that is familiar and
strange. The material presence of stuff recedes into the horizon
of a photograph uploaded to the internet and indexed by Google,
a Google search performed by the artist, a painting of the search
result. That horizon—that old dream of referentiality—is the cultural logic that intertwines psychic and political economies, the
boundaries between material and immaterial; rational and irrational; individual and aggregate; past, present, and future.

Notes

Preface

1. Examples include the documentaries *Packrat* (2004) by Kris Britt Montag and *My Mother's Garden* by Cynthia Lester; the feature films *Clutter* (2013) by Diane Crespo and *Hello, My Name Is Doris* (2015) by Michael Showalter; the novels *Homer and Langley* (2009) by E. L. Doctorow, *The Museum of Innocence* (2008) by Orhan Pamuk, and *Dirty Little Secrets* (2010) by C. J. Omololu; the memoirs *Collections of Nothing* (2008) by William Davies King, *Dirty Secret* (2010) by Jessie Sholl, *White Walls* (2016) by Judy Batallion, *Coming Clean* (2013) by Kimberly Rae Miller; *Mess* (2015) by Barry Yourgrau, *The Force of Things* (2013) by Alexander Stille; the plays *Keep* (2016) by Francesca Pazniokas and *The Loss Machine* (2012) by Kyle Loven; guides for mental health service and organizing professionals; self-help books; art installations; paintings; photographs; television forensic dramas; sitcoms; and stand-up and late-night comedy by Samantha Bee, Conan O'Brian, Kathy Griffin, and Ali Wong; Lauren Berlant's *Cruel Optimism* (Durham, NC: Duke University Press, 2011) includes a section on hoarding in Charles Johnson's short story, "Exchange Value," 35–43, and Jane Bennett makes the hoarder a paradigmatic vital materialist in "Powers of the Hoard: Further Notes on Material Agency," in *Animal, Vegetable, Mineral: Ethics and Objects*, ed. Jeffrey Jerome Cohen (Washington, DC: Oliphaunt Books, 2012): 237–69.

2. The primary support group run in the style of Alcoholics Anonymous is Clutterers Anonymous. See Barry Yourgrau, *Mess: One Man's Struggle to Clean Up His House and His Act* (New York: W. W. Norton, 2015) for a first-person account of a Clutterers Anonymous meeting in New York. The largest advocacy and support group for Children of Hoarders (COH) is Internet-based, though members have organized local meetups. The restricted Yahoo! COH group had more than 3,000 members.

3. The house is described by David Wallis in "Is It Normal to Hoard?": "On a tidy street in a resurgent New England mill town, where the trimmed bushes look like green thimbles mounted in mulch, Melvin's large Victorian house sticks out. Two bicycles, one missing the front wheel, lean against threadbare front steps; stacks of two-by-fours, rakes, and bicycle tires piled up on a desk surround the front door"; *Nautilus*, no. 10, "Mergers and Acquisitions," February 14, 2014, http://nautil.us/issue/10/mergers--acquisitions/is-it-normal-to-hoard.

4. Yi Chang, Lei Tang, Yoshiyuki Inagaki, and Yan Liu, "What Is Tumblr: A Statistical Overview and Comparison," *ACM SIGKDD Explorations Newsletter* 16, no. 1 (2014): 21–29.

Introduction to Hoardiculture

1. Helen Worden Erskine, *Out of This World* (New York: F. P. Putnam's Sons, 1953), 37.

2. Worden Erskine, *Out of This World*, 38.

3. Worden Erskine, *Out of This World*, 39.

4. Worden Erskine, *Out of This World*, 45.

5. "Collyer Mansion Yields Junk, Cats" *New York Times*, March 26, 1947.

6. "Collyer Mansion Yields Junk, Cats."

7. "Four Pianos Auctioned in Collyer Parlor," *New York Times*, June 21, 1947.

8. "200 Bid Spiritedly for Collyer Items," *New York Times*, June 11, 1947.

9. There is a serendipitous coda to the story of the sale of the Collyer brothers' stuff. In 2013, Barry Lubetkin, a collector and clinical psychologist, stumbled upon a photograph of the Collyer brothers' dilapidated drawing room and recognized the clock his father had purchased more than sixty years earlier. See Franz Lidz, "Owner of Forgotten Clock Finds a Name (and Hands) to Put with the Face," *New York Times*, December 26, 2013.

10. See Lidz, "The Paper Chase," *New York Times*, October 26, 2003. Lidz is also the author of a biographical memoir of the Collyer brothers and his uncle, *Ghosty Men: The Strange but True Story of the Collyer Brothers and My Uncle Arthur, New York's Greatest Hoarders* (New York: Bloomsbury, 2003).

11. Worden Erskine, *Out of This World*, 45.

12. Worden Erskine, *Out of This World*, 48.

13. See Patrick Moran, "The Collyer Brothers and the Fictional Lives of Hoarders," *MFS Modern Fiction Studies* 62, no. 2 (2016): 272–91 for the study of key topoi in literary representations of the Collyer brothers.

14. A notable work of cultural criticism is Scott Herring's *The Hoarders* (Chicago: University of Chicago Press, 2014), which examines the story of the Collyer brothers through the lens of urban history and locates origins of a distinctly contemporary equation of hoarding with "disorganization" in racializing discourses about "social disordering." Herring argues that the "material deviance"

of hoarders challenges the social order that sustains normative ideas about consumption.

15. Kristen Mack, "Alone and Buried by Possessions," *Chicago Tribune*, August 10, 2010, https://www.chicagotribune.com/news/ct-xpm-2010-08-10-ct-met-hoarders-0811-20100810-story.html and Ivanna Hampton, "Woman Found Dead in Garbage-Filled Home," *NBC Chicago*, July 20, 2010, https://www.nbcchicago.com/news/local/skokie-elderly-woman-hoarder-garbage-house-home-trash-98814974.html. In "Update: Family Hires Crew to Clean Out Hoarder's Home," George Slefo describes the aftermath of the Davis' death, and the work of the Skokie-based cleaning company, American Hoarders; *Skokie Patch*, August 2, 2010, https://patch.com/illinois/skokie/update-village-hires-crew-to-clean-out-hoarders-home.

Just two months earlier and less than twenty-five miles away, a similar tragedy unfolded. In May 2010, residents of the Grand Crossing neighborhood on the South Side of Chicago noticed that mail was piling up on Jesse and Thelma Gaston's porch and parking tickets were accumulating on their car. One neighbor called 911 and asked that someone check on the elderly couple. What firefighters found, after traversing the yard strewn with broken appliances and lawn furniture and knocking down the front door, was a tableau of American horror: the pair was "buried alive" amid their hoarded possessions. The Gastons were taken to Jackson Park Hospital, where Jesse died of cancer six weeks later. Thelma, who was blind and diabetic, was made a ward of the county, and was transferred to a North Side nursing home. See Mack, "Alone and Buried."

Other such examples abound. In February 2011, Richard Alan Meier of St. Paul, died in a residential fire exacerbated by hoarding; Mara Gottfried, "Man Found Dead Inside St. Paul Home's Burning Kitchen," *Twin Cities Pioneer Press*, February 8, 2011, http://www.twincities.com/2011/02/08/man-found-dead-inside-st-paul-homes-burning-kitchen/. Eunice Crowder of North Portland died in a house fire the following year; Anna Griffen, "Hoarder Killed in North Portland House Fire Lived in Plain Sight, Leaving a Trail of Questions," *Oregonian*, December 8, 2012, http://www.oregonlive.com/portland/index.ssf/2012/12/house_fire_that_killed_north_p.html. On March 26, 2009—seven years after family members had reported her missing—the remains of seventy-six-year-old Eunice Workman were found under piles of trash and debris in her Oakland home. See Angela Woodall, "Body of Woman Missing for Seven Years Found in Oakland House," *Oakland Tribune*, March 25, 2009, https://www.eastbaytimes.com/2009/03/25/body-of-woman-missing-for-seven-years-found-in-oakland-house/.

16. On the narrative formulas of the television series *Hoarders* (A&E) and *Hoarding: Buried Alive* (TLC), see Susan Lepselter, "The Disorder of Things. Hoarding Narratives in Popular Media," *Anthropological Quarterly* 84, no. 4 (2011): 919–47. Following the success of *Hoarders* other networks developed similar shows: from 2010 to 2014 TLC ran the popular *Hoarding: Buried Alive*, and from 2010 through 2012 Animal Planet aired *Confessions: Animal Hoarding.*

Other reality series from the same period touch on issues related to hoarding; for example, History's *American Pickers* (2010–) and *Pawn Stars* (2009–); A&E's *Storage Wars* (2010–19); TLC's *Extreme Couponing* (2010–12); the National Geographic Channel's *Doomsday Preppers* (2012–14); the Style Network's *Clean House* (2003–11); and Netflix's series *Tidying Up with Marie Kondo* (2019–).

17. American Psychiatric Association, *Diagnostic and Statistical Manual of Mental Disorders* (Arlington, VA: American Psychiatric Publishing, 2013); emphasis added.

18. In a seminal article in *RES*, William Pietz traces the origin of the fetish to the intersection of Christian feudal, African lineage, and merchant capitalist systems in sixteenth- and seventeenth-century West Africa. In this context, the fetish was an ethnocentric concept used by Portuguese traders to name inanimate objects to which natives attributed magic powers; Pietz explains, "The discourse about the fetish has always been a critical discourse about the false objective values of a culture from which the speaker is personally distanced." See "The Problem of the Fetish, I," *RES: Anthropology and Aesthetics* 9, no. 1 (1985): 5–17, 14.

19. *DSM-5*, "Use of the Manual," DSM-Psychiatryonline.org. On the expediency of fetishism, see Freud, "Fetishism," in *The Standard Edition of the Complete Psychological Works of Sigmund Freud (SE)*, trans. and ed. James Strachey (London: Hogarth Press, 1953–74); 21 (1961):147–58, 151.

20. *DSM-5*, "Use of the Manual," DSM-Psychiatryonline.org.

21. Freud, "Fetishism," *SE* 21, 152–53.

22. The elimination disorders, encopresis (fecal incontinence) and enuresis (bed-wetting) may be considered exceptions.

23. Randy O. Frost, Gail Steketee, David Tolin, and Stefanie Renaud, "Development and Validation of the Clutter Image Rating," *Journal of Psychopathology and Behavioral Assessment* 30, no. 3 (2008), 193–203; and Frost and Veselina Hristova, "Assessment of Hoarding," *Journal of Clinical Psychology* 67, no. 5 (2011): 456–66.

24. Carl Schmitt, *The Nomos of the Earth in the Ius Publicum Europaeum* (New York: Telos Press, 2003), 235. David Harvey, *A Brief History of Neoliberalism* (New York: Oxford University Press, 2007), 165.

25. Wendy Brown, *Undoing the Demos: Neoliberalism's Stealth Revolution* (New York: Zone Books, 2015), 9. Gary Becker, *An Economic Approach to Human Behavior* (Chicago: University of Chicago Press, 1990), 14.

26. Louis Paul Abeille, *Lettre d'un négociant sur la nature du commerce des grains* (S.n.1763); Bibliothèque nationale de France, département Réserve des livres rares.

27. On grain hoarding, see Rehman Sobhan, "The Politics of Hunger and Entitlement," in *The Political Economy of Hunger*, ed. Jean Drèze and Amartya Sen (Oxford: Oxford University Press, 2007), 1:79–113. On the meaning of "people" defined against "population," see Michel Foucault's discussion of Abeille in

Security, Territory, Population. Lectures at the Collège de France 1977–1978 (New York: Picador, 2004), 29–49. On the "people" and "bare life," or *zoo*, see Giorgio Agamben, "What Is a People," in *Means Without End: Notes on Politics* (Minneapolis and London: University of Minnesota Press, 2000), 29–34.

28. John Maynard Keynes understood such immobility—the hoarding of exchange value—as a "liquidity-preference" that can be analyzed in relation to interest rates, which can be adjusted to stimulate circulation and discourage hoarding. Interest was traditionally regarded as the reward for not spending, but Keynes viewed it as recompense for not hoarding.

29. Karl Marx, *A Contribution to the Critique of Political Economy*, trans. N. I. Stone (Chicago: Charles H. Kerr & Company, 1904), 178, 171, 179.

30. Marx, *Capital*, vol. 1, trans. Ben Fowkes (London and New York: Penguin Classics, 1990), 231.

31. Marx, *Capital*, 163.

32. In "Mediants, Materiality, Normativity," Arjun Appadurai argues that new theories of materiality are needed to parse the enmeshments of material entities in immaterial networks of bundled and rebundled financial products; see *Public Culture* 27, no. 2 (76) (2015): 221–37. See Annie McClanahan, *Dead Pledges: Debt, Crisis, and Twenty-First-Century Culture* (Palo Alto, CA: Stanford University Press, 2018), 5–16 for a concise history of the debt crisis in the United States and the deregulation that allowed investors to bundle unsecured debt into risky financial products.

33. See Fred Penzel, "Hoarding in History," in *Oxford Handbook of Hoarding and Acquiring*, ed. Frost and Steketee, 6–16.

34. The neologism "hoardiculture" is associated with the Elsewhere Project in Greensboro, North Carolina, a living museum, artist residency program, and creative re-use of a depression-era general store turned surplus warehouse turned hoard.

1. Psychologies

1. In the years leading up to the inclusion of hoarding disorder in the *DSM-V*, compulsive hoarding was common parlance in psychiatric and popular culture.

2. See Maurizio Lazzarato, *The Making of the Indebted Man: An Essay on the Neoliberal Condition* (New York: Semiotext(e), 2012) and *Governing by Debt* (New York: Semiotext(e), 2015). Building on Nietzsche's discussion of debt and guilt in *Genealogy of Morals*, and Gilles Deleuze and Félix Guattari's reading of it in *Anti-Oedipus*, Lazzarato proposes that the defining paradigm of the social rests not in an underlying equality that fosters the exchange of commodities and labor, but of relations of credit and debt.

3. In *The System of Objects* (New York: Verso, 1996), for example, Jean Baudrillard distinguishes between a collection and an accumulation on the basis of value.

"Collecting proper . . . has a door open onto culture, being concerned with differentiated objects which often have exchange value, which may also be 'objects' of preservation, trade, social ritual, exhibition - perhaps even generators of profit" (103).

4. A central preoccupation of new materialist thought—which includes Louis Althusser's aleatory materialism, Rosi Braidotti's Deleuzian postanthropocentric philosophy, Bill Brown's Heideggerian "thing theory," Graham Harman's Object-Oriented Ontology, Jane Bennett's vital materialism, and Maurizia Boscagli's stuff theory—is the way in which matter eludes human agency and even cognition. Two edited volumes, Diana Coole and Samantha Frost's *New Materialisms: Ontology, Agency, Politics* (Durham, NC: Duke University Press, 2010), and Iris van der Tuin and Rick Dolphijn's *New Materialism: Cartographies and Interviews* (Ann Arbor: Open Humanities Press, 2012), present the field and chart the range of theoretical approaches it encompasses. See also Maurizia Boscagli's *Stuff Theory: Everyday Objects, Radical Materialism* (New York: Bloomsbury Academic, 2014).

5. Brown, *Other Things* (Chicago: University of Chicago Press, 2015), 45.

6. See Steven Rasmussen and Jane L. Eisen, "The Epidemiology and Clinical Features of Obsessive-Compulsive Disorder," *Psychiatric Clinics* 15, no. 4 (1992): 743–58 and David Veale and Alison Roberts, "Obsessive-Compulsive Disorder," *British Medical Journal* 348 (2014), https://doi.org/10.1136/bmj.g2183.

Hoarding disorder is counted in the fifth edition of the *Diagnostic and Statistical Manual of Mental Disorders* (*DSM-5*). The other obsessive-compulsive and related disorders included in *DSM-5* are obsessive-compulsive disorder, body dysmorphic disorder, skin-picking disorder, and hair-pulling disorder. Hoarding is also listed among possible symptoms of depression, anorexia nervosa, schizophrenia, and dementia disorder.

7. Lennard Davis, *Obsession: A History* (Chicago: University of Chicago Press, 2008), 5.

8. Davis, *Obsession*, 4. Along with Davis, both Jennifer Fleissner and Paul Cefalu argue that there is a modern specificity to obsessive-compulsive disorders. Marina van Zuylen focuses on the nineteenth-century obsession with monomania, arguing that it expresses a desire to keep arbitrariness and contingency at bay. See Fleissner, *Women, Compulsion, Modernity: The Moment of American Naturalism* (Chicago: University of Chicago Press, 2004); Cefalu, "What's So Funny about Obsessive-Compulsive Disorder?" *PMLA* 124, no. 1 (2009): 44–58; and van Zuylen, *Monomania: The Flight from Everyday Life in Literature and Art* (Ithaca: Cornell University Press, 2005).

9. See Paula Findlen's, *Possessing Nature: Museums, Collecting, and Scientific Culture in Early Modern Italy* (Berkeley: University of California Press, 1994) for a study of curiosity cabinets and grand galleries in Italy.

10. On the vicissitudes of monomania in the nineteenth-century psychiatry, see Jan Goldstein's *Console and Classify: The French Psychiatric Profession in the Nineteenth Century* (Chicago: University of Chicago Press, 1989), 152–96.

11. Goldstein, *Console and Classify*, 153.

12. Partial insanity was introduced by Esquirol's teacher at the Salpêtrière hospital, Philippe Pinel; see Goldstein, *Console and Classify*, 122–28.

13. Simon During describes monomania as a disorder in which will, emotion, and reason become separated from each other. See "The Strange Case of Monomania: Patriarchy in Literature, Murder in *Middlemarch*, Drowning in *Daniel Deronda*," *Representations* 23 (1988): 86–104, 86.

14. Goldstein names Honoré de Balzac, de Tocqueville, and Charles de Bernard, and others who begin to use "monomania" in the 1830s. *Console and Classify*, 152.

15. Goldstein notes that the term virtually disappears from French psychiatry by around 1870. Nordau calls the proliferation of manias a "philologico-medical trifling" in *Degeneration* (London: Heinemann, 1895), 242.

16. "Disposophobia" (the fear of discarding) and "syllogomania" (the gathering of rubbish) were both coined more recently, though they evoke the phobias and manias of the nineteenth century. The first use of "syllogomania" I located was in A. N. G. Clark, G. D. Mankikar, and Ian Gray's "Diogenes Syndrome: A Clinical Study of Gross Neglect," published in *The Lancet* 305, no. 7903 (1975): 366–68. The term "disposophobia" was coined by Ron Alford, founder of the North Carolina-based Disaster Masters, a cleaning company that specializes in hoards. He defined the term in Ben McGrath's "Squished," which appeared in the January 12, 2004 issue of the *New Yorker*: "It's an affliction, it's really a disease. It starts in the head of the people and manifests somewhere on the floor and on horizontal surfaces in their dwelling units."

17. See, for example, Virginia Woolf's "Solid Objects," in *A Haunted House and Other Short Stories* (San Diego: Harcourt, Brace & World, 1972), 79–86; James Joyce's *Finnegans Wake* (New York: Penguin Classics, 1999); and Carlo Emilio Gadda's *L'Adalgisa. Disegni Milanesi* (Milan: Adelphi, 2012). In 1893, Giovanni Mingazzini, a neurologist and professor of medicine at the Sapienza University of Rome, published "Sul collezionismo nelle diverse forme psicopatiche" in *Rivista sperimentale di freniatria e medicina legale delle alienazioni mentali* (Reggio Emilia: Stefano Calderini & Sons), 19:541–73. Four years later, Sante de Sanctis, also based in Rome, published "Collezionismi e impulsi collezionistici," in *Bollettino della società Lancisiana degli ospedali* 17, no. 1 (1897): 3–30.

18. For a sustained discussion of the origin and endurance of debates between biological and psychodynamic perspectives, see Anne Harrington's *Mind Fixers. Psychiatry's Troubled Search for the Biology of Mental Illness* (New York: W. W. Norton, 2019).

19. Jean-Baptiste le Rond D'Alembert's entry on "Bibliomanie" was included in the second volume of the *Encyclopédie*, coedited with Denis Diderot, published in 1752.

20. Neil Kenny studies the thriving market for "livres rares et curieux" in France beginning in the mid-seventeenth century. See Kenny, "Books in Space

and Time: Bibliomania and Early Modern Histories of Learning and 'Literature' in France," *MLQ: Modern Language Quarterly* 61, no. 2 (June 2000): 253–86. "Bibliomanie" and "bibliomane" were first used during the period Kenny discusses. In a letter dated December 20, 1652, the French physician and book collector Guy Patin uses "bibliomanie" in light-hearted self-deprecation, urging the *destinataire*, Charles Spon, to seek reimbursement for books purchased on Patin's behalf: "You have enough other troubles from me without having to empty your purse for my fantasies and my capricious bibliomania, which should cause harm only to myself." Patin's letters, edited by Loïc Capron, are available at http://www.biusante.parisdescartes.fr/patin/.

On the distinction between the immateriality of the text and materiality of the book, see Carlo Ginzburg, "Clues: Roots of an Evidential Paradigm," in *Clues, Myths, and the Historical Method* (London: Hutchinson Radius, 1988), 106–8.

21. Walter Benjamin, *The Arcades Project* (Cambridge: Belknap Press of Harvard University Press, 2003), 204. Baudrillard, similarly, writes: "what is possessed is always an object *abstracted from its function and thus brought into relationship with the subject*"; *The System of Objects*, 91.

22. Francesco Petrarch's focus on the dangers of books rests in their abuse by over-consumption, that is, by drawing from them more than a mind can absorb: "Like our stomachs, our minds are hurt more often by overeating than by hunger, and as the use of food so is the use of books to be limited to the capacity of the user." See Conrad Rawski's translation of Petrarch's *De remediis utriusque Fortune; Remedies for Fortune Fair and Foul: A Modern English Translation of* De remediis utriusque Fortune (Bloomington: Indiana University Press, 1991), 1:138. See Henry W. Kent, "The Love of the Book," *Bulletin of the American Library Association* 9, no. 4 (July 1915): 94–101 for a survey of bibliomania that covers Petrarch, Ferriar, and Dibdin.

23. D'Alembert, "Bibliomania," *The Encyclopedia of Diderot & d'Alembert Collaborative Translation Project*, trans. Malcolm Eden (Ann Arbor: Michigan Publishing, University of Michigan Library, 2015), http://hdl.handle.net/2027/spo.did2222.0003.188.

24. D'Alembert, "Bibliomania."

25. D'Alembert, "Bibliomania." On the contrast between this ideal of a library and d'Alembert's work as the coeditor of the *Encyclopédie*, see Jennifer Tsien's discussion of the anonymously authored "Livres" article in the *Encyclopédie* in "Diderot's Battle against Books: Books as Objects during the Enlightenment and Revolution," *Belphégor. Littérature populaire et culture médiatique*, ed. Anthony Enns and Bernhard Metz, Special issue: *Distinctions That Matter/Fictions Économiques*, 13-1 (2015), https://doi.org/10.4000/belphegor.609.

26. Beccaria never published his poems; the manuscript of "Il bibliomane" is held at the Biblioteca Ambrosiana in Milan and has been published in the *Edizione nazionale delle opere di Cesare Beccaria*, vol. 2 (Milan: Mediobanca, 1984), edited

by Luigi Firpo. It is also included in Ugo Rozzo's *Furor bibliographicus ovvero la bibliomania* (Macerata: Biblohaus, 2011), 88–90.

27. "Che val, se in mezzo a così chiari lumi / Ei solo in folte tenebre si giaccia/ Se degli innumerevoli volume / Sol si contenta dell'esterna faccia, / E senza averli giammai letti o tocchi / Dei fregi e dei colori appaga gli occhi?" Rozzo, 90; translation mine.

28. Ferriar, *The Bibliomania: An Epistle to Richard Heber* (London: Cadell & Davies, 1809), 3.

29. Ferriar, *Bibliomania*, 4. On book collecting and sexuality, see Michael Robinson, "Ornamental Gentlemen: Thomas F. Dibdin, Romantic Bibliomania, and Romantic Sexualities," *European Romantic Review* 22, no. 5 (2011): 685–706. See also Mike Goode, "Dryasdust Antiquarianism and Soppy Masculinity: The Waverley Novels and the Gender of History," *Representations* 82, no. 1 (Spring 2003): 52–86.

30. See Marvin J. Taylor, "The Anatomy of Bibliography: Book Collecting, Bibliography and Male Homosocial Discourse," *Textual Practice* 14, no. 3 (2000): 457–77.

31. Ferriar, *Bibliomania*, 4.

32. Thomas Frognall Dibdin, *The Bibliomania; or Book-Madness; Containing Some Account of the History, Symptoms, and Cure of this Fatal Disease* (London: Longman, Hurst, Rees, and Orme, 1809), iii and 4.

33. Dibdin, *Bibliomania*, 4.

34. Althorp is more famous today as the burial site of Diana Spencer, of the same family.

35. Dibdin, *Bibliomania*, 4–8, 7.

36. Dibdin, *Bibliomania*, 82.

37. Dibdin, *Bibliomania*, 14–15.

38. See Francesco Orlando, *Obsolete Objects in the Literary Imagination* (New Haven: Yale University Press, 2006), 11–12.

39. Dibdin, *Bibliomania, or, Book Madness: A Bibliographical Romance, in Six Parts* (London: Chatto & Windus, 1876), 88.

40. Mercurius Rusticus (pseud. Dibdin), *Bibliophobia. Remarks on the present languid and depressed state of literature and the book trade. In a letter addressed to the author of the Bibliomania* (London: Bohn, 1832), 10.

41. Walter Scott and W. Powell Jones, "Three Unpublished Letters of Scott to Dibdin," *Huntington Library Quarterly*. 3, no. 4 (July 1940): 477–84.

42. Dibdin, *The Bibliographical Decameron: Or, Ten Days of Pleasant Discourse Upon Illuminated Manuscripts*, vol. 3, Day IX (London: Shakespeare Press, 1817), 62–117.

43. Dibdin, *Bibliophobia*, 10.

44. Dibdin, *Bibliographical Romance*, 123.

45. As quoted in Umberto Eco, "Collazione di un collezionista," *La memoria vegetale e altri scritti di bibliofilia* (Milan: Bompiani, 2011), 47–57; 47–48.

46. Eco, "Collazione," 48–49. In "Riflessioni sulla bibliofilia," Eco includes a section on stealing books. In *La memoria vegetale*, 32–34.

47. Dibdin, *Bibliographical Romance*, 118.

48. The exercise of discernment that enables the mischievous thrill Eco describes, or that results in the identification of a precious volume hidden at a Jesuit library, is different from the form of literary judgment that Giacomo Leopardi finds wanting in his 1824 "Parini, or On Glory." Leopardi argues that the true worth of a work of literature emerges only after multiple readings. The myriad new works published each year, therefore, hinder a young writer's chances of success. True judgment, for Leopardi, is the result of a decades- or centuries-long distillation process. Discerning readers serve as catalysts, but they cannot substitute the slow accumulation of successive generations of critical assessments.

49. See Gerry Max, "Gustave Flaubert: The Book as Artifact and Idea: *Bibliomanie* and Bibliology," *Dalhousie French Studies* 22 (1992) for a reading of the story, and of the relative lack of critical attention it has received.

50. Gustave Flaubert, "Bibliomania," in *A Passion for Books: A Book Lover's Treasury of Stories, Essays, Humor, Lore, and Lists on Collecting, Reading, Borrowing, Lending, Caring for and Appreciating Books*, ed. Harold Rabinowitz and Rob Kaplan (New York: Three Rivers Press, 1999): 64–76, 66.

51. Flaubert, "Bibliomania," 66.

52. Charles Nodier, "Bibliomane," in *L'Amateur de livres* (Le Pré-Saint-Gervais: Le Castor Astral, 1993), 27.

53. Nodier, "L'Amateur de livres," in *L'Amateur de livres*, 101.

54. Nodier, "L'Amateur," 102, 95.

55. Nodier, "L'Amateur," 95.

56. Nodier, "L'Amateur," 103.

57. Nodier, "L'Amateur," 101, 102.

58. Nodier, "L'Amateur," 102. It is no small irony that the phrenologists, with their collections of skulls and cranial measurements, were no less overwhelmed by their material accumulations than bibliomaniacs.

59. Jean Baptiste Félix Descuret, *La médecine des passions ou Les passions considérées dans leurs rapports avec les maladies, les lois et la religion*, Deuxième édition (Paris: Labé, 1844). For Descuret's account of Boulard's bibliomania, see 751–57.

60. Christina Rossetti's *Goblin Market* (1865) carries echoes of Descuret's account of Boulard's sickness and cure in warning of the deadly addiction that could result from giving in to the seductions of the market.

61. Flaubert, *Madame Bovary*, trans. Geoffrey Wall (New York: Penguin Classics, 2003), 198.

62. André Matthey, *Nouvelles recherches sur les maladies de l'esprit précédé de considérations sur les difficultés de l'art de guérir* (Paris: J. J. Paschoud, 1816). Other key writers on kleptomania include Charles Chrétien Henri Marc, *De la folie: considérée dans ses rapports avec les questions médico-judiciaires* vol. 2 (1840):

247–303, https://doi.org/12148/bpt6k85087q, and then, at the turn of the century Alexandre Lacassagne, "Les vols à l'étalage et dans les grands magasins," *Archives d'anthropologie criminelle, de criminologie et de psychologie normale et pathologique* 11 (1896): 560–65. See also Paul Dubuisson, who coins the term "magasinitis" in "Les voleuses des grands magasins," *Archives d'anthropologie criminelle, de criminologie et de psychologie normale et pathologique* 16 (1901): 1–20, and Wilhelm Stekel, "The Sexual Roots of Kleptomania," *Journal of Criminal Law and Criminology* 2, no. 2 (1911): 239–46.

63. Johann Caspar Lavater, *Essays on Physiognomy: Designed to Promote the Knowledge and the Love of Mankind*, trans. Thomas Holcroft (London: William Tegg & Co., 1858), 376–77.

64. Lavater's other examples of the powerful effects of the imagination of pregnant women on their children are still more astonishing. He writes, for example, of a pregnant woman who attended the execution of a man who had been sentenced to have his right hand cut off before being beheaded. She witnessed the be-handing but left before the beheading. "This lady bore a daughter, who is still living, and who had only one hand. The right hand came away with the after-birth." Lavater, *Essays on Physiognomy*, 376.

65. See Patricia O'Brien, "The Kleptomania Diagnosis: Bourgeois Women and Theft in Late Nineteenth-Century France," *Journal of Social History* 17, no. 1 (Autumn 1983): 65–77, and Tammy Whitlock, "Gender, Medicine, and Consumer Culture in Victorian England: Creating the Kleptomaniac," *Albion: A Quarterly Journal Concerned with British Studies* 31, no. 3 (Autumn 1999): 413–37.

66. Cesare Lombroso summarizes, in 1893: "Of eighty prisoners arrested for rebelling against or assaulting the guards, I found that only nine were not menstruating. Parisian women are likely to begin shoplifting while menstruating: among fifty-six such thieves studied by Legrand de Saulle, thirty-five were in the menstrual period, and for ten it had just ended. Legrand thus concluded that when hysterical young women steal bibelots, perfume, and the like, it is almost always during the menstrual period." In Lombroso and Guglielmo Ferrero, *Criminal Woman, the Prostitute, and the Normal Woman*, trans. Mary Gibson (Durham, NC: Duke University Press, 2004), 160.

67. See Whitlock, "Gender, Medicine, and Consumer Culture," 413.

68. W. Stekel, "The Psychology of Kleptomania," in *Twelve Essays on Sex and Psychoanalysis*, trans. S. A. Tannenbaum (New York: Critic and Guide, 1922), 301.

69. Valentin Magnan is best known for his treatise on dipsomania (alcoholism).

70. Magnan, *Leçons cliniques sur les maladies mentales: considérations générales sur la folie, les héréditaires ou dégénérés, les délirants chroniques, les intermittents* (Paris: A. Delahaye et E. Lecrosnier, 1887), 152.

71. Nordau, *Degeneration*, 27.

72. Nordau, *Degeneration*, 27. In addition to such female troubles and to degeneration, clinicians associated the urge to buy, steal, or gather, with

a distracted, unfocused state of mind that is matched by two disorders classi-fied in the *DSM-5* with obsessive-compulsive and related disorders: skin-pick-ing disorder and hair-pulling disorder. Not generally associated with obsessive thoughts, skin-picking and hair-pulling seem to be prompted by depression, anger, boredom, frustration, indecision, or fatigue. See Jonathan S Abramowitz, "Presidential Address: Are the Obsessive-Compulsive Related Disorders Related to Obsessive-Compulsive Disorder? A Critical Look at *DSM-5*'s New Category," *Behavior Therapy* 49, no. 1 (2018): 1–11. On states of inattention, Gertrude Stein's work on automatic writing is a key precursor; see "Cultivated Motor Automa-tism; a Study of Character in Its Relation to Attention," *Psychological Review* 5, no. 3 (1898): 295–306 and "Normal Motor Automatism," coauthored with Leon M. Solomons, in *Psychological Review* 3, no. 5 (1896): 492–512.

73. Mingazzini, "Sul collezionismo," 541.

74. Sante de Sanctis, "Collezionismo," 7.

75. Sante de Sanctis, "Collezionismo," 8.

76. Sante de Sanctis, "Collezionismo," 28.

77. In *The Interpretation of Dreams,* Freud acknowledges de Sanctis's work with a patient who suffered from paranoia but offers harsh words for the psy-chiatrist's monograph on dreams, published in 1899: "I have unfortunately been unable to escape the conclusion that his painstaking volume is totally deficient in ideas—so much so, in fact, that it would not even lead one to suspect the exis-tence of the problems with which I have dealt." *SE* 4 (1953), 93.

78. *Interpretation of Dreams, SE* 4, 177.

79. On Freud's collection of antiquities, see Stephen Barker, ed., *Excavations and Their Objects. Freud's Collection of Antiquity.* The number of objects cited is that given by Russel Belk and Melanie Wallendorf in "Of Mice and Men: Gender Identity in Collecting," in *Interpreting Objects in Collections,* ed. Susan M. Pearce (London: Routledge, 1994), 240–53, 242, and John Forrester, "'Mille e tre': Freud and Collecting," *Cultures of Collecting,* ed. John Elsner and Roger Cardinal (Lon-don: Reaktion Books, 1994), 224–51.

80. Freud, *The Psychopathology of Everyday Life, SE* 6 (1960), 167.

81. Freud, *Studies on Hysteria,* "The Case of Emmy von N.," *SE* 2 (1955), 87.

82. Freud, *Three Essays on the Theory of Sexuality, SE* 7 (1953), 138.

83. Freud, *Notes Upon a Case of Obsessional Neurosis, SE* 10 (1955), 157.

84. The "Rat Man" was identified as Ernst Lanzer by Patrick Mahoney in *Freud and the Rat Man* (New Haven: Yale University Press, 1986).

85. Freud, *Notes, SE* 10, 176.

86. The ultimate injustice of the case is the one Freud explains later, in a note added in 1923: "The patient's mental health was restored to him by the analysis which I have reported upon in these pages. Like so many other young men of value and promise, he perished in the Great War"; Freud, *Notes, SE* 10, 249.

87. Freud, *Notes, SE* 10, 206.

88. Freud, *Notes, SE* 10, 205.
89. Freud, *Notes, SE* 10, 206. So strong, so elemental, was the child's rage that the father declared, memorably: "The child will be either a great man or a great criminal" (205). Freud adds, in a note: "These alternatives did not exhaust the possibilities: His father had overlooked the commonest outcome of such premature passions—a neurosis" (205).
90. One of the most famous episodes in the Rat Man case history is a pedagogical moment in which Freud explains to his patient the way unconscious thoughts are preserved by comparing them to objects at Pompeii: "I then made some short observations upon *the psychological differences between the conscious and the unconscious,* and upon the fact that everything conscious was subject to a process of wearing-away, while what was unconscious was relatively unchangeable; and I illustrated my remarks by pointing to the antiques standing about in my room. They were, in fact, I said, only objects from a tomb, and their burial had been their preservation: the destruction of Pompeii was only beginning now that it had been dug up." Freud points out a key difference: "Every effort was made to preserve Pompeii, whereas people were anxious to be rid of tormenting ideas like his." Freud, *Notes, SE* 10, 176.
91. See Christian Metz, "Photography and Fetish," *October* 34 (1985): 81–90.
92. Although Freud uses the word *Verleugnung* sporadically throughout his writing, beginning in 1924 he develops a more precise understanding of the term, and from 1927 on he uses the concept almost exclusively in connection with fetishism. See J. Laplanche and J. B. Pontalis, *The Language of Psycho-Analysis,* trans. Donald Nicholson-Smith (New York: W. W. Norton, 1973).
93. James Strachey, editor's note to "Fetishism," *SE* 21 (1961), 149.
94. Freud, "Fetishism," *SE* 21, 156.
95. Freud, *Notes, SE* 10, 166, 167.
96. Adam Phillips, "Clutter: A Case History," in *Promises, Promises. Essays on Literature and Psychoanalysis* (New York: Basic Books, 2001), 69–71, 62.
97. Phillips, "Clutter," 68, 69, 66, 65, 64, 63.
On the legendary mess of Francis Bacon's South Kensington studio, see Ian Buchanan, "The Clutter Assemblage," *Drain Magazine* 7, no. 1, 2011, http://drain-mag.com/the-clutter-assemblage/.
98. Phillips, "Clutter," 65.
99. Elena Ferrante, *Frantumaglia: A Writer's Journey* (New York: Europa editions, 2016).
100. Phillips, "Clutter," 65.
101. Randy Frost and Gail Steketee, "Hoarding: Clinical Aspects and Strategies," in *Obsessive Compulsive Disorders: Practical Management,* ed. Michael Jenike, Lee Baer, and William E. Minichiello (St. Louis, MO: Mosby, 1998), 538.
102. Frost and Steketee, "Hoarding," 538.
103. Frost and Steketee, "Hoarding," 538.

104. Roman Jakobson, Linda Waugh, and Monique Monville-Burston, eds., *On Language* (Cambridge: Harvard University Press, 1990).

105. Michel Foucault, *The Order of Things* (New York: Routledge, 1994), xviii.

106. See, for example, Perminder S. Sachdev and Gin S. Malhi, "Obsessive–Compulsive Behaviour: A Disorder of Decision-Making," *Australian & New Zealand Journal of Psychiatry* 39, no. 9 (2005): 757–63.

See J. M. Harlow, "Recovery from the Passage of an Iron Bar Through the Head" (Boston: David Clapp & Son, 1869), U.S. National Library of Medicine Digital Collection, http://resource.nlm.nih.gov/66210360R. For an introduction to the significance of Harlow's report in psychiatry, see Edgar Miller's "Recovery from the Passage of an Iron Bar Through the Head," *History of Psychiatry* 4, no. 14 (1993): 274–81. On its relevance to hoarding, see Frost and Steketee, *Stuff*, 212.

107. On the linguistic axes that distinguish souvenir from collection, see Susan Stewart, *On Longing: Narratives of the Miniature, the Gigantic, the Souvenir, the Collection* (Durham, NC: Duke University Press, 1992), 132–50.

108. Stewart, *On Longing*, 132–50.

109. Alexander Stille describes his aunt Lally, a hoarder: "She was strangely lacking in a sense of proportion, of being able to tell the forest from the trees"; *The Force of Things* (New York: Macmillan, 2013), 73.

110. Mark Singer, "The Book Eater," *New Yorker*, February 5, 2001, 62–71.

111. Singer, "The Book Eater," 66.

112. The exchangeability of thoughts and things is a premise shared by the thriving organization industry, whose promises reach well beyond the prosaic tidy house to include happiness and health. The organization guru Marie Kondo, author of best-selling self-help books and star of the popular Netflix series *Tidying Up with Marie Kondo* even champions tidying-up as a life-changing magic: "When you put your house in order, you put your life and your past in order too." See Marie Kondó, *The Life-Changing Magic of Tidying-Up*, trans. Cathy Hirano (Berkeley: Ten Speed Press, 2014), 4.

In a 2010 episode of the Style Network's *Clean House* (2003–11), titled "Lindsay Lohan: I'm a Hoarder," the eponymous actress describes the psychological impact of her messy apartment: "It makes you feel like, the unorgana— . . . like how disheveled some of it is, and how much there is? Yes, the clutter. Um, it's . . . It takes up a lot of space, you know. Mentally." In such statements, thoughts, feelings, and things move fluidly between mind and dwelling, bound by a single causal chain. An abundance of objects can clutter the mind, and an emptiness of mind (or heart) can be filled with objects (with varying degrees of success). It is that equation that makes hoarding sometimes seem a form of mourning, an attempt to fill up the absence left by the death of a loved one with so much stuff.

113. On this use of "bizarre objects" to name abject matter (rotten food, nail clippings, hair), see Alberto Pertusa, Randy Frost, and David Mataix-Cols, "When Hoarding Is a Symptom of OCD: A Case Series and Implications for *DSM-5*," *Behavior Research and Therapy* 48 (2010): 1012–20, 1013.

2. Economies

1. Brian Vickers and Stephanie Preston note the burden of hoarding on healthcare, public services, and financial systems; "The Economics of Hoarding," in *The Oxford Handbook of Hoarding and Acquiring* (Oxford: Oxford University Press, 2014), 221–32.

2. See, for example, Vickers and Preston, "Economics," 221.

3. Vickers and Preston, "Economics," 221, and Susan Lepselter, "The Disorder of Things: Hoarding Narratives in Popular Media," *Anthropological Quarterly* 84, no. 4 (2011): 919–47.

4. See the introduction to James Cannon, *The Paris Zone: A Cultural History, 1840–1944* (New York: Routledge, 2016), 1–14.

5. Cannon, *The Paris Zone*, 1–14.

6. These materials were sorted and sold: the carcasses were used to make fertilizer and glue; glass and metal were melted down; cardboard and rags were pulped for paper production. Ragpickers who stumbled upon valuables—jewelry, silver spoons, banknotes—were required by law to turn them in at the nearest police station See Pierre Larousse, *Le Grand dictionnaire universel du XIXe siècle*, vol. 4 (Paris: Administration Du Grand Dictionnaire, 1866); and Jean Bedel, *Saut de "Puces" à Saint-Ouen* (Saint-Rémy-en-l'Eau: Monelle Hayot, 2012), 42–44. The Saint-Ouen market at the Porte de Clignancourt was officially established to mollify ragpickers whose labor had been hindered by the 1884 Poubelle law requiring landlords to provide covered garbage containers to their tenants. See Cannon, *The Paris Zone*.

7. On the contemporaneous development of marginalist theories in Britain, by William Jevons; Austria, by Karl Menger; France, by Léon Walras; and Italy, by Vilfredo Pareto, see Jean-Joseph Goux, *Symbolic Economies. After Marx and Freud*, trans. Jennifer Curtiss Gage (Ithaca: Cornell University Press, 1990), 198–202.

8. See "On the Economic Phenomenon: A Reply to Benedetto Croce," *Giornale degli economisti e annali di economia*, Nuova serie, 71, no. 2/3 (December 2012): 11–28.

9. Goux, *Symbolic Economies*, 202.

10. Walter Benjamin, "Notes on a Theory of Gambling," in *The Sociology of Risk and Gambling Reader*, ed. James Cosgrave (New York: Taylor & Francis, 2006), 212.

11. Phillips, "Clutter"; see also chapter 1 in this book.

12. Freud, "On Transience," *SE* 14 (1957), 303–7.

13. Charles Baudelaire, *The Painter of Modern Life* (London: Penguin UK, 2010).

14. Theodor Adorno, *Minima moralia. Reflections from a Damaged Life*, trans. E. F. N. Jephcott (New York: Verso, 2005; Apple ebook), 283.

15. Benjamin, "On the Concept of History," in *Selected Writings*, Vol. 4: *1938–1940*, ed. Howard Eiland and Michael Jennings (Cambridge: Belknap Press of Harvard University Press, 2003), 389–400, 392.

16. Benjamin, "On the Concept of History," 392.

17. See Susan Buck-Morss, *The Dialectics of Seeing: Walter Benjamin and the Arcades Project* (Cambridge: MIT Press, 1991), 94–95; and Kaja Silverman, *Flesh of My Flesh* (Palo Alto: Stanford University Press, 2009), 179–80, 211–13.

18. Bruno Latour, *We Have Never Been Modern* (Durham, NC: Duke University Press, 1993), 10. On the emergence of nostalgia as a distinctly modern ailment symptomatic of this philosophy of time, see also Svetlana Boym's *The Future of Nostalgia* (New York: Basic Books, 2001), 19–32.

19. Michael Thompson, "Introduction," in *Rubbish Theory: The Creation and Destruction of Value*, new ed. (London: Pluto Press, 2017), 1–18, 4.

20. See Ian Shapira, "Renoir Found at W.Va. Flea Market Likely to Fetch $100,000 at Auction," *Washington Post*, September 11, 2012, https://www.washingtonpost.com/local/renoir-found-at-wva-flea-market-likely-to-fetch-100000-at-auction/2012/09/11/2725710a-fc44-11e1-8adc-499661afe377_story.html. The naivete of those hoping to stumble upon overlooked treasure remains a persistent theme in writing about the market. In Carlo Fruttero and Franco Lucentini's 1972 *La donna della domenica* (*The Sunday Woman*), for example, a worldly character marvels that people still go to the flea market with the secret hope of finding a Van Gogh. In *The Collector's Whatnot: A Compendium, Manual, and Syllabus of Information and Advice on All Subjects Appertaining to the Collection of Antiques, Both Ancient and Not so Ancient*, ed. Booth Tarkington, Kenneth Lewis Roberts, Hugh MacNair Kahler, et al. (Boston: Houghton Mifflin, 1923), "Professor Charles A. Doolittle" warns against purchasing antiques in Italy: "There are so many Cinque Cento artisans still living in Florence" (85).

21. Thierry Bardini, *Junkware* (Minneapolis: University of Minnesota Press, 2011), 9.

22. Bardini, *Junkware*, 9.

23. David Trotter, *Cooking with Mud: The Idea of Mess in Nineteenth-Century Art and Fiction* (Oxford: Oxford University Press, 2000), 15.

24. Trotter, *Cooking*, 20.

25. Trotter, *Cooking*, 21.

26. Baudelaire, *The Flowers of Evil*, trans. James McGowan (Oxford: Oxford University Press, 1993), 56.

27. On Baudelaire's ragpicker as poet, see also his "Le soleil," in *The Flowers of Evil*, 168 Irving Wohlfarth, "Et Cetera? The Historian as Chiffonnier," *New*

German Critique, 39 (1986): 143–68. On the ragpicker as revolutionary in Breton's *Nadja*, see Margaret Cohen, *Profane Illumination: Benjamin and the Paris of Surrealist Revolution* (Berkeley: University of California Press, 1993). Other prominent literary portraits of the ragpicker include Félix Pyat's enormously successful play *Le Chiffonnier de Paris*, staged in 1847, and Mie d'Aghonne's 1880 *Les Mémoires d'un chiffonnier*. See also Barbara Schinman Fields, *Jean-Francois Raffaëlli (1850–1924): The Naturalist Artist* (PhD diss., Columbia University, 1979); and Louis Paulian, *La Hotte du chiffonnier* (Paris: Hachette, 1885).

28. Benjamin, *The Writer of Modern Life: Essays on Charles Baudelaire*, ed. Michael Jennings (Cambridge: Harvard University Press, 2006), 108.

29. David Harvey, *Paris: Capital of Modernity* (New York: Routledge, 2003), 214. Clive Scott, *Street Photography from Atget to Cartier-Bresson* (London: I.B. Tauris, 2007), 92.

30. On Raffaëlli's ragpickers, see Marnin Young, "Heroic Indolence: Realism and the Politics of Time in Raffaëlli's Absinthe Drinkers," *The Art Bulletin* 90, no. 2 (2008), 235–59; Fields, *Jean-Francois Raffaëlli*, and Cannon, *The Paris Zone*, 49–61.

31. Paulian, "Les Chiffonniers," *L'Illustration*, February 1, 1884, 75; my translation.

32. Paulian, "Les Chiffonniers," 75.

33. See Bedel, *Les Puces ont cent ans. Histoire des chiffonniers, brocanteurs et autres chineurs du Moyen Age à nos jours* (Cany: Presses de l'imprimerie Gabel, 1985), and *Saut de puces a Saint-Ouen* (Saint-Rémy-en-l'Eau: M. Hayot, 2012.

34. See Ian Walker, *City Gorged with Dreams* (Manchester: Manchester University Press, 2002), 118–21 on these two images.

35. First considered the elite of the profession of *chiffonnier*, *chineur* gradually took on negative connotations and became associated with trafficking in forgeries and stolen goods. On the tripartite structure of the profession, see Paulian, "Les Chiffonniers," 75, as well as Bedel, *Saut de puces*, 42–44, and Félicien Champsaur, "Les Chiffonniers," in *Les Types de Paris*, ed. Edmond de Goncourt et al. (Paris: E. Plon, Nourrit, 1889), 139–44.

36. The Saint-Ouen market at the Porte de Clignancourt was officially established to mollify ragpickers whose labor had been hindered by the 1884 Poubelle law requiring landlords to provide covered garbage containers to their tenants. See Cannon, *The Paris Zone*, 46–48.

37. See Bedel, *Saut de puces*, 57–58.

38. Office de Tourisme de Plaine Commune Grand Paris, "L'histoire du marché: Origine du nom marché aux puces," http://www.tourisme-plainecommune-paris.com/decouvrir/patrimoine-vivant-et-preserve/chinez-au-marche-aux-puces-de-saint-ouen/lhistoire-du-marche, n.d.

39. "Au 'Marché-aux-Puces,'" *La Lanterne*, June 24, 1891, http://gallica.bnf.fr/ark:/12148/bpt6k75293445.

40. "Au 'Marché-aux-Puces.'"

41. "Au 'Marché-aux-Puces.'"

42. André Warnod, *La Brocante et les petits marchés de Paris* (Paris: Figuière, 1914), 1.

43. "Les surprises du marché aux puces," *XIX*ᵉ *Siècle*, July 27, 1891, http://gallica. bnf.fr/ark:/12148/bpt6k7559759t; my translation.

44. "Les surprises du marché aux puces."

45. "La Terreur des Fortifs," *Le Zonier*, December 1, 1897, 2; as quoted in Cannon, 82. Cannon explains that suburban landowners played an outsized role in promoting the image of violence in the Zone.

46. The story, appeared on November 14, 1895 in *Le Journal*, with the title "150,000 Francs pour huit sous," http://gallica.bnf.fr/ark:/12148/bpt6k76212398, and in *Le Matin: derniers télégrammes de la nuit*, with the title "Une fortune inespérée," http://gallica.bnf.fr/ark:/12148/bpt6k5564864.

47. In these first two accounts of November 1895, the boy is referred to as Edouard F. In reports related to the legal proceedings in February of the following year, he is referred to as Henri Pouget.

48. On the flaneur at the flea market, see Warnod, *Les Plaisirs de la rue* (Paris: L'édition française illustrée, 1920), 10–11.

49. On "exposition narrative" as a genre that emphasizes spatial organization and visual perception, see Cristina Della Coletta, *World's Fairs Italian Style: The Great Exhibitions in Turin and Their Narratives, 1860–1915* (Toronto: University of Toronto Press, 2006), 6, 52.

50. Edmondo De Amicis, *Le tre capitali*, 8. De Amicis's description of the city was first published in the 999-page Roux & Favale 1880 guide to the city occasioned by (and contributing to) preparations for the 1884 exposition. The volume includes writings by Vittorio Bersezio, Nicomede Bianchi, Roberto Sacchetti, Corrado Corradino, and others. In 1884, the volume was republished in *Torino e l'esposizione Italiana del 1884: Cronaca illustrata della esposizione nazionale-industriale ed artistica del 1884* (Turin: Roux & Favale). De Amicis then included the guide to Turin in *Le tre capitali—Torino—Firenze—Roma* (Catania: Niccolò Giannotta, 1898).

51. De Amicis, *Tre capitali*, 19. Fueling the locally inflected patriotism of De Amicis's account is the lingering sense of injury at the transfer of the capital of the new Kingdom of Italy from Turin to Florence twenty years earlier. See Della Coletta, *World's Fairs*, 21.

52. *Balòn*, sometimes spelled *Balùn, Balôn*, or *Balûn*, is Piedmontese dialect for *pallone*, which can mean balloon or ball. The market takes its name from the nickname of the Borgo Dora, where it takes place. The neighborhood was once called the "Borgo del Pallone," probably after sporting events held there. Already by the seventeenth century, there was a restaurant in the neighborhood named Osteria del Pallone. In 2012, a hot-air balloon anchored by steel cables was raised over the market and began offering rides.

53. Della Coletta, *World's Fairs*, 20.

54. Della Coletta, *World's Fairs*, 23.

55. Della Coletta, *World's Fairs*, 44; Zola's *Trois Villes*—Lourdes, Rome, and Paris—were published between 1894 and 1898. His *Le Ventre de Paris* was published in 1873.

56. De Amicis, *Le tre capitali*, 49–50.

57. De Amicis, *Le tre capitali*, 50.

58. De Amicis, *Le tre capitali*, 50–51.

59. See Leo Spitzer's influential *Enumeración Caótica en la Poesía Moderna* (Buenos Aires: Imprenta y casa editora Coni, 1945) and "Explication de Texte Applied to Walt Whitman's Poem 'Out of the Cradle Endlessly Rocking,'" *ELH* 16, no. 3 (1949): 229–49.

60. On hypallage, see Barbara Spackman, *Fascist Virilities* (Minneapolis: University of Minnesota Press, 1995), 72. On the poetics of etcetera, see Eco, *The Infinity of Lists: An Illustrated Essay* (New York: Rizzoli Editions, 2009).

61. Modernist writers from Joyce, to Gadda, to Nanni Balestrini will torment this form of the list by subordinating signified to signifier so that the unifying logic, the reason for the grouping rests not in what is signified but in alliteration, meter, rhyme, and other properties of the signifier.

62. Francesco Orlando, *Obsolete Objects in the Literary Imagination: Ruins, Relics, Rarities, Rubbish, Uninhabited Places, and Hidden Treasures* (New Haven: Yale University Press, 2006).

63. De Amicis, *Le tre capitali*, 52.

64. Dante, *Inferno*, VII:22–23, trans. Charles S. Singleton (Princeton: Princeton University Press, 1970).

65. Dante, *Inferno*, VII:30, trans. Allan Mandelbaum, https://digitaldante. columbia.edu/dante/divine-comedy/inferno/inferno-7/. Dante's words are "perché tieni?" and "perché burli?"

66. Baudelaire describes Edgar Allan Poe's story as such in *The Painter of Modern Life*. He asks: "Do you remember a picture (for indeed it is a picture!) written by the most powerful pen of this age entitled *The Man of the Crowd*?," 10.

67. E. A. Poe, *The Collected Works of Edgar Allan Poe. Tales and Sketches, 1831–1842*, ed. Thomas Ollive Mabbott, with the assistance of Eleanor D. Kewer and Maureen C. Mabbott (Cambridge: Belknap Press of Harvard University Press, 1978), 506–18, 511.

68. Poe, *Collected Works*, 511.

69. Paul Hurh, "'The Creative and the Resolvent': The Origins of Poe's Analytical Method," *Nineteenth Century Literature* 66, no. 4 (2012): 466–93, 485; emphasis added.

70. On the origin of "la capitale morale," see Paolo Papi, "Perché Milano è considerate la capitale morale," *Panorama*, October 29, 2015, https://www.panorama. it/news/cronaca/perche-milano-e-considerata-la-capitale-morale/. Giovanni Verga

called Milan the "la città più città d'Italia" in his essay about the surrounding area, "I dintorni di Milano," in *Milano 1881* (Milano: Ottino, 1881), 423. In addition to exposition catalogs and the commissioned volumes *Mediolanum* (Milan: Vallardi, 1881) and *Milano 1881*, numerous similar collections, including *Milano e i suoi dintorni* (Milan: Civelli, 1881) and *Conferenze sulla Esposizione nazionale del 1881* (Milan: Hoepli, 1881) were published for the occasion of the exposition.

71. Pietro Virtuani, "Nota introduttiva e bibliografica," in *Il ventre di Milano: Fisiologia della Capitale morale, per cura di una società di letterati*, ed. Cletto Arrighi (Milan: Ledizioni, 2016), 13. See also Giovanna Rosa, "La 'città più città d'Italia' e l'esposizione del 1881," in *1881–2015: Milano città di esposizioni* (Milan: Istituto Lombardo, 2016).

The palombari, or "divers," were so named because they sought to dive into the depths of social problems through investigative journalism. Key figures included Paolo Valera and Lodovico Corio, cofounders of the literary movement associated with the journal *La plebe*. The name may also bear some relationship to the famous passage in Verga's "Fantasticheria": the most interesting story to an oyster is of the perfidy of crayfish, or the knife of the diver (*palombaro*) who tears it from the reef.

72. See Virtuani, "Nota introduttiva," 13. See also Giovanna Rosa's "La 'città più città d'Italia' e l'esposizione del 1881," in *1881–2015*.

73. Other contributors include Leo Speri, Gustavo Macchi, Oleardo Bianchi, Neo Cirillo, Otto Cima, Mario Colombo, Aldo Barilli, Ferdinando Fontana (Milan: Aliprandi, 1888). Arrighi was a prominent figure of the *Scapigliatura*—a word meaning unkempt or disheveled, something like an Italian equivalent of bohemianism. The name comes from Arrighi's *La scapigliatura e il 6 febbraio*, after the date of an 1853 revolt against the Austrians in Milan.

Arrighi was openly contemptuous of Valera, calling him "Paolino." Arrighi was the director of the Teatro Milanese, and Valera had included an attack on the morality of the theater's leading lady, Emma Ivon (stage name of Emma Allis), who was also a former lover of Vittorio Emanuele II and current consort of Edoardo Ferravilla, another star actor. See Gioia Sebastiani, "Emma Ivon in un'alba editoriale," *Belfagor* 46, no. 5 (1991): 567–75.

74. Arrighi, *Ventre*, 7.

75. Matilde Serao's *Il ventre di Napoli*, often translated as *The Bowels* (rather than *The Belly*) *of Naples*, appeared in 1884—months after the visit to Naples by the Italian prime minister, Agostino Depretis, who declared, "Naples must be disemboweled" ("bisogna sventrare Napoli").

76. Arrighi, *Ventre*, 7.

77. Arrighi, *Ventre*, 7.

78. Arrighi, "La fiera di Senigallia," in *Ventre*, 58. Senigallia is often spelled Sinigallia or Sinigaglia. I have regularized the varied spellings in this chapter, using "Senigallia" throughout, even though Arrighi uses "Sinigallia"; Lattuada and Gadda use "Sinigallia."

79. Arrighi, *Ventre*, 58–59.
80. Arrighi, *Ventre*, 53, 56, 57.
81. F. T. Marinetti, "The Manifesto of Futurism," in *Futurism: An Anthology*, ed. Lawrence Rainey, Christine Poggi, and Laura Whitman (New Haven: Yale University Press, 2009), 52.
82. Marinetti, "Manifesto," 52.
83. On the futurist rejection of D'Annunzio, see "We Abjure Our Symbolist Masters," where Marinetti writes: "One must at all costs combat Gabriele D'Annunzio, because with all his great skill he has distilled the four intellectual poisons that we want to abolish forever," which include "the profound passion for the past and the mania for antiquity and collecting," in Rainey et al., *Futurism*, 94.
84. Marinetti, "We Abjure," 93.
85. See Margaret Iverson, "Encounter: Breton Meets Lacan," in *Beyond Pleasure, Freud, Lacan, Barthes* (Philadelphia: University of Pennsylvania Press, 2007), 62, on the flea market as a site for the meeting of a sewing machine and an umbrella, as in Conte de Lautréamont's formulation in *Les Chants de Maldoror*.
86. Flea market purchases—curious objects, primitive sculptures, and books—figured prominently in Breton's collection, which was housed at the 42 rue Fontaine apartment where he lived from 1922 until his death in 1966. Composed of more than 15,000 items, the collection was auctioned off amid controversy after the death of Breton's third wife, Elisa, in 2000. On the significance of Breton's collection, see Christina Helena Rudosky, *Breton the Collector: A Surrealist Poetics of the Object* (PhD diss., University of Colorado, 2015). In a work included in the 2013 Venice Biennale, the video-artist Ed Atkins describes the dispersed objects using an aquatic metaphor like those of De Amicis's account of the flea market: "These objects. Bobbing on the glassy surface of a becalmed sea at night. All that's left of the shipwreck." The transcript of the video is included in Massimiliano Gioni and Natalie Bell, *The Keeper* (New York: New Museum, 2016), 61.
87. André Breton, *Nadja* (New York: Grove Press, 1960), 52.
88. Breton, *Nadja*, 52.
89. See Rosalind Krauss, "The photographic conditions of surrealism," *October* 19 (1981): 3–34, 23.
90. Krauss, "Photographic Conditions," 23.
91. Krauss, "Photographic Conditions," 23.
92. Sontag, *On Photography* (New York: Picador, 1977), 69. In *City*, Walker studies documentary surrealist photography—long overlooked, he argues, despite the critical interest in movement's collage and manipulated photographic images after Krauss and Jane Livingston's 1985 Corcoran Gallery of Art exhibition, *Amour Fou: Photography and Surrealism*. See R. Krauss, Jane Livingston, and Dawn Ades. *L'Amour Fou: Photography & Surrealism. With an Essay by Dawn Ades* (New York: Abbeville Press, 1985).

93. Breton, *Nadja*, 52.
94. Breton, *Nadja*, 55.
95. See Cohen's discussion of this episode in *Profane Illumination*,113–19.
96. Walker, *City*, 55–63 and 123. Walker studies the documentary-style surrealist photographs that, he argues, have been neglected in the spate of studies inspired by Krauss.
97. Breton, *Mad Love* (Lincoln: University of Nebraska Press, 1988), 28.
98. Breton, *Mad Love*, 28.
99. Breton, *Mad Love*, 32.
100. Goux, *Symbolic Economies*, 201.
101. Atget's work began to circulate among a wider, international community of artists and critics only after Berenice Abbott's publication of the first collection of his work in 1930. In his review essay of *Atget: Photographe de Paris* in 1930, Benjamin writes that the photographer seeks out all that is "unremarked, forgotten, cast adrift" and finds in his work the beginnings of the emancipation of the object from the aura, defined, in that essay, as a weave of space and time. The "uniqueness and duration" intertwined in the object, Benjamin writes, is alienated by the "transience and reproducibility" of photographic images. See "A Little History of Photography," in *Walter Benjamin: Selected Writings, Volume 2, Part 2: 1931–1934*, ed. Eiland, Jennings, and Gary Smith, trans. Rodney Livingstone et al. (Cambridge: Belknap Press of Harvard University Press, 2005), 507–30, 519.
102. The indifference of the vendor resembles that Arrighi notes in *Il ventre di Milano*, as well as that of the antique dealers Rainer Maria Rilke describes in *The Notebooks of Malte Laurids Brigge* (New York: Penguin, 2009): "The shops of antique dealers, or small antiquarian booksellers, or dealers in engravings, the windows overcrowded. Not a soul ever enters these shops. Plainly they do no business. But if you look in, there they sit, reading, without a care; they take no thought for tomorrow, they are unconcerned about success" ([17], 28).
103. Longanesi founded *L'italiano. Rivista settimanale della gente fascista* (*Weekly Magazine of the Fascist People*) in 1926, the same year he authored the *Vademecum del perfetto fascista* (*Vademecum of the perfect fascist*), which included such aphorisms as "Mussolini ha sempre ragione" ("Mussolini is always right"). Despite his initial enthusiasm for fascism, and Longanesi's editorial projects were increasingly marked by irony, disdain, and even opposition to the regime. In 1930 Longanesi changed the subtitle of *L'italiano* to *Periodico della rivoluzione fascista* (*Periodical of the Fascist Revolution*).
104. The photograph appeared in *L'italiano. Periodico della rivoluzione fascista* 7, no. 14 (September 1932): 195.
105. On the disquieting effect of dolls, mannequins, and other lifeless objects that arouse doubts about whether they are indeed inanimate, see Freud's "The Uncanny," in *SE* 17 (1955), 217–56. Dario Lanzardo's *Dame e cavalieri nel Balo n di Torino: sguardo fotografico sul mercato dell'usato* (Milan: Mondadori, 1984).

106. See Ennery Taramelli, *Viaggio nell'Italia del neorealismo* (Turin: Società editrice internazionale, 1995), 96.

107. Cesare Barzacchi, *L'Italia di Longanesi*. *Memorie fotografiche di Cesare Barzacchi* (Rome: Edizioni del Borghese, 1964), 36.

108. Taramelli, *Viaggio*, 97.

109. On the antifascism of *Occhio quadrato*, see David Forgacs, *Italy's Margins: Social Exclusion and Nation Formation since 1861* (Cambridge: Cambridge University Press, 2014), 53–56; Martina Caruso, *Italian Humanist Photography from Fascism to the Cold War* (London: Bloomsbury Academic, 2016), 66–69; and Antonella Russo, *Storia culturale della fotografia italiana. Dal neorealismo al postmoderno* (Turin: Einaudi, 2011).

See Gioia Sebastiani, *I libri di Corrente* (Bologna: Edizioni Pendragon, 1998) on the history of the small publishing house, an offshoot of the Milanese review of art and literature *Corrente di Vita giovanile*, founded by Ernesto Treccani in 1938 and closed by fascist police in 1940. The review and the publishing house became important venues for a generation of young and largely antifascist artists—Treccani, Lucio Fontana, Renato Guttuso, and Carlo Carrà; and writers—Luciano Anceschi, Salvatore Quasimodo, Vittorio Sereni. I libri di Corrente also published a special volume of writings about the city titled *La luna nel corso*. Edited by Anceschi in 1941, the volume contained writings by Giuseppe Ungaretti, Riccardo Bacchelli, Ugo Foscolo, Gianfranco Contini, Sereni, Emilio De Marchi, Carlo Cattaneo, Alfonso Gatto, and Gadda.

110. Taramelli, *Viaggio*, 76. Taramelli explains that *American Photographs*, published in connection with the MoMA exhibit, circulated clandestinely in Italy soon after and that its influence was quickly evident in publications like *Corrente* as well as the architecture and design magazine *Domus*.

111. Piero Berengo Gardin, *Alberto Lattuada: fotografo: dicci anni di occhio quadrato 1938–1948* (Florence: Alinari, 1982), 5.

112. The roots of neorealist cinema in documentary photography including Lattuada's *Occhio quadrato* are emphasized by the title of Berengo Gardin's introduction: "Alberto Lattuada. Interno. Giorno." Germano Celant writes: "Lattuada can be said to have anticipated the style of neorealism, which came to dominate the style of Italian photography for at least a decade." See *The Italian Metamorphosis, 1943–1968* (New York: Guggenheim Museum, 1994), 317.

113. Caruso, *Italian Humanist Photography*, 68.

114. Gardin, *Alberto Lattuada*, 15.

115. *Panorama* was founded soon after Longanesi's *Omnibus*. *Settimanale di attualità politica e letteraria* (*Omnibus. Political and Literary News Weekly*) was shut down by the Minculpop and was similar in its scope. The first issue of *Panorama* was published on April 27, 1939; it too was shut down by the Minculpop after an article by Indro Montanelli in the September 12, 1940 issue was declared "disfattista" (against the war efforts). Other prominent contributors include

Alfonso Gatti, Leonardo Sinisgalli, Elsa Morante, Carlo Linati, and Giovanni Comisso.

Gadda published two more essays in *Panorama*, both accompanied by photographs. "Terra lombarda" on April 12, 1940 and "L'uomo e la macchina" on April 27, 1940. The photographs accompanying the first two articles were unattributed; those appearing in "L'uomo e la macchina" were credited to Bruno Stefani. Stefani also photographed the Fiera di Senigallia beginning in the mid-1930s. See Stefani and Roberto Campari, *Bruno Stefani* (Parma: Università di Parma, 1976).

116. Pagano edited the architectural magazine *Casabella* with Edoardo Persico from 1933 to 1935. He returned to the magazine as sole editor in 1943, after working briefly for *Domus*. In 1944, he was arrested for his participation in the resistance and deported to Mauthausen, where he died.

117. The antifascism of the publication is particularly evident in the April 12, 1940 issue, which included a photo-essay by Raffaello Giolli, who was deported with Pagano and also died at Mauthausen. The essay, titled "Donne nude in piazza" ("Naked Women in the Square") accompanies photographs by Pagano of urban statues of naked women, photographed from angles that emphasize their bare buttocks and pudenda. The same issue also included an essay by Giulia Veronesi titled "La fotografia contro l'obbiettivo: pittura con la luce" ("Photography against the Objective Lens: Painting with Light"), which discusses works by Atget, Dadaist photographer and collage-artist John Heartfield, surrealists E. L. T. Mesens and Man Ray, Bauhaus photographer and painter László Moholy-Nagy, Bruno Munari, and abstract photogram artist and painter Luigi Veronesi, her brother. See also G., "Il codice dei mendicanti" (The Beggars' Code; April 27, 1940), 22–23.

118. The pictures in Panorama accompanying Gadda's essay are uncredited, but one of them appears in Giuseppe Pagano, fotografo (Milano: Electra, 1979), edited by Cesare de Seta. De Seta also includes several other pictures by Pagano of the Senigallia market, which appear to be taken at the same stalls on the same day.

119. Gadda had long been interested in photography; in the July 18, 1916 entry of his Giornale di guerra e di prigionia he enthuses about the arrival of a package containing a longed-for Vest Pocket Kodak camera. On Gadda's interest in photography, and his collaboration with Panorama, see Giulio Ungarelli, "Le occasioni di Gadda," Edinburgh Journal of Gadda Studies Supplement, no. 5 (2007), and Liliana Orlando's note in Saggi, giornali, favole, e altri scritti (Milan: Garzanti, 1991), 1264.

120. Pagano would go on to publish a photo-essay critical of the bombast of such expositions just one month later in the same magazine, titled "Arte e tecnica alla Fiera di Milano" ("Art and Technology at the Fiera di Milano"). The essay begins: "When the Fiera di Milano began, it steeped Postwar Europe with an air of superficial optimism." See *Panorama* 2, no. 8 (April 27, 1940): 32–33, 32. Gadda had also already published the similarly titled article, "Alla fiera di Milano," about an exposition in Milan in *L'Ambrosiano* (April 24, 1936), 3.

121. See C. De Seta, *Giuseppe Pagano fotografo*, and Daria De Seta, *Giuseppe Pagano: vocabulario de ima genes = images alphabet* (Madrid: Lampreave & Millán. Flavia Marcello, 2008).

122. See De Seta, *Giuseppe Pagano*, 11.

123. Gadda, "Fiera a Milano," 30; my translation.

124. Gadda, "Fiera," 29.

125. Gadda, "Fiera," 29.

126. Gadda, "Fiera," 30. On the slowness of flea markets, see also Warnod's *Les Plaisirs*, which describes the vendors at Saint-Ouen holding vigil over their knickknacks, unconcerned by the passage of time. Warnod interviews a vendor at the Saint-Ouen flea market who appears indifferent to the imminent demolitions of the Thiers Wall that threatened to upend his livelihood: "He shrugged his shoulders slightly and murmured, 'It's not like an old man like me will live to see that time,'" 36.

127. Gadda, "Fiera," 32.

128. Gadda, "Fiera," 29–30.

129. "Carabattole a Porta Ludovica" was published without Pagano's photographs in the volume *Gli anni* in 1943, and then in *Verso la Certosa* in 1961.

130. Gadda, "Fiera," 30.

131. Gadda, "Fiera," 30.

132. Gadda, "Fiera," 30.

3. Epistemologies

1. Walter Benjamin, "A Little History of Photography," 527.

2. Poe, "The Man of the Crowd," in *The Collected Works of Edgar Allan Poe*, 506–18, 511.

3. Benjamin, "Little History," 527. On Benjamin's urban flaneur-detective, see Carlo Salzani, "The City as Crime Scene: Walter Benjamin and the Traces of the Detective," *New German Critique*, no. 100, "Arendt, Adorno, New York, and Los Angeles" (Winter 2007): 165–87.

4. Arthur Conan Doyle, "The Adventure of the Musgrave Ritual," *Strand Magazine: An Illustrated Monthly* 5 (January 1893): 479–89, 484.

5. Frost and Steketee, *Stuff*, 203. Bad storytelling is not unique to hoarding disorder. It is frequently cited in connection with autism, as in Amit Pinchevski's "Bartleby's Autism: Wandering Along Incommunicability," *Cultural Critique* 78, no. 1 (2011): 27–59.

6. Frost and Steketee, *Stuff*, 203. The *Oxford Handbook of Hoarding and Acquiring* includes the chapter "Information Processing," 100–19, by Kiara R. Timpano, Ashley M. Smith, Julia C. Yang, and Demet Çek, which deals with cognitive disorders related to hoarding but does not specifically address the question of the speech and writing of hoarders.

7. Alexander Stille, *The Force of Things: A Marriage in War and Peace* (New York: Macmillan, 2013), 73.

8. Frost and Steketee, *Stuff*, 15. When the book was released, the Children of Hoarders Yahoo! Group listserv, where such extreme doctrines as the criminalization of hoarding are occasionally advocated, was peppered with angry messages maligning Frost and Steketee for what was considered excessive admiration for hoarders.

9. Frost and Steketee, *Stuff*, 202.

10. Ginzburg, "Clues: Roots of an Evidential Paradigm," in *Myths, Emblems, Clues* (New York: Radius, 1990), 98–125, 103.

11. Ginzburg, "Clues," 103. Ginzburg contrasts the paradigm with the Galilean method, which is concerned with mathematical laws and repeatable phenomena.

12. Ginzburg, "Clues," 103.

13. Gerard Genette, *Narrative Discourse: An Essay in Method* (Ithaca: Cornell University Press, 1980), 234. On the psychoanalytic concept of transference as metalepsis, see Giuseppe Civitarese, "Metalepsis, or the Rhetoric of Transference Interpretation," *The Intimate Room: Theory and Technique of the Analytic Field* (New York: Routledge, 2007): 50–71; see also Liviu Lutas, "Narrative Metalepsis in Detective Fiction," *Metalepsis in Popular Culture*, ed. Karin Kukkonen and Sonja Klimek (Berlin: De Gruyter, 2011), 41–64.

14. Tzvetan Todorov, "The Typology of Detective Fiction," in *The Poetics of Prose* (Ithaca: Cornell University Press, 1977), 42–52.

15. Giorgio Agamben, *Stanzas: Word and Phantasm in Western Culture* (Minneapolis: University of Minnesota Press, 1992), 141.

16. Agamben, *Stanzas*, 141.

17. Freud, *SE* 18 (1955), 16.

18. Jacques Lacan, "Function and Field of Speech and Language in Psychoanalysis," in *Écrits. A Selection*, trans. Bruce Fink (New York: W. W. Norton, 2002), 57–106, 100.

19. Lacan, "Function and Field," 100.

20. See "Thing Theory," Bill Browns' introduction to *Things*, which he edited (Chicago: University of Chicago Press, 2004), 1–16.

21. In Roland Barthes, "The Reality Effect," in *The Rustle of Language*, trans. Richard Howard (New York: Hill & Wang, 1975), 141–48.

22. Barthes, "Reality Effect," 142.

23. As quoted in Barthes, "Reality Effect," 141.

24. Brown, *The Material Unconscious: American Amusement, Stephen Crane and the Economies of Play* (Cambridge: Harvard University Press, 1996), 15–16.

25. Brown, *Material Unconscious*, 15–16.

26. Naomi Schor, *Reading in Detail: Aesthetics and the Feminine* (New York: Routledge, 2007), 101. See 100–104 for her discussion of "The Reality Effect."

27. In "The Realist Floor-Plan," in *On Signs*, ed. by Marshall Blonsky (Baltimore: Johns Hopkins University Press, 1985), Fredric Jameson makes a metronome of the barometer: "I find that my own reading is perturbed by a very peculiar slippage from barometer to metronome" (379).

28. Barthes, "The Reality Effect," 141. With *S/Z* (New York: Hill and Wang, 1975), he takes up the challenge with still greater zeal.

29. Frost and Steketee, *Stuff*, 61; and Fred Penzel, "Hoarding in History," *Oxford Handbook of Hoarding and Acquiring*, 11.

30. Doyle, "Musgrave Ritual," 479.

31. Doyle, "Musgrave Ritual," 479.

32. Doyle, "Musgrave Ritual," 479–80.

33. Doyle, "Musgrave Ritual," 481.

34. Doyle, "Musgrave Ritual," 484.

35. Doyle, "Musgrave Ritual," 484, 481.

36. Peter Brooks, *Reading for the Plot* (Cambridge: Harvard University Press, 1984), 24.

37. Doyle, "Musgrave Ritual," 489.

38. Doyle, "Musgrave Ritual," 479.

39. Doyle, *A Study in Scarlet*, ed. Owen Dudley Edwards (Oxford: Oxford University Press, 1993), 15.

40. Doyle, *Study in Scarlet*, 15.

41. Doyle, "The Five Orange Pips," *Strand Magazine: An Illustrated Monthly* 2 (July 1891): 481–91, 488.

42. In *The Novel and the Police* (Berkeley: University of California Press, 1988), D. A. Miller argues that the Victorian realist novel internalizes this system; in the absence of *actual* police, he sees a more rooted, diffuse presence of law enforcement. Even in the detective novel—whether it features professional or amateur sleuths, the ritual purging of guilt restores society to a *normal* state of a world in which police are not necessary: "Along with the criminal, criminology itself is deported elsewhere" (3). What emerges in their place is the detective, whose genius obscures the more futile labor of positivist criminologists and their close cousins, hoarders.

43. Allan Sekula, "The Body and the Archive," *October* 39 (1986): 3–64, 29. On the role of statistics and in positivist government and criminology, see Ian Hacking, *The Taming of Chance* (Cambridge: Cambridge University Press, 1990). On the place of statistics in nation formation in Italy, see Silvana Patriarca, *Numbers and Nationhood. Writing Statistics in Nineteenth-Century Italy* (Cambridge: Cambridge University Press, 2009).

44. Sekula, "The Body and the Archive," 29. On Mantegazza's photographic archive, see Rhiannon Welch, *Vital Subjects: Race and Biopolitics in Italy, 1860–1920* (Liverpool: Liverpool University Press, 2016), 89–92.

45. On Lombroso's collecting, see Gina Ferrero-Lombroso, *Cesare Lombroso: Storia della vita e delle opere narrata dalla figlia* (Turin: Bocca, 1915), 355.

46. The tally of Lombroso's work is from Marco Villa, *Il deviante e i suoi segni: Lombroso e la nascita dell'antropologia criminale* (Milan: Franco Angeli, 1985), 283; cited in Mary Gibson and Nicole Hahn Rafter's introduction to Cesare Lombroso, *Criminal Man*, trans. Gibson and Rafter (Durham, NC: Duke University Press, 2007), 3. See Elena Past, "Cesare Lombroso Vivisects the Criminal," *Methods of Murder: Beccarian Introspection and Lombrosian Vivisection in Italian Crime Fiction* (Toronto: University of Toronto Press, 2012), 135–70, on the contradictions inherent in Lombroso's focus on the criminal in place of the crime, and his oscillations between individuating and generalizing paradigms. See also Suzanne Stewart-Steinberg's discussion of Lombroso's "style" in "In a Dark Continent: Lombroso's 'Other' Italy," in *The Pinocchio Effect. On Making Italians, 1860–1920* (Chicago: University of Chicago Press, 2007), 229–88.

47. Like Herman Melville's "Bartleby, the Scrivener," Jorge Luis Borges's "Funes the Memorious" has been interpreted as a portrait of disability, with Funes described as an "idiot savant" or "autistic savant." See, for example, Patricia Novillo-Corvalán, "Literature and Disability: The Medical Interface in Borges and Beckett," *Medical Humanities* 37, no. 1 (2011): 38–43.

48. Jorge Luis Borges, "Funes the Memorious," in *Labyrinths: Selected Stories and Other Writings* trans. James E. Irby (New York: New Directions, 1964), 59.

49. Borges, "Funes," 63, 65, 64.

50. Adriana Cavarero, *For More Than One Voice: Toward a Philosophy of Vocal Expression* (Stanford: Stanford University Press, 2005), 48.

51. A study by Tamara L. Hartl and colleagues of twenty-two individuals with severe hoarding symptoms and twenty-four matched control subjects found that the compulsive hoarders recalled less information and used less effective organizational strategies than the control subjects. The individuals displaying hoarding symptoms also reported "significantly less confidence in their memory, more catastrophic assessments of the consequences of forgetting, and a stronger desire to keep possessions in sight." See Hartl et al., "Actual and Perceived Memory Deficits in Individuals with Compulsive Hoarding," *Depression and Anxiety* 20, no. 2 (2004): 59–69.

52. Carlo Emilio Gadda, *That Awful Mess on the Via Merulana*, trans. William Weaver (New York: New York Review of Books Classics, 2000), 66, 69.

53. Gadda, *That Awful Mess*, 182.

54. Gadda, *"Per favore, mi lasci nell'ombra": Interviste 1950–1972*, ed. Claudio Vela (Milan: Adelphi, 1993), 172.

55. Gadda, *That Awful Mess*, 5. On the "tragic incompleteness," see Robert Rushing, "La sua tragica incompiutezza": Anxiety, Mis-Recognition and Ending in Gadda's *Pasticciaccio*," *MLN* 116, no. 1 (2001): 130–49.

56. Gadda, *Meditazione milanese*, in *Scritti vari e postumi* (SVP), ed. Andrea Silvestri, Claudio Vela, Isella, Paola Italia, and Pinotti (Milan: Garzanti, 2009), 614–894, 650; translation mine. *Meditazione milanese* was composed in Milan between February 1928 and May of the following year.

57. Gadda, "L'egoista," in *Saggi, giornali, favole e altri scritti I* (*SGF I*), ed. Liliana Orlando, Clelia Martignoni, and Isella (Milan: Garzanti, 2008), 654–67, 654; translation mine. On the ways in which Gadda's oeuvre itself—a dense knot of recurring character types, topoi, and even passages repeated verbatim—resembles the *grovigli* everywhere within it, see Gian Carlo Roscioni, *La disarmonia prestabilita: Studio su Gadda* (Turin: G. Einaudi, 1969), 43.

58. Rushing, *Resisting Arrest: Detective Fiction and Popular Culture* (New York: Other Press, 2007), 137.

59. Roscioni, *La disarmonia*, 43.

60. Gadda, *That Awful Mess*, 323. On the ways in which this passage engages theories of posthumanism, see Deborah Amberson and Elena Past, "Gadda's *Pasticciaccio* and the Knotted Posthuman Household," *Beyond Anthropocentrism* 4 (2016), https://doi.org/10.7358/rela-2016-001-ambe.

61. Gadda, *That Awful Mess*, 322.

62. Gadda, *That Awful Mess* 322, 323.

63. Italo Calvino, *Six Memos for the New Millennium*, trans. Geoffrey Brock (New York: Haughton Mifflin, 1988), 144.

64. Guglielmi refers to the ongoing seismic impact of Ferdinand de Saussure's posthumous *Course in General Linguistics* (1916). Angelo Guglielmi, "Avanguardia e sperimentalismo," in *Gruppo '63. Critica e teoria*, ed. Renato Barilli and Guglielmi (Turin: Controsegni, 2003), 331–38, 331.

65. Luigi Malerba, *La scoperta dell'alfabeto. Le parole abbandonate* (Milan: Mondadori, 2017), 5.

66. Malerba, *La scoperta*, 5.

67. Marilyn Schneider, "To Know Is to Eat: A Reading of *Il serpente*," *Yale Italian Studies*, 2 (1978): 71–84, 72.

68. Malerba, *Diario di un sognatore* (Turin: Einaudi, 1981), 3; translation mine.

69. JoAnn Cannon, "Intervista con Luigi Malerba," *MLN* 104, no. 1 (1989): 226–37, 235; translation mine.

70. See Guido Almansi, "Malerba and the Art of Story-Telling," *Quaderni d'italianistica*, 1, no. 2 (1980): 157–70, 163.

71. Brian Richardson, *Unnatural Voices: Extreme Narration in Modern and Contemporary Fiction* (Columbus: Ohio State University Press, 2006), 91.

72. Malerba, *The Serpent*, trans. William Weaver (New York: Farrar, Straus and Giroux, 1968), 15.

73. Malerba, *Serpent*, 15.

74. Richardson, *Unnatural Voices*, 93.

75. Malerba, *Serpent*, 121.

76. Malerba, *Serpent*, 151.

77. Malerba, *Serpent*, 186.

78. Malerba, *Serpent*, 12.

79. Stamp collecting became a speculator's market in the late 1800s, and was frequently described by waffling between psychological and economic paradigms, making philately now obsession, now inopportune investment. William Roberts explains that whereas the value of a book depends on several principles, the value of a stamp is assessed solely on the basis of rarity. He puts the number of people who earn a living through this "eccentric calling" "well into the five figures." Like the flea market flaneur, the stamp collector is haunted by the logic of belatedness. Although Roberts names several lucky speculators and amateurs who made fortunes, he imagines the heyday of stamp collecting to have passed. Whereas once stamps may have seemed like a good investment, the hobby has become so popular that little opportunity for profit remains. He concludes: "Stamps are either very rare or very common—very expensive or very cheap. The dozen or so rarities to which allusion has already been made will soon be absorbed by public institutions, the proper sepulchers of so many useless antiquities! In the future, therefore, mediocrity must become the bane of stamp collections, and who will care to ride a hobby in which the best can only be fifth-rate?" Roberts, "The Stamp-Collecting Craze," *Fortnightly Review* 55, no. 329 (May 1894): 662–68.

80. Malerba, *Serpent*, 43.

81. Malerba, *Serpent*, 43.

82. The genre of detective fiction is referred to as "*giallo*" (yellow) in Italy because of a Mondadori imprint launched in 1929 featuring bright yellow covers. On the history of the imprint and its censure under Fascism, see Past, *Methods of Murder*, 3, and Jane Dunnett "Crime and the Critics: On the Appraisal of Detective Novels in 1930s Italy," *Modern Language Review* 106, no. 3 (July 2011): 745–64, 749.

83. "Autarky" refers to the period of relative isolation and economic autonomy of fascist Italy following the 1935 invasion of Ethiopia and the sanctions imposed by the League of Nations in response to the attack on the member nation. Economic autonomy from Western Europe and colonial expansion were pivotal to the fascist strategy before the invasion of Ethiopia.

84. Malerba, *Serpent*, 5. The perceived danger of traditional gelato made with real eggs was the subject of a series of newspaper articles in the 1950s. Motta ice cream capitalized on this fear with an advertising campaign launched in 1959 that emphasized the hygienic modernity of their products. The imposing Motta sign in Piazza Barberini is mentioned in the novel. See Maria Chiara Liguori, "Have You Had Your Daily Drug? The Italian Motta Ice-Cream Campaign in 1959," in *Advertising & Society Review* 15, no. 5 (2015), https://doi.org/10.1353/asr.2015.0002.

85. In "Self and the City: A Psychoanalytical Reading of Luigi Malerba's *Il serpente*," in *Italica* 83, no. 3/4 (2006): 609–28, Ruth Glynn finds the interpretive stakes of the novel in the first chapter. Glynn proposes that one episode, the narrator's encounter with Alfonso, represents a screen memory. Referencing Michel de Certeau's "Walking in the City," Glynn understands Parma as a maternal space, and, relying on a Lacanian developmental model, she diagnoses the narrator's disorder as resulting from difficulties surrounding entry into the symbolic.

86. The chapter uses a sort of shorthand to evoke the period of autarky; the soldiers in the street singing "that song that everyone knows" and "the voice on the radio." Without naming the song or identifying the voice, the text conjures a distinct time and place that would be unmistakable to a contemporary Italian reader. This is because just one year before the publication of *Il serpente*, Angelo Del Boca's *La guerra d'Abissinia* (Milan: Feltrinelli, 1965), caused an uproar among veterans' associations and raised public awareness about the atrocities committed during the invasion of Ethiopia.

87. The draft is at the Fondo Manoscritti in Pavia; translation mine.

88. Malerba, *Serpent*, 3. Cork was among the materials that remained readily available during the period of economic autarky. When metals used to make traditional high-heeled shoes became unavailable, Salvatore Ferragamo invented the cork- and wood-based platform shoe. See Natalia Aspesi, *Il lusso & l'autarchia: storia dell'eleganza italiana, 1930–1944* (Milan: Rizzoli, 1982).

89. Jean-Baptiste Pontalis and Jean Laplanche, "Fantasy and the Origins of Sexuality," *International Journal of Psycho-Analysis* 49 (1968): 1–18.

90. Malerba, *Serpent*, 6.

91. Malerba, *Serpent*, 78, 163.

92. Malerba, *Serpent*, 169, 165, 166.

93. "The Beginning in the End" aired on May 20, 2010; "House of Hoarders" aired on October 21 of the same year.

94. Ginzburg, "Clues," 124.

95. There is no medical definition of "level five disposophobic." The term is perhaps intended to evoke the clutter image rating (composed of nine photographs) as well as cancer staging systems.

96. Frost and Steketee use "clutter blindness" to describe the obliviousness of many hoarders to the impediments, including squalor and stench, of their dwellings. Frost and Steketee offer no example of a "clutter blindness" so extreme that, as in the *CSI: Las Vegas* episode, a corpse goes unnoticed. A Norman Bates worthy ghoulishness does pop up in a March 8, 2011 story in the *St. Louis Post Dispatch*. The paper reported that mummified remains were found in the home of Gladys Jean Bergmeier, who had passed away on February 7 at age seventy-five. Three weeks later, a relative cleaning out the home of the deceased stumbled upon remains that are believed to be those of Bergmeier's "long-unseen" mother, Gladys Stansbury. See https://www.stltoday.com/news/local/metro/mummified-remains-found-in-jennings-home-after-owner-s-death/article_22a7e62f-f70b-5f3d-b069-cbc01d3e0b64.html.

97. Frost and Steketee, *Stuff*, 30.

98. On Andy Warhol's *Time Capsules* and his collecting, see Herring, *The Hoarders*, 51–84, and Jonathan Flatley, *Like Andy Warhol* (Chicago: University of Chicago Press, 2017), 53–88.

4. Ecologies

1. Mitchell Dean's "The Malthus Effect: Population and the Liberal Government of Life" is an excellent study of the imbrication of discourses of scarcity and "overpopulation." *Economy and Society* 44, no. 1 (2015): 18–39.

2. Rachel Carson's 1962 *Silent Spring,* which exposed the dangers of chemical pesticides, was decisive in this shift, as were two subsequent disasters: the dioxin leak at a chemical plant in the northern Italian town of Seveso in 1976, and then the Chernobyl nuclear disaster of 1986.

3. See Max Liboiron, "Modern Waste as an Economic Strategy," *Lo Squaderno: Explorations in Space and Society,* no. 29, "Garbage and Wastes" (2013): 9–12.

4. Christiana Bratiotis, Cristina Sorrentino Schmalisch, and Gail Steketee, *The Hoarding Handbook: A Guide for Human Service Professionals* (Oxford: Oxford University Press, 2011), 181.

5. Roberto Esposito, *Persons and Things: From the Body's Point of View* (Cambridge: Polity Press, 2015), 22.

6. Waste is the subject of several excellent scholarly monographs in the last decade. See William Viney's *Waste: A Philosophy of Things* (London: Bloomsbury Academic, 2014); Susan Signe Morrison's *The Literature of Waste: Material Ecopoetics and Ethical Matter* (New York: Palgrave, 2015), Rachele Dini's *Consumerism, Waste, and Re-Use in Twentieth-Century Fiction* (New York: Palgrave, 2016). These studies build on the classical interventions of Mary Douglas, *Purity and Danger: An Analysis of Concept of Pollution and Taboo* (New York: Routledge, 1966), Thompson, *Rubbish Theory,* and Julia Kristeva, *Powers of Horror: An Essay of Abjection* (New York: Columbia University Press, 1984). Other key works of cultural anthropology include Susan Strasser's *Waste and Want: A Social History of Trash* (New York: Palgrave, 2000) and Samantha McBride's *Recycling Reconsidered: The Promise and Failure of Environmental Action in the United States* (Cambridge: MIT Press, 2011). See David Boarder Giles, "The Anatomy of a Dumpster. Abject Capital and the Looking Glass of Value," *Social Text* 32, no. 1 (2014): 93–113, for an ethnographic account of the community of dumpster divers in Seattle. Through this ethnographic research, Giles theorizes "abject value"; that is, the value produced by waste. Joshua Ozias Reno's "Toward a New Theory of Waste: From 'Matter out of Place' to Signs of Life" attempts to bring waste studies into line with new materialism, departing from the "social constructivism" of Douglas, Kristeva, and Thompson, by presenting a theory of waste that is rooted in posthuman relationality; *Theory, Culture & Society* 31, no. 6 (2014): 3–27. My own position is much closer to the social constructivist theories. Indeed, the basic premise that hoarding is produced by clashing perspectives means that it is inherently socially constructed and relational.

7. See Freud, "On the Antithetical Meaning of Primal Words," in *SE* 11 (1957), 155–61. In *The Future of Nostalgia,* Boym notes the similarly paired antitheses

of the primal words tradition and revolution: "The modern opposition between tradition and revolution is treacherous. Tradition means both delivery—handing down or passing on a doctrine—and surrender, or betrayal. Traduttore, traditore, translator, traitor. The word revolution, similarly, means both cyclical repetition and the radical break" (19).

8. The first use of "ecology" (or oecology) listed in the *Oxford English Dictionary* is in 1875.

9. Randy Frost and Rachel Gross find no evidence to suggest that hoarding is related to material deprivation, though they did find a correlation between hoarding and anxieties about the possibility of future deprivation. The authors write: "The hypothesis that hoarders are overly concerned with being without possessions when they are needed was supported by these data. For the three questions regarding 'just-in-case' items, hoarders were significantly different from non-hoarders." They also found no support for the hypothesis that hoarding is related to material deprivation early in life: "There were no differences in the responses to the question 'When you were young, was there a period of time when you had very little money?'" Hoarding seems to have less to do with material deprivation than with increased anxiety about economic contingencies. Frost and Gross, "The Hoarding of Possessions," *Behaviour Research and Therapy* 33, no. 4 (1993), 367–81, 377.

In "The Immorality of Waste: Depression-Era Perspectives in the Digital Age," Samantha MacBride describes the attitudes she encountered among participants at a 2007 e-cycling event in Manhattan. She found that the people who had gone through the considerable trouble of bringing their old computers, printers, and other electronics to Union Square to be recycled were dismayed to learn that rather than being redistributed to those in need, the devices would be crushed and sorted into component parts. She interprets their disappointment as a holdover from the Depression-era liberal ideology of rugged individualism. The danger of their thinking is that it masks structural inequalities that make self-sufficiency impracticable: "Self-sufficiency is not possible once land is enclosed and owned by a few; goods can only be bought with wages; and commodities are priced to absorb most of a working-household's income." *SubStance* 37, no. 2 (2008): 71–77, 73.

10. Nikolai Gogol calls Pliushkin "human detritus." The formula "matter out of place" seems to have been first used by Lord Palmerston in a toast delivered at the annual banquet of the Royal Agricultural Society in 1852. Palmerston celebrates a boundlessness that makes waste impossible: "Well, it is a law of nature that nothing is destroyed. Matter is decomposed, but only for the purpose of again assuming some new form, useful for the purposes of the human race." Gogol, *Dead Souls*, trans. Donald Rayfield (New York: New York Review of Books Classics, 2008).

See also Richard Fardon, "Citations Out of Place, or, Lord Palmerston Goes Viral in the Nineteenth Century but Gets Lost in the Twentieth," *Anthropology Today* 29, no. 1 (2013): 25–27. Freud also includes the formulation in English in

"Character and Anal Erotism," though he does not name the source. *The Standard Edition,* 9:169–75.

11. Pliushkin is among the hoarders frequently named in the twenty-first-century social science writing, including Fred Penzel's "Hoarding in History," in *The Oxford Handbook of Hoarding and Acquiring,* ed. Frost and Gail Steketee (Oxford: Oxford University Press, 2014), 6–16, 10, and Frost and Steketee's, *Stuff. Compulsive Hoarding and the Meaning of Things* (New York: Houghton Mifflin Harcourt, 2010), 61–62.

12. Penzel, "Hoarding in History," 10. Other synonyms in popular usage include Diogenes syndrome, syllogomania, and disposophobia. "Compulsive hoarding" was in popular use before hoarding disorder was included in the *DSM-V.*

13. Gogol, *Dead Souls,* 125, 122.

14. On Langley Collyer's scavenging, see Helen Worden Erskine, *Out of This World* (New York: Putnam, 1953), 7.

15. Gogol, *Dead Souls,* 125.

16. Francesco Orlando, *Obsolete Objects in the Literary Imagination* (New Haven: Yale University Press, 2006), 31.

17. This foreclosure of future use is decisive because of Pliushkin's severed bonds with his heirs. As such, Pliushkin's "material deviance," to use Herring's term, takes the form of a repudiation of reproductive heteronormativity that Lee Edelman theorizes in *No Future: Queer Theory and the Death Drive* (Durham, NC: Duke University Press, 2004).

18. Gogol, *Dead Souls,* 127–28.

19. Boym, *Future,* 13.

20. Gogol, *Dead Souls,* 137–38.

21. On the relationship between economic dematerialization of value and modernism, see Jean-Joseph Goux, *Symbolic Economies: After Marx and Freud* (Ithaca: Cornell University Press, 1990), and "Banking on Signs," *Diacritics* 18, no. 2 (Summer, 1988): 15–25; as well as Walter Benn Michaels, *The Gold Standard and the Logic of Naturalism* (Berkeley: University of California Press, 1987).

22. Gogol, *Dead Souls,* 118.

23. Gogol, *Dead Souls,* 142–43.

24. This mention of Gogol appears in a footnote to the first version of *Quer pasticciaccio brutto de' via Merulana,* which was serialized in nonconsecutive issues of *Letteratura* in 1946–47. The note rages against the fascist demographic campaign, which included a tax on unwed men. The note was removed from the final version of the novel, published by Garzanti in 1957; see *Romanzi e racconti* (Milan: Garzanti, 1988), 307.

25. Gadda owned both the 1932 and the 1941 editions of Margherita Silvestri Lapenna's two-volume translation of *Le avventure di Cicikov ovvero Le anime morte (Dead Souls),* as well as *The Squabble, Taras Bulba,* and *Petersburg Tales.*

Gadda's library is inventoried in Andrea Cortellessa and Giorgio Patrizi, eds., *La Biblioteca di Don Gonzalo*, vol. 1 (Rome: Bulzoni, 2001); Gogol's texts are listed on 140.

26. Gadda, *Romanzi e racconti I*, 839; "L'Adalgisa" was first published in *"Tesoretto" Almanacco dello Specchio 1941* (Milan: Mondadori, 1940), 449–78; the letter is cited in the Adelphi edition of 2012; my translation.

27. So much for the wisdom Benjamin attributes to Anatole France that the only exact knowledge is publication date and format of books. See "Unpacking my Library: A Talk about Book Collecting," in *Illuminations: Essays and Reflections*, ed. Hannah Arendt (New York: Schocken Books, 1969), 60.

28. On waste as "matter out of time," see Viney, *Waste*, 2.

29. Gadda, *L'Adalgisa. Disegni milanesi*, ed. Claudio Vela (Milan: Adelphi, 2017), 367; all translations from *L'Adalgisa* are mine.

30. Gadda, *L'Adalgisa*, 367.

31. Adalgisa is the name of the character; the definite article is often used in Northern Italy before women's names.

32. Gadda, *L'Adalgisa*, 367.

33. Gian Carlo Roscioni, *Il Duca di Sant'Aquila* (Milan: Mondadori, 1997), 35; my translation; the italicized words were in French in the original.

34. Gadda, *L'Adalgisa*, 271, 281.

35. Gadda, *L'Adalgisa*, 278. An Atheucus is a type of scarab beetle, so named because by adding the privative "a" from Latin to the Greek τεύχω, or "to make" so as to form "not made," in accordance with the ancient Egyptian belief that scarab beetles were autogenetic.

36. Gadda, *L'Adalgisa*, 278.

37. Gadda, *L'Adalgisa*, 278–79.

38. For an excellent analysis of the narrator's coming out as a fictional character, see Cristina Savettieri, "Self-Reflection and Ambivalence in Carlo Emilio Gadda's *L'Adalgisa*," *Italianist* 35, no. 3 (October 2015): 412–25.

39. The narrator derides the locution, explaining that by "portraits," Carlo meant "photographs," and that "landscapes of Libya" is pleonastic. Gadda, *L'Adalgisa*, 313, 279.

40. Gadda, *L'Adalgisa*, 280.

41. Even the glorious scarab becomes an example of extraneousness. After Gadda described the beetle in the 1940 story, his friend, the more successful writer Roberto Bacchelli (whose posthumous fortune, however, cannot compete with that of Gadda) described a Scarabaeus sacer in his novel *Il fiore della mirabilis*, glossing the beetle as a marvel of nature—in much the same way as Carlo. Gadda defends his own use of the beetle in a footnote in the 1943 publication, explaining that his scarab appeared before that of Bacchelli, and is put to a different use. Bacchelli was also an admirer of Gogol; his 1936 *Rabdomante* was inspired by *Dead Souls*.

42. Gadda, *L'Adalgisa*, 314, 319, 318.

43. Gadda, *L'Adalgisa*, 318.

44. Gadda, *L'Adalgisa*, 318.

45. Hampton's documentary film, *Possessed*, was discussed in chapter 1.

46. On the narrative formulas of *Hoarders* and *Hoarding: Buried Alive*, see Susan Lepselter, "The Disorder of Things. Hoarding Narratives in Popular Media," *Anthropological Quarterly* 84, no. 4 (2011): 919–47. After the success of *Hoarders*, other networks developed similar shows: TLC ran the popular *Hoarding: Buried Alive* (2010–14), and Animal Planet aired *Confessions: Animal Hoarding* (2010–12). Other reality series from the same period are rooted in the unpredictable vicissitudes of value: History's *American Pickers* (2010–) and *Pawn Stars* (2009–); A&E's *Storage Wars* (2010–); TLC's *Extreme Couponing* (2010–12); the National Geographic Channel's *Doomsday Preppers* (2012–14), and the Style Network's *Clean House* (2003–11).

47. Herring, Lepselter, Moran, and Bennett all discuss the segment featuring Jill.

48. Milwaukee was one of the cities hit particularly hard by the financial crisis. Matthew Desmond writes that in Milwaukee, a city of fewer than 105,000 renter households, sixteen families are evicted through the court system every day. The actual number of evictions is considerably higher since many landlords remove tenants using cheaper, quicker ways like offering small payouts rather than going through the court system. *Evicted: Poverty and Profit in the American City* (New York: Crown, 2016).

49. Lepselter, "Hoarding Narratives," 941.

50. The intrinsic properties of the pumpkin that mark its transformation into an aesthetic object in the episode update are the same ones that, for Susan Stewart, cross the threshold that distinguishes human forms of collecting. According to Susan Stewart: "The objects collected by the wood rat are intrinsic objects; objects complete in themselves because of the sensory qualities that have made them attractive to the rat." *On Longing* (Durham, NC Duke University Press, 1993), 153. On the association between hoarding and nonhuman animal behavior in contemporary representations, see Patrick W. Moran, "The Collyer Brothers and the Fictional Lives of Hoarders," *MFS Modern Fiction Studies* 62, no. 2 (2016), 272–91, 284–87.

51. See Bratiotis et al., *Hoarding Handbook*, 4.

52. Lars Eighner, "On Dumpster Diving," *Threepenny Review* 47 (1991): 6–8.

53. Giorgio Agamben, *Profanations* (New York: Zone Books, 2007), 30.

54. Agamben, *Profanations*, 30.

55. The installation was displayed from September 20 through October 23, 2005. It then traveled to Korea, Germany, England, and America.

56. Dacher Keltner and Jonathan Haidt, "Approaching Awe, a Moral, Spiritual, and Aesthetic Emotion," *Cognition & Emotion* 17, no. 2 (2003): 297–314.

57. Song Dong and Zhao Xiangyuan, *Waste Not: Zhao Xiangyuan & Song Dong = Wu jin qi yong: Zhao Xiangyuan & Song Dong*, ed. Wu Hung (Ginza, Chuo-Ku, Tokyo: Tokyo Gallery + BTAP and Wu Hung, 2009), 15.

58. Song and Zhao, *Waste Not*, 16, 5.

59. Song and Zhao, *Waste Not*, 14, 4, 19.

60. Song and Zhao, *Waste Not*, 177.

61. Benjamin, "Unpacking my Library," 67.

62. This is the title of a radio show dedicated to Christian Guienne. See http://www.franceculture.fr/emission-sur-les-docks-10-11-portraits-24-le-diogene-des-baronnies-2011-04-26.

63. Frost and Steketee explain that hoards are often composed of valuables mixed in with worthless stuff, though hoarders usually know where things are. *Stuff*, 97.

64. In Martin Hampton and Leonie Hampton, *The Collector*, pt. 2, 2009, http://www.leoniehampton.com/films/the-collector-part-ii/.

65. Patricia Yaeger, "Editor's Column: The Death of Nature and the Apotheosis of Trash; or, Rubbish Ecology," *PMLA* 123, no. 2 (2008): 321–39.

66. Bruno Latour, *Facing Gaia: Eight Lectures on the New Climactic Regime*, trans. Catherine Porter (Cambridge: Polity Press, 2017), 8.

Conclusion

1. Franz Lidz, *Ghosty Men: The Strange but True Story of the Collyer Brothers, New York's Greatest Hoarders* (New York: Bloomsbury, 2003), 8.

2. Even hoards of pure exchange value in paper form carry certain hazards. As anthropologist Jack Weatherford explains, "That is a problem you have with paper money. Insects, rats and other animals gnaw at it." Cited in Graham Bowly, "Personal Finance for Dictators: Where to Stash the Cash," *New York Times*, March 12, 2011.

3. The report is from the "morning paper" quoted in William James, *Principles of Psychology* (New York: Dover, 1890), 2:425.

4. James, *Principles*, 425.

5. Agamben, *Stanzas*, 141.

6. Jacques Derrida, *Paper Machine* (Palo Alto, CA: Stanford University Press, 2005), 43.

7. In 2001, the *New York Times* paid $60,000 to install new Metro-North recycling bins designed to prevent commuters from helping themselves to discarded papers. See Arianne Chernock, "New Recycle Bins Stop a Long Habit," *New York Times*, August 19, 2001, 14 and Samantha MacBride, "The Immorality of Waste: Depression-Era Perspectives in the Digital Age," *SubStance* 37, no. 2 (2008): 71–77.

8. Barry Yourgrau, *Mess: One Man's Struggle to Clean Up His House and His Act* (New York: Norton, 2016), 200–212.

9. Staving off death may be no less necessary for Wallace than for Scheherazade. Frost and Steketee report "several cases" of hoarders have committed suicide after their homes were subjected to "forced clean-outs." *Stuff*, 97.

10. Benjamin, "Unpacking My Library," 59.

11. Frost and Steketee, *Stuff,* 14.

12. *Ten Characters* was installed at the Ronald Feldman Gallery in New York in 1988. See Matthew Jesse Jackson's introduction to Ilya Kabakov, *On Art,* ed. M. J. Jackson, trans. Antonina W. Bouis and Cynthia Martin, with M. J. Jackson (Chicago: University of Chicago Press, 2018), 5–6.

13. First published in *Ilya Kabakov: Ten Characters* (London: Institute of Contemporary Art, 1989). The quotation is from a short 1981 essay, "Nozdrev and Pliushkin," in which Kabakov compares the two characters from Gogol's *Dead Souls,* making them at once immortal types and specific social characters, representing extroversion and introversion, openness and secrecy, the West and the Soviet Union; in Kabakov, *On Art.*

14. Kabakov, "The Man Who Never Threw Anything Away," in *The Archive,* ed. Charles Merewether (London: Whitechapel, 2006), 32–37, 32.

15. Kabakov, "Man Who Never Threw Anything Away," 33.

16. Kabakov, "Man Who Never Threw Anything Away," 33.

17. Kabakov, "Man Who Never Threw Anything Away," 33.

18. E. L. Doctorow, *Homer and Langley* (New York: Random House, 2009), 13.

19. Doctorow, *Homer and Langley,* 48.

20. Doctorow, *Homer and Langley,* 48.

21. Fredric Jameson, "The Realist Floor-Plan," in *On Signs,* ed. Marshall Blonsky (Baltimore: Johns Hopkins University Press, 1985), 373–83.

22. "A Note upon the 'Mystic Writing-Pad,'" *SE* 19: 225–32.

23. Freud, "A Note," *SE* 19, 230. Giuseppe Civitarese observes that the words "in suitable lights" (*bei geeigneter Belichtung lesbar*), seem to suggest the whole of psychoanalysis. See "From the mystic writing pad to the α function: metaphors of text and translation in Freud and Bion," in *The Violence of Emotions: Bion and Post-Bionian Analysis* (New York: Routledge, 2012), 173–90, 173.

24. Freud, "A Note," *SE* 19:232.

Bibliography

"150,000 Francs pour huit sous." *Le Journal*, November 14, 1895. http://gallica.bnf.fr/ark:/12148/bpt6k76212398.

"200 Bid Spiritedly for Collyer Items." *New York Times*, June 11, 1947.

Abeille, Louis Paul. *Lettre d'un négociant sur la nature du commerce des grains.* Bibliothèque nationale de France, département Réserve des livres rares. http://catalogue.bnf.fr/ark:/12148/cb30000620n.

Abramowitz, Jonathan S. "Presidential Address: Are the Obsessive-Compulsive Related Disorders Related to Obsessive-Compulsive Disorder? A Critical Look at DSM-5's New Category," *Behavior Therapy* 49, no. 1 (2018): 1–11.

Adorno, Theodor. *Minima moralia. Reflections from a Damaged Life.* Translated by E. F. N. Jephcott. New York: Verso, 2005.

Agamben, Giorgio. *Means without End: Notes on Politics* Minneapolis: University of Minnesota Press, 2000.

———. *Profanations.* New York: Zone Books, 1992.

———. *Stanzas: Word and Phantasm in Western Culture.* Minneapolis: University of Minnesota Press, 1992.

Alighieri, Dante. *The Divine Comedy.* Translated by Charles S. Singleton. Princeton: Princeton University Press.

———. *Inferno.* Translated by Allan Mandelbaum. *Digital Dante.* Columbia University. https://digitaldante.columbia.edu/dante/divine-comedy/inferno/inferno-7/.

Almansi, Guido. "Malerba and the Art of Story-Telling." *Quaderni d'italianistica* 1 (1980): 157–70.

Amberson, Deborah, and Elena Past. "Gadda's Pasticciaccio and the Knotted Posthuman Household." *Relations: Beyond Anthropocentrism* 4, no. 1 (2016), https://doi.org/10.7358/rela-2016-001-ambe.

American Psychiatric Association. *Diagnostic and Statistical Manual of Mental Disorders: DSM-5.* Arlington, VA: American Psychiatric Association, 2013.

Anceschi, Luciano, ed. *La luna nel corso: Pagine milanesi.* Milan: Edizioni di corrente, 1941.

Appadurai, Arjun. "Mediants, Materiality, Normativity." *Public Culture*, 27, no. 2 (May 2015): 221–37.

Arrighi, Cletto. *La scapigliatura e il 6 febbraio.* Milan: Francesco Sanvito, 1862.

Arrighi, Cletto, Aldo Barilli, Ferdinado Fontana, Leo Speri, Otto Cima, Francesco Giarelli, Pinzo, Oleardo Bianchi, Gustavo Macchi, Mario Colombo et al. *Il ventre di Milano: Fisiologia della capitale morale.* Milan: Aliprandi, 1888.

Aspesi, Natalia. *Il lusso e l'autarchia: storia dell'eleganza italiana 1930–1944.* Milan: Rizzoli, 1982.

Atkins, Ed. *The Trick Brain.* Video transcript in *The Keeper.* Edited by Massimiliano Gioni and Natalie Bell. New York: New Museum, 2016.

"Au 'Marché-aux-Puces.'" *La Lanterne*, June 24, 1891.

Bardini, Thierry. *Junkware.* Minneapolis: University of Minnesota Press, 2011.

Barker, Stephen, ed. *Excavations and Their Objects: Freud's Collection of Antiquity.* Albany: State University of New York Press, 1996.

Barthes, Roland. *The Rustle of Language.* Translated by Richard Howard. New York: Hill & Wang, 1975.

———. *S/Z.* New York: Hill and Wang, 1975.

Barzacchi, Cesare. *L'Italia di Longanesi. Memorie fotografiche di Cesare Barzacchi.* Rome: Edizioni del Borghese, 1964.

Batalion, Judy. *White Walls. A Memoir about Motherhood, Daughterhood, and the Mess in Between.* New York: Random House, 2016.

Baudelaire, Charles. *The Flowers of Evil.* Translated by James McGowan. Oxford: Oxford University Press, 1993.

———. *The Painter of Modern Life.* London: Penguin, 2010.

Baudrillard, Jean. *The System of Objects.* New York: Verso, 1996.

Becker, Gary. *An Economic Approach to Human Behavior.* Chicago: University of Chicago Press, 1990.

Bedel, Jean. *Les Puces ont cent ans. Histoire des chiffonniers, brocanteurs et autres chineurs du Moyen Age à nos jours.* Cany: Presses de l'imprimerie Gabel, 1985.

———. *Saut de puces à Saint-Ouen.* Saint-Rémy-en-l'Eau: M. Hayot, 2012.

Belk, Russel, and Melanie Wallendorf. "Of Mice and Men: Gender Identity in Collecting." In *Interpreting Objects and Collections*, edited by Susanne M. Pearce, 240–53. New York: Routledge, 1994.

Benjamin, Walter. *The Arcades Project.* Cambridge: Harvard University Press, 1999.

———. "A Little History of Photography." In *Selected Writings, Vol. 2, Part 2: 1931–1942*. Edited by Michael W. Jennings, Howard Eiland, and Gary Smith, translated by Rodney Livingstone et al., 507–30. Cambridge: Belknap Press of Harvard University Press, 2005.

———. "Notes on a Theory of Gambling." In *The Sociology of Risk and Gambling Reader*, edited by J. F. Cosgrove, 209–11. New York: Routledge, 2006.

———. "On the Concept of History." In *Selected Writings, Vol. 4: 1938–1940*, edited by Howard Eiland and Michael W. Jennings. Cambridge: Belknap Press of Harvard University Press, 2003.

———. *The Writer of Modern Life. Essays on Charles Baudelaire*. Edited by Jennings, translated by Eiland. Cambridge: Belknap Press of Harvard University Press, 2006.

Bennett, Jane. "Powers of the Hoard: Further Notes on Material Agency." In *Animal, Vegetable, Mineral: Ethics and Objects*, edited by Jeffrey Jerome Cohen, 237–69. Washington, DC: Oliphaunt Books, 2012.

———. *Vibrant Matter: A Political Ecology of Things*. Durham, NC: Duke University Press, 2010.

Berlant, Lauren Gail. *Cruel Optimism*. Durham, NC: Duke University Press, 2011.

Bersezio, Vittorio, E. De Amicis, N. Bianchi, R. Sacchetti, A. Arnulfi, S. Carlevaris, D. Busi-Aime, G. Gloria, G. Giacosa, V. Carrera, et al. *Torino*. Turin: Roux e Favale, 1880. http://books.google.com/books?id=m9Q7AQAAIAAJ.

———. *Torino e l'esposizione italiana del 1884. Cronaca illustrata della esposizione nazionale-industriale ed artistica del 1884*. Turin: Roux e Favale, 1884.

Borges, Jorge Luis. *Labyrinths: Selected Stories and Other Writings*. Translated by James E. Irby. New York: New Directions, 1964.

Boscagli, Maurizia. *Stuff Theory: Everyday Objects, Radical Materialism*. New York: Bloomsbury Academic, 2014.

Boym, Svetlana. *The Future of Nostalgia*. New York: Basic Books, 2001.

Bratiotis, Christiana, Cristina Sorrentino Schmalisch, and Gail Steketee. *The Hoarding Handbook: A Guide for Human Service Professionals*. Oxford: Oxford University Press, 2011.

Breton, André. *Mad Love*. Translated by Mary Ann Caws. Lincoln: University of Nebraska Press, 1987.

———. *Nadja*. Translated by Richard Howard. New York: Grove Press, 1960.

Brooks, Peter. *Reading for the Plot*. Cambridge: Harvard University Press, 1984.

Brown, Bill. *The Material Unconscious: American Amusement, Stephen Crane & the Economies of Play*. Cambridge: Harvard University Press, 1996

——. *Other Things*. Chicago: University of Chicago Press, 2019.

——. *Things*. Chicago: University of Chicago Press, 2004.

Brown, Wendy. *Undoing the Demos: Neoliberalism's Stealth Revolution*. New York: Zone Books, 2015.

Buchanan, Ian. "The Clutter Assemblage." *Drain Magazine* 7, no. 1 (2011). http://drainmag.com/the-clutter-assemblage/.

Buck-Morss, Susan. *The Dialectics of Seeing: Walter Benjamin and the Arcades Project*. Cambridge: MIT Press, 1991.

Calvino, Italo. *Six Memos for the Next Millennium*. Translated by Geoffrey Brock. Boston: Houghton Mifflin Harcourt, 2016.

Cannon, James. *The Paris Zone: A Cultural History, 1840–1944*. New York: Routledge, 2016.

Cannon, JoAnn. "Intervista con Luigi Malerba," *MLN* 104, no. 1 (1989): 226–37.

Carson, Rachel. *Silent Spring*. Boston: Houghton Mifflin Harcourt, 2002.

Caruso, Martina. *Italian Humanist Photography from Fascism to the Cold War*. London: Bloomsbury Academic, 2016.

Cavarero, Adriana. *For More Than One Voice: Toward a Philosophy of Vocal Expression*. Palo Alto: Stanford University Press, 2005.

Cefalu, Paul. "What's So Funny about Obsessive-Compulsive Disorder?" *PMLA* 124, no. 1 (2009): 44–58.

Celant, Germano. *The Italian Metamorphosis, 1943–1968*. New York: Guggenheim Museum, 1994.

Chang, Yi, Lei Tang, Yoshiyuki Inagaki, and Yan Liu. "What Is Tumblr: A Statistical Overview and Comparison." *ACM SIGKDD Explorations Newsletter* 16, no. 1 (2014): 21–29.

Chernock, Arianne. "New Recycle Bins Stop a Long Habit." *New York Times*, August 19, 2001.

Civitarese, Giuseppe, *The Intimate Room: Theory and Technique of the Analytic Field*. New York: Routledge, 2010.

——. *The Violence of Emotions: Bion and Post-Bionian Analysis*. New York: Routledge, 2012.

Clark, A. N.G., G. D. Mankikar, and Ian Gray. "Diogenes Syndrome: A Clinical Study of Gross Neglect in Old Age." *The Lancet* 305, no. 7903 (1975): 366–68.

Cohen, Margaret. *Profane Illumination: Walter Benjamin and the Paris of Surrealist Revolution*. Berkeley: University of California Press, 1995.

"Collyer Mansion Yields Junk, Cats." *New York Times*, March 26, 1947.

Coole, Diana, and Samantha Frost. *New Materialisms: Ontology, Agency, and Politics*. Durham, NC: Duke University Press, 2010.

Cortellessa, Andrea, and Giorgio Patrizi, eds. *La biblioteca di Don Gonzalo.* Vol. 1. Rome: Bulzoni, 2001.

Crespo, Diane, dir. 2015. *Clutter.* Filmbuff. DVD.

D'Alembert, Jean-Baptiste le Rond. "Bibliomania." In *The Encyclopedia of Diderot & d'Alembert Collaborative Translation Project.* Translated by Malcolm Eden. Ann Arbor, MI: University of Michigan Library, 2015. http://hdl.handle.net/2027/spo.did2222.0003.188. (Originally published as "Bibliomanie," *Encyclopédie ou Dictionnaire raisonné des sciences, des arts et des métiers.* Paris, 1752.)

Davenport, Marcia. *My Brother's Keeper.* London: Collins, 1954.

Davis, Lennard J. *Obsession: A History.* Chicago: University of Chicago Press, 2009.

De Amicis, Edmondo. *Le tre capitali: Torino, Firenze, Roma.* Catania: N. Giannotta, 1898.

De Sanctis, Sante. "Collezionismi e impulsi collezionistici." *Bollettino della società Lancisiana degli ospedali* 17, no. 1 (1897): 3–30.

De Seta, Cesare. *Giuseppe Pagano, fotografo.* Milano: Electra, 1979.

De Seta, Daria. *Giuseppe Pagano: vocabulario de ima genes = images alphabet.* Madrid: Lampreave & Millán, 2008.

Dean, Mitchell. "The Malthus Effect." *Economy and Society* 44, no. 1 (2015): 18–39.

Del Boca, Angelo. *La guerra d'Abissinia: 1935–1941.* Milano: Feltrinelli, 1965.

Della Coletta, Cristina. *World's Fairs Italian-Style: The Great Expositions in Turin and Their Narratives, 1860–1915.* Toronto: University of Toronto Press, 2006.

Derrida, Jacques. *Paper Machine.* Palo Alto: Stanford University Press, 2005.

Descuret, Jean-Baptiste-Félix. *La médecine des passions: ou les passions considérées dans leurs rapports avec les maladies, les lois et la religion.* Paris: Labé, 1844.

Desmond, Matthew. *Evicted: Poverty and Profit in the American City.* New York: Crown, 2016.

Dibdin, Thomas Frognall. *The Bibliographical Decameron, or, Ten Days Pleasant Discourse upon Illuminated Manuscripts, and Subjects Connected with Early Engraving, Typography, and Bibliography.* London: Printed for the author by W. Bulmer and Co., Shakespeare Press, 1817.

——. *Bibliomania, or, Book Madness: A Bibliographical Romance, in Six Parts,* London: H. G. Bohn, 1842.

——. *The Bibliomania; or Book-Madness; Containing some Account of the History, Symptoms, and Cure of This Fatal Disease.* London: Longman, Hurst, Rees, and Orme, 1809.

————. *Bibliophobia. Remarks on the Present Languid and Depressed State of Literature and the Book Trade. In a Letter Addressed to the Author of the Bibliomania. By Mercurius Rusticus [pseud.] With notes by Cato Parvus.* London, H. Bohn, 1832. http://hdl.handle.net/2027/uc2.ark:/13960/t5cc19d4s.

Dini, Rachele. *Consumerism, Waste, and Re-Use in Twentieth-Century Fiction Legacies of the Avant-Garde.* New York: Palgrave, 2016.

Doctorow, E. L. *Homer & Langley: A Novel.* New York: Random House, 2009.

Dolphijn, Rick, and Iris van der Tuin. *New Materialism Interviews and Cartographies.* Ann Arbor: Open Humanities Press, University of Michigan Library, 2012.

Domotor, Zoltana [Rebecca Falkoff]. 2010. *If I Were a Hoarder.* http://ifiwereahoarder.com.

Douglas, Mary. *Purity and Danger: An Analysis of Concept of Pollution and Taboo.* New York: Routledge, 1966.

Doyle, Arthur Conan. "The Adventure of the Musgrave Ritual." *Strand Magazine: An Illustrated Monthly* 5 (January 1893): 479–89.

————. "The Five Orange Pips." *Strand Magazine: An Illustrated Monthly* 2 (July 1891): 481–91.

————. *A Study in Scarlet,* ed. Owen Dudley Edwards. Oxford: Oxford University Press, 1993.

Dubuisson, Paul. "Les voleuses dans les grands magasins." *Archives d'anthropologie criminelle, de criminologie et de psychologie normale et pathologique* 16 (1901): 1–20.

Dunnett, Jane. "Crime and the Critics: On the Appraisal of Detective Novels in 1930s Italy." *Modern Language Review* 106, no. 3 (July 2011): 745–64.

During, Simon. "The Strange Case of Monomania: Patriarchy in Literature, Murder in *Middlemarch,* Drowning in *Daniel Deronda.*" *Representations* 23 (1988): 86–104.

Eco, Umberto. *The Infinity of Lists: An Illustrated Essay.* New York: Rizzoli, 2009.

————. *La memoria vegetale e altri scritti.* Milan: Bompiani, 2011.

Edelman, Lee. *No Future: Queer Theory and the Death Drive.* Durham, NC: Duke University Press, 2004.

Eighner, Lars. "On Dumpster Diving." *Threepenny Review* 47 (Autumn 1991) 6–8.

Esposito, Roberto. *Persons and Things: From the Body's Point of View.* Translated by Zakiya Hanafi. Cambridge: Polity Press, 2015.

Fardon, Richard. "Citations Out of Place: Or, Lord Palmerston Goes Viral in the Nineteenth Century but Gets Lost in the Twentieth." *Anthropology Today* 29, no. 1 (2013): 25–27.

Ferrante, Elena. *Frantumaglia. A Writer's Journey.* New York: Europa editions, 2016.

Ferriar, John. *The Bibliomania: An Epistle, To Richard Heber, Esq.* London: Printed for T. Cadell and W. Davies by J. Haddock, 1809.

Fields, Barbara Schinman. "Jean-François Raffaëlli (1850–1924): The Naturalist Artist." PhD diss., Columbia University, 1979.

Findlen, Paula. *Possessing Nature: Museums, Collecting, and Scientific Culture in Early Modern Italy.* Berkeley: University of California Press, 1994

Flatley, Jonathan. *Like Andy Warhol.* Chicago: University of Chicago Press, 2017.

Flaubert, Gustave. "Bibliomania." In *A Passion for Books: A Book Lover's Treasury of Stories, Essays, Humor, Lore, and Lists on Collecting, Reading, Borrowing, Lending, Caring for and Appreciating Books*, edited by Harold Rabinowitz and Rob Kaplan. New York: Three Rivers Press, 1999.

———. *Bibliomanie et autres textes 1836–1839.* Paris: Jean-Cyrille Godefroy, 1982.

———. *Madame Bovary: Provincial Lives.* Translated by Geoffrey Wall. New York: Penguin Classics, 2014.

Fleissner, Jennifer L. "Obsessional Modernity: The 'Institutionalization of Doubt.'" *Critical Inquiry* 34, no. 1 (2007): 106–34.

Forgacs, David. *Italy's Margins: Social Exclusion and Nation Formation since 1861.* Cambridge: Cambridge University Press, 2014.

Forrester, John. "'Mille e tre': Freud and Collecting." In *Cultures of Collecting.* edited by John Elsner and Roger Cardinal, 224–51. London: Reaktion Books, 1994.

Foucault, Michel. *The Order of Things.* London: Routledge, 1994.

———. *Security, Territory, Population. Lectures at the Collège de France, 1977–1978.* New York: Picador, 2004.

"Four Pianos Auctioned in Collyer Parlor." *New York Times*, June 21, 1947.

Freud, Sigmund. *Beyond the Pleasure Principle.* In *SE* 18 (1955), 1–64.

———. "Character and Anal Erotism." In *SE* 9 (1959), 169–75.

———. "Fetishism." In *SE* 21 (1961), 147–58.

———. "Frau Emmy von N." In *SE* 2 (1955), 48–105.

———. *The Interpretation of Dreams. SE* 4–5 (1953).

———. *Notes Upon a Case of Obsessional Neurosis.* In *SE* 10 (1955), 151–318.

———. "A Note upon the 'Mystic Writing-Pad.'" In *SE* 19 (1961), 225–32.

———. "On the Antithetical Meaning of Primal Words." In *SE* 11 (1957), 155–61.

———. "On Transience." In *SE* 14 (1957), 303–7.

———. *The Psychopathology of Everyday Life. SE* 6 (1960).

———. *The Standard Edition of the Complete Psychological Works of Sigmund Freud (SE).* Translated and edited by James Strachey. London, Hogarth Press, 1953–74.

———. *Three Essays on the Theory of Sexuality*. In *SE* 7 (1953), 123–246.

———. "The Uncanny." In *SE* 17 (1955), 217–56.

Frost, R., and Rachel C. Gross. "The Hoarding of Possessions." *Behaviour Research and Therapy* 31, no. 4 (1993): 367–81.

Frost, R., and Veselina Hristova. "Assessment of Hoarding," *Journal of Clinical Psychology* 67, no. 5 (2011): 456–66.

Frost, R., and G. Steketee. "Hoarding: Clinical Aspects and Treatment Strategies." In *Obsessive Compulsive Disorders: Practical Management*, edited by Jenike, Michael A., Lee Baer, and William E. Minichiello, 533–54. St. Louis, MO: Mosby, 1998.

———. *Stuff. Compulsive Hoarding and the Meaning of Things*. Boston: Houghton Mifflin Harcourt, 2010.

Frost, Randy O., Gail Steketee, David Tolin, and Stefanie Renaud. "Development and Validation of the Clutter Image Rating." *Journal of Psychopathology and Behavioral Assessment* 30, no. 3 (2008): 193–203.

G. "Il codice dei mendicanti." *Panorama* 2, no. 8 (April 27, 1940): 22–23.

Gadda, Carlo Emilio. "Alla fiera di Milano." *L'Ambrosiano* (April 24, 1936): 3.

———. "Fiera a Milano." *Panorama* 2, no. 6 (March 27, 1940): 29–33.

———. *L'Adalgisa. Disegni milanesi*. Edited by Claudio Vela. Milan: Adelphi, 2017.

———. "L'egoista." In *Saggi, giornali, favole e altri scritti I* (*SGF I*), edited by Liliana Orlando, Clelia Martignoni, and D. Isella, 654–67. Milan: Garzanti, 2008.

———. "L'uomo e la macchina." *Panorama* 2, no. 8 (April 27, 1940): 28–31.

———. *Meditazione milanese*. In *Scritti vari e postumi* (*SVP*). Edited by Andrea Silvestri, Claudio Vela, Dante Isella, Paola Italia, and Giorgio Pinotti, 614–894. Milan: Garzanti, 2009.

———. "Terra Lombarda." *Panorama* 2, no. 7 (April 12, 1940): 46–48.

———. *"Per favore, mi lasci nell'ombra": Interviste 1950–1972*. Edited by Claudio Vela. Milan: Adelphi, 1993.

———. *That Awful Mess on the Via Merulana*. Translated by William Weaver. New York: NYRB Classics, 2000.

Gardin, Piero Berengo. *Alberto Lattuada: fotografo: Dieci anni di occhio quadrato 1938–1948*. Florence: Alinari, 1982.

Genette, Gerard. *Narrative Discourse*. Ithaca: Cornell University Press, 1980.

Giles, David Boarder. "The Anatomy of a Dumpster. Abject Capital and the Looking Glass of Value." *Social Text* 32, no. 1 (2014): 93–113.

Ginzburg, Carlo. *Clues, Myths, and the Historical Method*. New York: Hutchinson Radius, 1990.

Giolli, Raffaello. "Donne nude in piazza." *Panorama* 2, no. 7 (April 12, 1940): 20–24.

Glynn, Ruth. "Self and the City: A Psychoanalytical Reading of Luigi Malerba's *Il serpente.*" *Italica* 83, no. 3/4 (2006): 609–28.

Gogol, Nikolai. *Dead Souls: An Epic Poem.* Translated by Donald Rayfield. New York: New York Review Books, 2012.

Goldstein, Jan E. *Console and Classify: The French Psychiatric Profession in the Nineteenth Century.* Chicago: University of Chicago Press, 2001.

Goncourt, Edmond de, Jean-François Raffaëlli, and Albert Wolff. *Les Types de Paris.* Paris: E. Plon, Nourrit et Cie, 1889.

Goode, Mike. "Dryasdust Antiquarianism and Soppy Masculinity: The Waverley Novels and the Gender of History." *Representations* 82, no. 1 (2003): 52–86.

Gottfried, Mara. "Man Found Dead Inside St. Paul Home's Burning Kitchen" *Twin Cities Pioneer Press,* February 8, 2011. http://www.twincities.com/2011/02/08/man-found-dead-inside-st-paul-homes-burning-kitchen/.

Goux, Jean-Joseph. "Banking on Signs." *Diacritics* 18, no. 2 (Summer 1988): 15–25.

———. *Symbolic Economies: After Marx and Freud.* Translated by Jennifer Gage. Ithaca: Cornell University Press, 2016.

Griffin, Anna. "Hoarder Killed in North Portland House Fire Lived in Plain Sight, Leaving a Trail of Questions." *Oregonian,* December 8, 2012. https://www.oregonlive.com/portland/2012/12/house_fire_that_killed_north_p.html.

Guglielmi, Angelo. "Avanguardia e sperimentalismo." In *Gruppo '63. Critica e teoria,* edited by Renato Barilli and A. Guglielmi, 331–38. Turin: Controsegni, 2003.

Hacking, Ian. *Mad Travelers: Reflections on the Reality of Transient Mental Illnesses.* Charlottesville: University of Virginia Press, 1998.

———. *The Taming of Chance.* Cambridge: Cambridge University Press, 1990.

Hampton, Ivanna. "Woman Found Dead in Garbage-Filled Home." *NBC Chicago,* July 20, 2010. https://www.nbcchicago.com/news/local/skokie-elderly-woman-hoarder-garbage-house-home-trash-98814974.html.

Hampton, Martin, dir. *The Collector.* 2005. http://www.martinhampton.com/MPH_FILMS_films_THE_COLLECTOR.html.

———. *Possessed.* 2008. www.possessed.me.uk.

Hampton, Martin, and Leonie Hampton, dirs. *The Collector, Part II.* 2009. http://www.leoniehampton.com/films/the-collector-part-ii.

Harlow, John M. "Recovery from the Passage of an Iron Bar through the Head." *History of Psychiatry* 4, no. 14 (1993): 274–81.

Harrington, Anne. *Mind Fixers: Psychiatry's Troubled Search for the Biology of Mental Illness.* New York: W. W. Norton, 2019.

Hartl, Tamara L., Randy O. Frost, George J. Allen, Thilo Deckersbach, Gail Steketee, Shannon R. Duffany, and Cary R. Savage. "Actual and Perceived Memory Deficits in Individuals with Compulsive Hoarding." *Depression and Anxiety* 20, no. 2 (2004): 59–69.

Harvey, David. *A Brief History of Neoliberalism*. New York: Oxford University Press, 2007.

Herring, Scott. *The Hoarders*. Chicago: University of Chicago Press, 2014.

Hurh, Paul. "'The Creative and the Resolvent': The Origins of Poe's Analytical Method." *Nineteenth Century Literature* 66, no. 4 (2012): 466–93.

Iversen, Margaret. *Beyond Pleasure: Freud, Lacan, Barthes*. University Park: Pennsylvania State University Press, 2007.

Jakobson, Roman. *On Language*. Cambridge: Harvard University Press, 1990.

James, William. *Principles of Psychology*, vol. 2. New York: Dover, 1890.

Jameson, Fredric. "The Realist Floor-Plan." In *On Signs*, edited by Marshall Blonsky, 373–83. Baltimore: Johns Hopkins University Press, 1985.

Kabakov, Ilya. *Ilya Kabakov. Ten Characters*. London: Institute of Contemporary Art, 1989.

———. "The Man Who Never Threw Anything Away." In *The Archive*, edited by Charles Merewether, 32–37. London: Whitechapel, 2006.

———. *On Art*. Edited by M. J. Jackson and translated by Antonina Bouis, Cynthia Martin, and M. J. Jackson. Chicago: University of Chicago Press, 2018.

Keltner, Dacher, and Jonathan Haidt. "Approaching Awe, a Moral, Spiritual, and Aesthetic Emotion." *Cognition and Emotion* 17, no. 2 (2003): 297–314.

Kenny, Neil. "Books in Space and Time: Bibliomania and Early Modern Histories of Learning and" Literature" in France." *MLQ: Modern Language Quarterly* 61, no. 2 (2000): 253–86.

Kent, Henry W. "The Love of the Book." *Bulletin of the American Library Association* 9, no. 4 (1915): 94–101.

King, William Davies. *Collections of Nothing*. Chicago: University of Chicago Press, 2008.

Kondó, Marie. *The Life-Changing Magic of Tidying Up: The Japanese Art of Decluttering and Organizing*. New York: Ten Speed Press, 2014.

Krauss, Rosalind. "The Photographic Conditions of Surrealism." *October* 19 (1981): 3–34.

Krauss, R., Jane Livingston, and Dawn Ades. *L'Amour Fou: Photography & Surrealism*. New York: Abbeville Press, 1985.

Kristeva, Julia. *Powers of Horror: An Essay of Abjection*. New York: Columbia University Press, 1984.

Lacan, Jacques. "Function and Field of Speech and Language in Psychoanalysis." In *Écrits. A Selection*, edited and translated by Bruce Fink, 57–106. New York: W. W. Norton, 2002.

Lacassagne, Alexandre. "Les Vols à l'étalage et dans les grands magasins." *Archives d'anthropologie criminelle, de criminologie et de psychologie normale et pathologique* 11 (1896): 560–65.

Lanzardo, Dario, Gianni Carchia, Albino Galvano, and Liliana Lanzardo. *Dame e cavalieri nel Balôn di Torino: sguardo fotografico sul mercato dell'usato.* Milano: Mondadori, 1984.

Laplanche, Jean, and Jean-Bertrand Pontalis. *The Language of Psycho-Analysis.* Translated by Donald Nicholson-Smith." New York: W. W. Norton, 1973.

Latour, Bruno. *Facing Gaia: Eight Lectures on the New Climatic Regime.* Medford, MA: Polity Press, 2017.

———. *We Have Never Been Modern.* Cambridge: Harvard University Press, 1993.

———. "Why Has Critique Run Out of Steam? From Matters of Fact to Matters of Concern." *Critical Inquiry* 30, no. 2 (2004): 225–48.

Lavater, Johann Caspar. *Essays on Physiognomy: Designed to Promote the Knowledge and the Love of Mankind.* Translated and edited by Thomas Holcroft, Georg Gessner, John E. Rothensteiner, and William S. Bogart. London: William Tegg and Co., 1858.

Lazzarato, Maurizio. *Governing by Debt.* New York: Semiotext(e), 2015.

———. *The Making of the Indebted Man: An Essay on the Neoliberal Condition.* New York: Semiotext(e), 2012.

Lepselter, Susan. "The Disorder of Things. Hoarding Narratives in Popular Media," *Anthropological Quarterly* 84, no. 4 (2011): 919–47

Lester, Cynthia, dir. 2008. *My mother's Garden: A Film.* www.MyMothers GardenMovie.com.

Liboiron, Max. "Modern Waste as Strategy." *Lo Squaderno: Explorations in Space and Society,* no. 29, "Garbage and Wastes" (2013): 9–12.

Lidz, Franz. *Ghosty Men: The Strange but True Story of the Collyer Brothers, New York's Greatest Hoarders: An Urban Historical.* New York: Bloomsbury, 2003.

———. "Owner of Forgotten Clock Finds a Name (and Hands) to Put with the Face." *New York Times,* December 26, 2013.

———. "The Paper Chase." *New York Times,* October 26, 2003.

Liguori, Maria Chiara. "Have You Had Your Daily Drug? The Italian Motta Ice-Cream Campaign in 1959." *Advertising & Society Review* 15, no. 5 (2015), https://doi.org/10.1353/asr.2015.0002.

Lombroso, Cesare, *Criminal Man.* Translated and edited by Mary Gibson and Nicole Hahn Rafter. Durham, NC: Duke University Press, 2006.

Lombroso, Gina. *Cesare Lombroso: storia della vita e delle opere.* Turin: Fratelli Bocca, 1915.

Loven, Kyle. *Loss Machine*. Seattle, WA: On the Boards, 2012.

Lutas, Liviu. "Narrative Metalepsis in Detective Fiction." In *Metalepsis in Popular Culture*, edited by Karin Kukkonen and Sonja Klimek, 41–64. Berlin: De Gruyter, 2011.

MacBride, Samantha. "The Immorality of Waste: Depression-Era Perspectives in the Digital Age." *SubStance* 37, no. 2 (2008): 71–77.

——. *Recycling Reconsidered: The Present Failure and Future Promise of Environmental Action in the United States*. Cambridge: MIT Press, 2013.

Mack, Kristen. "Alone and Buried by Possessions." *Chicago Tribune*, August 10, 2010. https://www.chicagotribune.com/news/ct-xpm-2010-08-10-ct-met-hoarders-0811-20100810-story.html.

Magnan, Valentin. *Leçons cliniques sur les maladies mentales . . . par V. Magnan*. Paris: A. Delahaye et E. Lecrosnier, 1887.

Mahony, Patrick J. *Freud and the Rat Man*. New Haven: Yale University Press, 1986.

Malerba, Luigi. *Diario di un sognatore*. Turin: Einaudi, 1981.

——. *La scoperta dell'alfabeto. Le parole abbandonate* (Milan: Mondadori, 2017)

——. *The Serpent*. Translated by William Weaver. New York: Farrar, Straus and Giroux, 1968.

Marc, C-C-H. *De la Folie. Ses rapports avec les questions médico-judiciaires*. Baillière, 1840.

Marinetti, F. T. "Founding and Manifesto of Futurism." In *Futurism: An Anthology*, edited by Lawrence Rainey, Christine Poggi, and Laura Whitman, 49–54. New Haven: Yale University Press, 2009.

——. "We Abjure Our Symbolist Masters." In *Futurism: An Anthology*, edited by Lawrence Rainey, Christine Poggi, and Laura Whitman, 93–95. New Haven: Yale University Press, 2009.

Martin, Emily. *Bipolar Expeditions: Mania and Depression in American Culture*. Princeton University Press, 2009.

Marx, Karl. *Capital*, vol. I. Translated by Ben Fowkes. New York: Penguin Classics, 1990.

——. *A Contribution to the Critique of Political Economy*. Translated by N. I. Stone. Chicago: Charles H. Kerr & Company, 1904.

Matthey, André. *Nouvelles recherches sur les maladies de l'esprit: précédées de considérations sur les difficultés de l'art de guérir*. Paris: Paschoud, 1816.

Max, Gerry. "Gustave Flaubert: The Book as Artifact and Idea: Bibliomanie and Bibliology." *Dalhousie French Studies* 22 (1992): 9–22.

McClanahan, Annie. *Dead Pledges: Debt, Crisis, and Twenty-First-Century Culture*. Palo Alto, CA: Stanford University Press, 2018.

McGrath, Ben. "Squished." *New Yorker*, January 12, 2004.

Metz, Christian. "Photography and Fetish." *October* 34 (1985): 81–90.

Michaels, Walter Benn. *The Gold Standard and the Logic of Naturalism: American Literature at the Turn of the Century.* Berkeley: University of California Press, 1987.

Miller, D. A. *The Novel and the Police.* Berkeley: University of California Press, 1988.

Miller, Edgar. "Recovery from the Passage of an Iron Bar Through the Head," *History of Psychiatry* 4, no. 14 (1993): 274–81.

Miller, Kimberly Rae. *Coming Clean. A Memoir.* Boston: New Harvest, 2013.

Mingazzini, Giovanni. *Rivista sperimentale di freniatria e medicina legale delle alienazioni mentali,* vol. 19, 541–73. Reggio Emilia: Stefano Calderini & Sons, 1893.

Montag, Kris Britt, dir. *Packrat.* 2004. http://docuseek2.com/fn-pack.

Moran, Patrick. "The Collyer Brothers and the Fictional Lives of Hoarders." *MFS Modern Fiction Studies* 62, no. 2 (2016): 272–91.

Morrison, Susan. *The Literature of Waste: Material Ecopoetics and Ethical Matter.* New York: Palgrave, 2015.

"Mummified Remains Found in Jennings Home." *St. Louis Post Dispatch,* March 8, 2011.

Nodier, Charles. *L'Amateur de livres.* Bordeaux: Le Castor Astral, 1993.

Nordau, Max Simon. *Degeneration.* New York: D. Appleton and Co., 1912.

Novillo-Corvalán, Patricia. "Literature and Disability: The Medical Interface in Borges and Beckett." *Medical Humanities* 37, no. 1 (2011): 38–43.

O'Brien, Patricia. "The Kleptomania Diagnosis: Bourgeois Women and Theft in Late Nineteenth-Century France." *Journal of Social History* 17, no. 1 (1983): 65–77.

Office de Tourisme de Plaine Commune Grand Paris. "L'histoire du marché: Origine du nom marché aux puces." n.d. http://www.tourisme-plainecommune-paris.com/decouvrir/patrimoine-vivant-et-preserve/chinez-au-marche-aux-puces-de-saint-ouen/lhistoire-du-marche.

Omololu, C. J. *Dirty Little Secrets.* New York: Walker, 2010.

Orlando, Francesco. *Obsolete Objects in the Literary Imagination: Ruins, Relics, Rarities, Rubbish, Uninhabited Places, and Hidden Treasures.* New Haven: Yale University Press, 2006.

Pagano, Giuseppe. "Arte e tecnica alla Fiera di Milano." *Panorama* 2, no. 8 (April 27, 1940), 32–33.

Pamuk, Orhan. *The Museum of Innocence: A Novel.* Translated by Maureen Freely. London: Faber and Faber, 2009.

Papi, Paolo. "Perché Milano è considerate la capitale morale." *Panorama* (October 29, 2015). https://www.panorama.it/news/cronaca/perche-milano-e-considerata-la-capitale-morale/.

Pareto, Vilfredo. "On the Economic Phenomenon: A Reply to Benedetto Croce." Translated by F. Priuli. *Giornale degli economisti e annali di economia* 71, no. 2/3 (2012): 11–28.

Past, Elena. *Methods of Murder: Beccarian Introspection and Lombrosian Vivisection in Italian Crime Fiction*. Toronto: University of Toronto Press, 2012.

Patriarca, Silvana. *Italian Vices: Nation and Character from the Risorgimento to the Republic*. Cambridge: Cambridge University Press, 2010.

Paulian, Louis. "Les Chiffonniers." *L'Illustration*, February 2, 1884.

———. *La hotte du chiffonnier*. Paris: Hachette, 1885.

Pazniokas, Francesca. *Keep*. New York: Wide Eyed Productions/Mastodon, 2016.

Penzel, Fred. "Hoarding in History." In *The Oxford Handbook of Hoarding and Acquiring*, edited by R. Frost and G. Steketee, 6–16. Oxford: Oxford University Press, 2014.

Pertusa, Alberto, Randy Frost, and David Mataix-Cols. "When Hoarding Is a Symptom of OCD: A Case Series and Implications for DSM-V." *Behaviour Research and Therapy* 48, no. 10 (2010): 1012–20.

Petrarch, Francesco. *Petrarch's Remedies for Fortune Fair and Foul: A Modern English Translation of De remediis utriusque Fortune, with a Commentary*. Translation and commentary by Conrad H. Rawski. Bloomington: Indiana University Press, 1991.

Phillips, Adam. "Clutter: A Case History." In *Promises, Promises: Essays on Psychoanalysis and Literature*, 59–71. New York: Basic Books, 2001.

Pietz, William. "The Problem of the Fetish, I." *RES: Anthropology and Aesthetics* 9, no. 1 (1985): 5–17.

Pinchevski, Amit. "Bartleby's Autism: Wandering along Incommunicability." *Cultural Critique* 78 (2011): 27–59.

Poe, E. A. 1978. *The Collected Works of Edgar Allan Poe. Tales and Sketches, 1831–1842*. Edited by Thomas Ollive Mabbott, with the assistance of Eleanor D. Kewer and Maureen C. Mabbott. Cambridge: Belknap Press of Harvard University Press, 1978.

Pontalis, Jean-Baptiste, and Jean Laplanche. "Fantasy and the Origins of Sexuality." *International Journal of Psycho-Analysis* 49 (1968): 1–18.

Rasmussen, Steven A., and Jane L. Eisen. "The Epidemiology and Clinical Features of Obsessive Compulsive Disorder." *Psychiatric Clinics* 15, no. 4 (1992): 743–58.

Reno, Joshua Ozias. "Toward a New Theory of Waste: From 'Matter out of Place' to Signs of Life." *Theory, Culture & Society* 31, no. 6 (2014): 3–27.

Richardson, Brian. *Unnatural Voices: Extreme Narration in Modern and Contemporary Fiction*. Columbus: Ohio State University Press, 2006.

Rilke, Rainer Maria. *The Notebooks of Malte Laurids Brigge* New York: Penguin, 2009.

Roberts, William. "The Stamp-Collecting Craze." *Fortnightly Review* 55, no. 329 (May 1894): 662–68.

Robinson, Michael. "Ornamental Gentlemen: Thomas F. Dibdin, Romantic Bibliomania, and Romantic Sexualities." *European Romantic Review* 22, no. 5 (2011): 685–706.

Rosa, Giovanni. "La 'città più città d'Italia' e l'esposizione del 1881." In *1881–2015: Milano città di esposizioni*. Milan: Istituto Lombardo, 2016.

Roscioni, Gian Carlo. *Il Duca di Sant'Aquila*. Milan: Mondadori, 1997.

——. *La disarmonia prestabilita*. Turin: Einaudi, 1969.

Rozzo, Ugo. *Furor bibliographicus, ovvero La bibliomania*. Edited by Massimo Gatta. Macerata: Biblohaus, 2011.

Rudosky, Christina Helena. "Breton the Collector: A Surrealist Poetics of the Object." PhD diss., University of Colorado at Boulder, 2015.

Rushing, Robert A. "'La sua tragica incompiutezza': Anxiety, Mis-Recognition and Ending in Gadda's *Pasticciaccio*." *MLN* 116, no. 1 (2001): 130–49.

——. *Resisting Arrest: Detective Fiction and Popular Culture*. New York: Other Press, 2007.

Russo, Antonella. *Storia culturale della fotografia italiana: dal neorealismo al postmoderno*. Turin: Einaudi, 2011.

Sachdev, Perminder S., and Gin S. Malhi. "Obsessive–Compulsive Behaviour: A Disorder of Decision-Making." *Australian & New Zealand Journal of Psychiatry* 39, no. 9 (2005): 757–63.

Salzani, Carlo. "The City as Crime Scene: Walter Benjamin and the Traces of the Detective." *New German Critique* 100 (2007): 165–87.

Savettieri, Cristina, "Self-Reflection and Ambivalence in Carlo Emilio Gadda's *L'Adalgisa*." *Italianist* 35, no. 3 (October 2015) 412–25.

Scott, Andrew. London: *The Dazzle*. London: Found 111 Theater, 2015.

Scott, Walter, and W. Powell Jones. "Three Unpublished Letters of Scott to Dibdin." *Huntington Library Quarterly* 3, no. 4 (1940): 477–84.

Schor, Naomi. *Reading in Detail: Aesthetics and the Feminine*. New York: Routledge, 2013.

Schmitt, Carl. *The Nomos of the Earth in the Ius Publicum Europaeum*. New York: Telos Press, 2003.

Schneider, Marilyn. "To Know Is To Eat. A Reading of *Il serpente*." *Yale Italian Studies* 2 (1978): 71–84.

Sebastiani, Gioia. "Emma Ivon in un'alba editoriale." *Belfagor* 46, no. 5 (1991): 567–75.

——. *I libri di Corrente*. Bologna, Edizioni Pendragon, 1998.

Sekula, Allan. "The Body and the Archive." *October* 39 (1986): 3–64.

Serao, Matilde. *Il ventre di Napoli*. Milan: Treves, 1884.

Shapira, Ian. "Renoir Found at W.Va. Flea Market Likely to Fetch $100,000 at Auction." *Washington Post*, September 11, 2012.

Sholl, Jessie. *Dirty Secret: A Daughter Comes Clean about Her Mother's Compulsive Hoarding*. New York: Gallery Books, 2010.

Showalter, Michael, 2016. *Hello, My Name Is Doris*. Culver City, CA: Sony Pictures Home Entertainment. DVD.

Silverman, Kaja. *Flesh of My Flesh*. Palo Alto, CA: Stanford University Press, 2009.

Singer, Mark. "The Book Eater." *New Yorker*, February 5, 2001, 62–71.

Slefo, George. "Update: Family Hires Crew to Clean Out Hoarder's Home." *Skokie Patch*, August 2, 2010.

Sobhan, Rehman. "The Politics of Hunger and Entitlement." In *The Political Economy of Hunger*, edited by Jean Drèze and Amartya Sen, vol. 1, 79–113. Oxford: Oxford University Press, 2007.

Sontag, Susan. *On Photography*. New York: Picador, 1977.

Spackman, Barbara. *Fascist Virilities: Rhetoric, Ideology, and Social Fantasy in Italy*. Minneapolis: University of Minnesota Press, 1996.

Spitzer, Leo. *La enumeración caótica en la poesía moderna*. Buenos Aires: Imprenta y casa editora Coni, 1945.

——. "Explication de Texte Applied to Walt Whitman's Poem, 'Out of the Cradle Endlessly Rocking.'" *ELH* 16, no. 3 (1949): 229–49.

Stefani, Bruno. *Bruno Stefani*. Edited by Roberto Campari. Parma: Università di Parma, 1976.

Stein, Gertrude. "Cultivated Motor Automatism: A Study of Character in Its Relation to Attention." *Psychological Review* 5, no. 3 (1898): 295–306.

Solomons, Leon M., and Gertrude Stein. "Normal Motor Automatism." *Psychological Review* 3, no. 5 (1896): 492–512.

Song Dong and Xiangyuan Zhao. *Waste Not: Zhao Xiangyuan & Song Dong = Wu jin qi yong: Zhao Xiangyuan & Song Dong*. Edited by Wu Hung. Tokyo: Tokyo Gallery + Beijing Tokyo Art Projects, 2009.

Stekel, Wilhelm. "The Sexual Roots of Kleptomania." *Journal of Criminal Law and Criminology* 2, no. 2 (1911): 239–46.

——. *Twelve Essays on Sex and Psychoanalysis*. Translated by S. A. Tannenbaum. New York: Critic and Guide Company, 1922.

Stewart, Susan. *On Longing: Narratives of the Miniature, the Gigantic, the Souvenir, the Collection*. Durham, NC: Duke University Press, 1993.

Stewart-Steinberg, Suzanne. *The Pinocchio Effect: On Making Italians, 1860–1920*. Chicago: University of Chicago Press, 2007.

Stille, Alexander. *The Force of Things: A Marriage in War and Peace.* New York: Farrar, Straus and Giroux, 2013.

Strasser, Susan. *Waste and Want: A Social History of Trash.* New York: Metropolitan Books, 2000.

Taramelli, Ennery. *Viaggio nell'Italia del neorealismo: la fotografia tra letteratura e cinema.* Torino: SEI, 1995.

Tarkington, Booth, Kenneth Lewis Roberts, and Hugh MacNair Kahler. *The Collector's Whatnot; A Compendium, Manual, and Syllabus of Information and Advice on All Subjects Appertaining to the Collection of Antiques, Both Ancient and Not so Ancient.* Watkins Glen, NY: American Life Foundation & Study Institute, 1969.

Taylor, Marvin J. "The Anatomy of Bibliography: Book Collecting, Bibliography and Male Homosocial Discourse." *Textual Practice* 14, no. 3 (2000): 457–77.

Thompson, Michael. *Rubbish Theory: The Creation and Destruction of Value.* New ed. London: Pluto Press, 2017.

Timpano, Kiara R., Ashley M. Smith, Julia C. Yang, and Demet Çek. "Information Processing." In *The Oxford Handbook of Hoarding and Acquiring*, edited by R. Frost and G. Steketee, 100–19. Oxford: Oxford University Press, 2014.

Todorov, Tzvetan. "The Typology of Detective Fiction." In *The Poetics of Prose*, 42–52. Ithaca: Cornell University Press, 1977.

Trent Jr., James W. *Inventing the Feeble Mind: A History of Mental Retardation in the United States.* Berkeley: University of California Press, 1994.

Trotter, David. *Cooking with Mud: The Idea of Mess in Nineteenth-Century Art and Fiction.* Oxford: Oxford University Press, 2000.

Tsien, Jennifer. "Diderot's Battle against Books: Books as Objects during the Enlightenment and Revolution." *Belphégor. Littérature populaire et culture médiatique* 13-1 (2015), https://doi.org/10.4000/belphegor.609.

"Une fortune inespérée." *Le Matin: derniers télégrammes de la nuit*, November 14, 1895; http://gallica.bnf.fr/ark:/12148/bpt6k5564864.

Ungarelli, Giulio. "Le occasioni di Gadda." In *Le ragioni del dolore*, edited by Emilio Manzotti, 53–71. Lugano: Edizioni Cenobio, 1993.

Van Zuylen, Marina. *Monomania: The Flight from Everyday Life in Literature and Art.* Ithaca: Cornell University Press, 2005.

Veale, David, and Alison Roberts. "Obsessive-Compulsive Disorder." *BMJ* 348 (2014), https://doi.org/10.1136/bmj.g2183.

Verga, Giovanni. "I dintorni di Milano." In *Milano 1881*, 421–28. Milan: Ottino, 1881.

Veronesi, Giulia. "La fotografia contro l'obbiettivo: pittura con la luce." *Panorama* 2, no. 7 (April 12, 1940): 35–39.

Vickers, Brian D., and Stephanie D. Preston. "The Economics of Hoarding." In *The Oxford Handbook of Hoarding and Acquiring*, edited by R. Frost and G. Steketee, 221–32. Oxford: Oxford University Press, 2014.

Villa, Renzo. "Il deviante e suoi segni." In *Lombroso e la nascita dell'antropologia criminale* 11–36. Milan: *Franco Angeli*, 1985.

Viney, William. *Waste: A Philosophy of Things*. London: Bloomsbury Academic, 2014.

Virtuani, Pietro "Nota introduttiva e bibliografica." In *Il ventre di Milano: Fisiologia della Capitale morale, per cura di una società di letterati*, 11–15. Milan: Ledizioni, 2016.

Walker, Ian. *City Gorged with Dreams: Surrealism and Documentary Photography in Interwar Paris*. Manchester: Manchester University Press, 2002.

Wallis, David. "Is It Normal to Hoard?" *Nautilus*, no. 10, "Mergers and Acquisitions," February 14, 2014. http://nautil.us/issue/10/mergers--acquisitions/is-it-normal-to-hoard.

Warnod, André. *La Brocante et les petits marchés de Paris*. Paris: E. Figuière, 1914.

———. *Les Plaisirs de la rue*. Paris: L'édition française illustrée, 1920.

Welch, Rhiannon Noel. *Vital Subjects: Race and Biopolitics in Italy, 1860–1920*, vol. 1. Liverpool: Liverpool University Press, 2016.

Whitlock, Tammy. "Gender, Medicine, and Consumer Culture in Victorian England: Creating the Kleptomaniac." *Albion* 31, no. 3 (1999): 413–37.

Wohlfarth, Irving. "Et Cetera? The Historian as Chiffonnier." *New German Critique* 39 (1986): 143–68.

Woodall, Angela. "Body of Woman Missing for Seven Years Found in Oakland House." *Oakland Tribune*, March. 25, 2009. https://www.eastbaytimes.com/2009/03/25/body-of- woman-missing-for-seven-years-found-in-oakland-house/.

Worden Erskine, Helen. *Out of This World: A Collection of Hermits and Recluses*. New York: Putnam, 1953.

Yaeger, Patricia. "Editor's Column: The Death of Nature and the Apotheosis of Trash; Or, Rubbish Ecology." *PMLA* 123, no. 2 (2008): 321–39.

Yourgrau, Barry. 2015. *Mess: One Man's Struggle to Clean Up His House and His Act*. New York: W. W. Norton.

Index

Italicized page numbers indicate photos.

CPSIA information can be obtained
at www.ICGtesting.com
Printed in the USA
LVHW111718020421
683324LV00007B/173